50 Speeches That Made the Modern World

50 Speeches That Made the Modern World

Editor

Andrew Burnet

With contributions by

Nancy E M Bailey

Allan Burnett

Andrew Campbell

Steve Cramer

Catherine Gaunt

First published in Great Britain in 2016 by Chambers. An Hachette UK company.

Based on material previously published in *The Chambers Book of Great Speeches,* 2013

British Library Cataloguing in Publication Data: a catalogue record for this title is available from the British Library.

Library of Congress Catalog Card Number: on file.

Hardback: 9781473640948

Paperback: 9781473640979

eBook: 9781473640955

3

The publisher has used its best endeavours to ensure that any website addresses referred to in this book are correct and active at the time of going to press. However, the publisher and the author have no responsibility for the websites and can make no guarantee that a site will remain live or that the content will remain relevant, decent or appropriate.

The publisher has made every effort to mark as such all words which it believes to be trademarks. The publisher should also like to make it clear that the presence of a word in the book, whether marked or unmarked, in no way affects its legal status as a trademark.

Every reasonable effort has been made by the publisher to trace the copyright holders of material in this book. Any errors or omissions should be notified in writing to the publisher, who will endeavour to rectify the situation for any reprints and future editions.

Typeset by Cenveo Publisher Services.

Printed and bound in Germany by Mohn Media GmbH.

Chambers Publishing Ltd policy is to use papers that are natural, renewable and recyclable products and made from wood grown in sustainable forests. The logging and manufacturing processes are expected to conform to the environmental regulations of the country of origin.

Carmelite House
50 Victoria Embankment
London EC4Y 0DZ
www.chambers.co.uk

Contents

Introduction

When we consider the phrase 'the modern world', the mind is soon swarming with ideas. Living in today's culture can feel like being surrounded by dozens of television screens, all tuned to different channels. Each one bombards us with its sound and images; each demands our attention.

Technology advances so rapidly that few of us can keep pace with the possibilities it offers – and many of us worry about their implications. Religious and political divides appear to grow ever wider and more perilous. Poverty worsens while vast wealth accumulates. Climate change; collapse of financial systems; the continuation of war. And all of this presents itself to us amid a relentless tide of entertainment, advertising and brash 'celebrity culture'.

But, amid this noise and haste, one skill remains as essential as it was in Greek and Roman times – and presumably long before. It is the art of oratory, the business of persuasion, in which one person commands the attention of many others to put across an argument. Nowadays, the audience may number in its millions, but a truly effective speaker can hold a crowd of any size.

This book cannot attempt to trace the history of public speaking, or consistently map it onto the turning points of history. Instead, it is a collection of 50 modern representative examples, arising from many different circumstances.

The speakers collected here embrace numerous agendas, some a great deal more laudable than others. Many of them deal with eternal issues, such as war and peace, inequality and justice, repression and revolution. Others address concerns peculiar to the modern age, such as AIDS and the atom bomb, technology and terrorism. All of them have something unique to say, and have said it in an original and compelling way.

In presenting these speeches, we have tried to place the reader in a ringside seat by describing the immediate circumstances, the historical background and, where possible, the audience's reactions. We have provided an introduction to each speech, and notes to explain references which may not be obvious. In some cases, we have abridged the speeches to remove material of less immediate interest to the reader.

But none of this should distract from the transcripts of the orators' own words. They are included here because they speak supremely well for themselves.

Andrew Burnet

Editor

'The more one thinks about the importance of the vote for women, the more one realizes how vital it is.'

— *Emmeline Pankhurst*

1

Emmeline Pankhurst

British suffragette

Emmeline Pankhurst née Goulden (1857–1928) was one of the significant voices of the women's suffrage movement of the late 19th and early 20th century. She fought for women's suffrage with tenacity and extreme militancy, and was later joined by her daughters Christabel (1880–1958) and Sylvia (1882–1960). Her 40-year-campaign reached a peak of success shortly before her death, when the Representation of the People Act was finally passed (1928), establishing voting equality for men and women.

'The laws that men have made'

24 March 1908, London, England

Formed in 1887 from 17 separate groups, the National Union of Women's Suffrage Societies had campaigned persistently but unsuccessfully to gain the vote for women. A growing sense of frustration drove Emmeline and her daughter Christabel Pankhurst to form breakaway groups: the Women's Social and Political Union in 1903 and the more militant Women's Freedom League in 1907.

Tactics pursued by members of these organizations included heckling political speeches and provoking the police to arrest them for disturbing the peace. Their activities attracted the desired attention, though they were also delightedly lampooned by cartoonists and mainstream newspapers. In 1907, the law was changed to allow women ratepayers to vote in local elections – but this did not satisfy Pankhurst.

In 1908, she gave a series of lectures under the umbrella title *The Importance of the Vote*. This one was given in the Portman Rooms during the Putney by-election of that year, which added urgency to its message. In her bald but patiently reasoned attack on the status quo, Pankhurst recites men's legislative shortcomings, condemning them for their failure to improve ordinary women's lives.

" What I am going to say to you tonight is not new. It is what we have been saying at every street corner, at every by-election during the last 18 months. It is perfectly well known to many members of my audience, but they will not mind if I repeat, for the benefit of those who are here for the first time tonight, those arguments and illustrations with which many of us are so very familiar.

In the first place, it is important that women should have the vote in order that in the government of the country the women's point of view should be put forward.

It is important for women that in any legislation that affects women equally with men, those who make the laws should be responsible to women, in order that they may be forced to consult women and learn women's views when they are contemplating the making or the altering of laws.

Very little has been done by legislation for women for many years – for obvious reasons. More and more of the time of Members of Parliament is occupied by the claims which are made on behalf of the people who are organized in various ways in order to promote the interests of their industrial organizations or their political or social organizations. So the Member of Parliament, if he does dimly realize that women have needs, has no time to attend to them, no time to give to the consideration of those needs. His time is fully taken up by attending to the needs of the people who have sent him to Parliament.

While a great deal has been done, and a great deal more has been talked about for the benefit of the workers who have votes, yet so far as women are concerned, legislation relating to them has been practically at a standstill. Yet it is not because women have no need, or because their need is not very urgent. There are many laws on the statute-book today which are admittedly out of date, and call for reformation; laws which inflict very grave injustices on women. I want to call the attention of women who are here tonight to a few acts on the statute-book which press very hardly and very injuriously on women.

Men politicians are in the habit of talking to women as if there were no laws that affect women. 'The fact is,' they say, 'the home is the place for women. Their interests are the rearing and training of children. These are the things that interest women. Politics have nothing to do with these things, and therefore politics do not concern women.' Yet the laws decide how women are to live in marriage, how their children are to be trained and educated, and what the future of their children is to be. All that is decided by act of Parliament. Let us take a few of these laws, and see what there is to say about them from the women's point of view.

First of all, let us take the marriage laws. They are made by men for women. Let us consider whether they are equal, whether they are just, whether they are wise. What security of maintenance has the married woman? Many a married woman, having given up her economic independence in order to marry, how is she compensated for that loss? What security does she get in that marriage for which she gave up economic independence? Take the case of a woman who has been earning a good income. She is told that she ought to give up her employment when she becomes a wife and a mother. What does she get in return?

All that a married man is obliged by law to do for his wife is to provide for her shelter of some kind, food of some kind and clothing of some kind. It is left to his good pleasure to decide what the shelter shall be, what the food shall be, what the clothing shall be. It is left to him to decide what money shall be spent on the home, and how it shall be spent; the wife has no voice legally in deciding any of these things. She has no legal claim upon any definite portion of his income. If he is a good man, a conscientious man, he does the right thing. If he is not, if he chooses almost to starve his wife, she has no remedy. What he thinks sufficient is what she has to be content with.

I quite agree, in all these illustrations, that the majority of men are considerably better than the law compels them to be … but since there are some bad men, some unjust men, don't you agree with me that the law ought to be altered so that those men could be dealt with?

Take what happens to the woman if her husband dies and leaves her a widow, sometimes with little children. If a man is so insensible to his duties as a husband and father when he makes his will, as to leave all his property away from his wife and children, the law allows him to do it. That will is a valid one. So you see that the married woman's position is not a secure one. It depends entirely on her getting a good ticket in the lottery. If she has a good husband, well and good: if she has a bad one, she has to suffer, and she has no remedy. That is her position as a wife, and it is far from satisfactory.

Now let us look at her position if she has been very unfortunate in marriage, so unfortunate as to get a bad husband, an immoral husband, a vicious husband, a husband unfit to be the father of little children. We turn to the divorce court. How is she to get rid of such a man? If a man has got married to a bad wife, and he wants to get rid of her, he has but to prove against her one act of infidelity. But if a woman who is married to a vicious husband wants to get rid of him, not one act nor a thousand acts of infidelity entitle her to a divorce. She must prove either bigamy, desertion or gross cruelty, in addition to immorality, before she can get rid of that man.

Let us consider her position as a mother. We have repeated this so often at our meetings that I think the echo of what we have said must have reached many.

By English law, no married woman exists as the mother of the child she brings into the world. In the eyes of the law she is not the parent of her child.

The child, according to our marriage laws, has only one parent who can decide the future of the child, who can decide where it shall live, how it shall live, how much shall be spent upon it, how it shall be educated and what religion it shall profess. That parent is the father.

These are examples of some of the laws that men have made, laws that concern women. I ask you, if women had had the vote, should we have had such laws? If women had had the vote, as men have the vote, we should have had equal laws. We should have had equal laws for divorce, and the law would have said that as nature has given to children two parents, so the law should recognize that they have two parents.

I have spoken to you about the position of the married woman who does not exist legally as a parent, the parent of her own child. In marriage, children have one parent. Out of marriage children have also one parent. That parent is the mother – the unfortunate mother. She alone is responsible for the future of her child; she alone is punished if her child is neglected and suffers from neglect.

But let me give you one illustration. I was in Herefordshire during the by-election. While I was there, an unmarried mother was brought before the bench of magistrates, charged with having neglected her illegitimate child. She was a domestic servant, and had put the child out to nurse. The magistrates – there were colonels and landowners on that bench – did not ask what wages the mother got; they did not ask who the father was or whether he contributed to the support of the child. They sent that woman to prison for three months for having neglected her child.

I ask you women here tonight: if women had had some share in the making of laws, don't you think they would have found a way of making all fathers of such children equally responsible with the mothers for the welfare of those children?

… The man voter and the man legislator see the man's needs first, and do not see the woman's needs. And so it will be until women get the vote.

It is well to remember that, in view of what we have been told of what is the value of women's influence. Woman's influence is only effective when men want to do the thing that her influence is supporting.

Now let us look a little to the future. If it ever was important for women to have the vote, it is ten times more important today, because you cannot take up a newspaper, you cannot go to a conference, you cannot even go to church, without hearing a great deal of talk about social reform and a demand for social legislation. Of course, it is obvious that that kind of legislation – and the Liberal government tell us that if they remain in office long enough we are going to have a great deal of it – is of vital importance to women.

If we have the right kind of social legislation it will be a very good thing for women and children. If we have the wrong kind of social legislation, we may have the worst kind of tyranny that women have ever known since the world began. We are hearing about legislation to decide what kind of homes people are to live in. That surely is a question for women. Surely every woman, when she seriously thinks about it, will wonder how men by themselves can have the audacity to think that they can say what homes ought to be without consulting women.

Then take education. Since 1870 men have been trying to find out how to educate children.[1] I think they have not yet realized that if they are ever to find out how to educate children,

---

[1] The Education Act of 1870 created school districts, each with its own elected board, and allowed women both to vote and to stand as candidates.

they will have to take women into their confidence, and try to learn from women some of those lessons that the long experience of ages has taught to them. One cannot wonder that whole sessions of Parliament should be wasted on education bills …

The more one thinks about the importance of the vote for women, the more one realizes how vital it is. We are finding out new reasons for the vote, new needs for the vote every day in carrying on our agitation.

I hope that there may be a few men and women here who will go away determined at least to give this question more consideration than they have in the past. They will see that we women, who are doing so much to get the vote, want it because we realize how much good we can do with it when we have got it. We do not want it in order to boast of how much we have got. We do not want it because we want to imitate men or to be like men. We want it because without it we cannot do that work which it is necessary and right and proper that every man and woman should be ready and willing to undertake in the interests of the community of which they form a part. 〞

'To the workers, everything;
to the toilers, everything!'
– *Vladimir Ilich Lenin*

2

Vladimir Ilich Lenin

Russian revolutionary leader

Shrewd, dynamic, pedantic and implacable, the Marxist political activist Vladimir Ilich Lenin (1870–1924) spearheaded the October Revolution of 1917 and inaugurated the 'dictatorship of the proletariat' that was to rule Russia for more than seven decades. Despite the ultimate failure of Soviet communism, his influence endures in Russia and beyond.

'To the workers, everything; to the toilers, everything!'

30 August 1918, Moscow, Russia

The occasion of this speech was a mass meeting in the hand-grenade shop of Moscow's Michelson Factory.

Much had changed in Russia after the February Revolution (in March 1917, by modern dating), which had forced Tsar Nicholas II's abdication and established a provisional government of moderate reformists. Although Lenin – unwilling to compromise his careful plans to reorganize the government and economy – had not taken advantage of anti-government demonstrations in July 1917, he had led the successful October Revolution a few months later. He allowed elections for a constituent assembly in November, but dissolved it in January 1918 after the Socialist Revolutionary Party won a majority of seats. Russia withdrew from World War I in March 1918, ceding vast areas of land and economic resources to Germany under the Treaty of Brest-Litovsk.

On 15 August, Lenin severed diplomatic relations with the USA and two weeks later he gave this speech discrediting the moderate provisional government (established after the February Revolution) and attacking the American concept of democracy. In it, he expresses his anger at the course of the war and the treatment of workers in other countries.

As he was leaving the meeting, a member of the Socialist Revolutionary Party, Fanya Kaplan, ran towards him and fired at close range. Lenin refused to go to hospital for fear that further assassins were waiting for him there, and was treated at home. He never fully recovered from his injuries.

" We Bolsheviks are constantly accused of violating the slogans of equality and fraternity. Let us go into this question in detail.

What was the authority which took the place of the Tsar's authority?[1] It was the authority of Guchkov[2] and Milyukov,[3] which began to prepare for a constituent assembly in Russia. What was it that really lay behind this work in favour of a liberation of the people from its yoke of a thousand years? Simply the fact that Guchkov and the other leaders gathered around them a host of capitalists who were pursuing their own imperialist purposes.

And when the clique of Kerensky,[4] Chernov,[5] etc, gained power, this new government, hesitating and deprived of any base to stand on, fought only for the basic interests of the bourgeoisie, closely allied to it. The power actually passed into the hands of the kulaks,[6] and nothing into those of the toiling masses.

We have witnessed the same phenomenon in other countries also. Let us take America, the freest and most civilized country. America is a democratic republic. And what is the result? We have the shameless rule of a clique not of millionaires but of multi-millionaires, and the entire nation is enslaved and oppressed. If the factories and works, the banks and all the riches of the nation belong to the capitalists; if, by the side of the democratic republic we observe a perpetual enslavement of millions of toilers and a continuous poverty, we have a right to ask: where is all your lauded equality and fraternity?

Far from it! The rule of democracy is accompanied by an unadulterated savage banditry. We understand the true nature of so-called democracies.

The secret treaties of the French Republic, of England and of the other democracies,[7] have clearly convinced us of the real nature, the underlying facts of this business. Their aims and interests are just as criminally predatory as are those of Germany. The war has opened our eyes. We now know very well that the 'defender of the fatherland' conceals under his skin a vile bandit and thief. This attack of the bandit must be opposed with a revolutionary action, with revolutionary creativeness.

To be sure, it is very difficult, at an exceptional time like this, to bring about a union, particularly of the peasant revolutionary elements. But we have faith in the creative energy and the social zeal of the vanguard of the revolution – the proletariat of the factories and shops. The workers have already well grasped the fact that, as long as they permit their

---

[1] The Romanov dynasty ruled Russia from 1613. Constitutional reforms took place in 1905 but after the February Revolution, the Tsar abdicated, ending imperial rule. The provisional government was established to rule the country until the formation of an elected constituent assembly.
[2] The Russian politician Aleksandr Guchkov (1862–1936) was Minister of War in the provisional government. He supported the war and opposed far-reaching land reform. He left office in May 1917.
[3] The Russian politician Pavel Miliukov (1859–1943) was Minister of Foreign Affairs in the provisional government until May 1917, having supported the war.
[4] The Russian socialist politician Aleksandr Kerensky (1881–1970) became Minister of War in the provisional government in May 1917, then Prime Minister in July 1917. Under Bolshevik pressure he fled Russia later that year.

[5] The Russian politician Viktor Chernov (c.1873–1952) helped to found the Socialist Revolutionary Party (SRP) in 1901. In 1917, he became Minister of Agriculture in the provisional government. He briefly chaired the constituent assembly following SRP election success, before Lenin dissolved the assembly.
[6] A pejorative term for landowning peasants who had acquired property following the emancipation of the serfs in 1905. The kulaks opposed Lenin's land reform.
[7] The rapid escalation of events leading to World War I was largely due to a network of treaties and pacts negotiated (often secretly) between the various European powers.

minds to revel in the phantasms of a democratic republic and a constituent assembly, they will have to hand out 50 million roubles a day in advance for military aims that will be destructive to themselves, and for just so long will it be impossible for them to find any outlet from the capitalist oppression.

Having grasped this, the workers created their soviets.[8] It was life itself, real, actual life, which taught the workers to understand that as long as the landholders had entrenched themselves so well in palaces and magic castles, freedom of assembly would be a mere fiction and would only perhaps be found in the other world. To promise freedom to the workers and at the same time to leave the castles, the land, the factories and all the resources in the hands of the capitalists and landowners – that this has nothing to do with liberty and equality.

We have only one slogan, one watchword: everyone who works has a right to enjoy the good things of life.

Idlers, parasites, those who suck out the blood of the toiling masses, must be deprived of these blessings. And our cry is: to the workers, everything; to the toilers, everything!

We know that all this is difficult to bring about. We know what savage opposition we shall encounter on the part of the bourgeoisie; but we believe in the final victory of the proletariat; for once it has freed itself from the terrible quandary of the threats of military imperialism and once it has erected, on the ruins of the structure it has overthrown, the new structure of the socialist republic, it cannot but gain the victory.

And, as a matter of fact, we find a merging of forces in progress everywhere. Owing to our abolition of private property in land, we now find an active fraternization going on between the proletariat of the city and of the village. The clarification of the class-consciousness of the workers is also advancing apace in a far more definite manner than before.

In the West too: the workers of England, France, Italy and other countries are responding more and more to the appeals and demands which bear witness to the early victory of the cause of international revolution. And our task of the day is this: that of performing our revolutionary work, regardless of all the hypocrisy, the base shouts of rage and the sermons delivered by the murderous bourgeoisie. We must turn all our efforts on the Czecho-Slovak front,[9] in order to disperse at once this band of cut-throats which cloaks itself in the slogans of liberty and equality and shoots down hundreds and thousands of workers and peasants.

We have only one recourse: victory or death!

---

8 Workers' and soldiers' councils, elected by popular vote.
9 Following the success of the October Revolution, the new regime came under attack from various anti-Bolshevik factions in a civil war between communist 'Reds' and a coalition of conservatives, monarchists and liberals known as 'Whites'. These included the Czecho-Slovak Legion in Siberia.

'I hold that non-cooperation is a just and religious doctrine; it is the inherent right of every human being and it is perfectly constitutional ...'

– *Mahatma Gandhi*

3

Mahatma Gandhi

Indian lawyer and statesman

As leader of the Congress Movement, Mohandas Karamchand Gandhi, known as Mahatma ('Great Soul') (1869–1948), led a non-violent campaign for Indian independence in the decades following World War I, eventually realized in the Partition of August 1947. Venerated by many as a moral teacher, reformer and patriot, his critics considered him a victim of self-delusion, which blinded him to the bloodshed provoked by his supposedly non-violent campaigns. Gandhi was assassinated in Delhi by a Hindu fanatic on 30 January 1948.

'Why do we want to offer this non-cooperation?'

12 August 1920, Madras (now Chennai), India

Gandhi made this speech near the very beginning of his long struggle. Following violent campaigns for Indian independence, the Anarchical and Revolutionary Crimes Act of 1919, popularly known as the Rowlatt Act, made permanent the suspension of civil liberties enacted during World War I. These developments prompted Gandhi to organize a peaceful, principled resistance movement known as *satyagraha* ('firmness in truth'). However, this was accompanied by violence in places, leading to the imposition of martial law in the Punjab, and the Amritsar Massacre of April 1919, at which British troops fired into a crowd gathered for a religious festival, killing at least 379.

The peace terms presented to Turkey by the Allies following World War I in the Treaty of Sèvres angered Indian Muslims, who launched the Khilafat movement in September 1919 to protect the Turkish Khilafa and save the Ottoman Empire from dismemberment by Britain and her allies. Gandhi supported this movement, and in June 1920 he wrote to the viceroy announcing his intention to start a non-cooperation movement in protest against the treaty. In his letter, he referred to the right of the subject 'to refuse to assist a ruler who misrules'. Supporters of the non-cooperation movement were instructed to refuse to perform government duties, withdraw their children from schools and colleges and establish national schools and colleges. They were to boycott British courts and establish private courts. They were to advocate truth and non-violence at all times and wear Indian home-spun cloth.

Gandhi formally launched his non-cooperation movement on 1 August 1920. Soon afterwards, he spoke to a crowd of 50,000 gathered on the beach at Madras. In the speech he explains the importance of the Khilafat movement and the principles of the non-violence movement.

Mr Chairman and friends …

I have sat here to address you on a most important question … I have come to ask every one of you whether you are ready and willing to give sufficiently for your country's sake, for you country's honour and religion …

What is this non-cooperation, about which you have heard much, and why do we want to offer this non-cooperation? I wish to go for the time being into the way. There are two things before this country: the first and the foremost is the Khilafat question. On this the heart of the Mussulmans[1] of India has become lacerated. British pledges given after the greatest deliberation by the prime minister of England[2] in the name of the English nation, have been dragged into the mire. The promises given to Muslim India … have been broken, and the great religion of Islam has been placed in danger.

The Mussulmans hold – and I venture to think they rightly hold – that, so long as British promises remain unfulfilled, so long is it impossible for them to tender whole-hearted fealty and loyalty to the British connection; and if it is to be a choice for a devout Mussulman between loyalty to the British connection and loyalty to his Code and Prophet, he will not require a second to make his choice – and he has declared his choice. The Mussulmans say frankly, openly, and honourably to the whole world that if the British ministers and the British nation do not fulfil the pledges given to them … it will be impossible for them to retain Islamic loyalty.

It is a question, then, for the rest of the Indian population to consider whether they want to perform a neighbourly duty by their Mussulman countrymen, and if they do, they have an opportunity of a lifetime, which will not occur for another 100 years, to show their goodwill, fellowship and friendship and to prove what they have been saying for all these long years, that the Mussulman is the brother of the Hindu. If the Hindu regards that before the connection with the British nation comes his natural connection with his Muslim brother, then I say to you that if you find that the Muslim claim is just … you cannot do otherwise than help the Mussulman through and through …

These are the plain conditions which the Indian Mussulmans have accepted; and it was when they saw that they could accept the proffered aid of the Hindus, that they could always justify the cause and the means before the whole world, that they decided to accept the proffered hand of fellowship.

It is then for the Hindus and Mohammedans[3] to offer a united front to the whole of the Christian powers of Europe and tell them that weak as India is, India has still got the capacity for preserving her self-respect …

That is the Khilafat in a nut-shell; but you have also got the Punjab. The Punjab has wounded the heart of India as no other question has for the past century. I do not exclude from my calculation the Mutiny of 1857. Whatever hardships India had to suffer during the Mutiny, the insult that was attempted to be offered to her during the passage of the Rowlatt

---

[1] An archaic term for Muslims.
[2] David Lloyd George (1863–1945) served as prime minister, 1916–22.
[3] Another term for Muslims.

legislation and that which was offered after its passage were unparalleled in Indian history … The House of Commons, the House of Lords, Mr Montagu,[4] the Viceroy of India,[5] every one of them knows what the feeling of India is on this Khilafat question and on that of the Punjab … [but] they are not willing to give the justice which is India's due and which she demands.

I suggest that … unless we have gained a measure of self-respect at the hands of the British rulers in India, no connection and no friendly intercourse is possible between them and ourselves. I therefore venture to suggest this beautiful and unanswerable method of non-cooperation.

I have been told that non-cooperation is unconstitutional. I venture to deny that it is unconstitutional. On the contrary,

> *I hold that non-cooperation is a just and religious doctrine; it is the inherent right of every human being…*

and it is perfectly constitutional … I do not claim any constitutionality for a rebellion, successful or otherwise, so long as that rebellion means in the ordinary sense of the term, what it does mean – namely wresting justice by violent means. On the contrary, I have said it repeatedly to my countrymen that violence, whatever end it may serve in Europe, will never serve us in India.

My brother and friend Shaukat Ali[6] believes in methods of violence … but because he recognizes as a true soldier that means of violence are not open to India, he sides with me, accepting my humble assistance, and pledges his word that so long as I am with him and so long as he believes in the doctrine, so long will he not harbour even the idea of violence against any single Englishman or any single man on earth …

As soon as India accepts the doctrine of the sword, my life as an Indian is finished. It is because I believe in a mission special to India and it is because I believe that the ancients of India, after centuries of experience, have found out that the true thing for any human being on earth is not justice based on violence, but justice based on sacrifice of self, justice based on Yagna and Kurbani.[7] I cling to that doctrine and I shall cling to it for ever. It is for that reason I tell you that whilst my friend believes also in the doctrine of violence and has adopted the doctrine of non-violence as a weapon of the weak, I believe in the doctrine of non-violence as a weapon of the strongest …

I say to my countrymen: so long as you have a sense of honour and so long as you wish to remain the descendants and defenders of the noble traditions that have been handed to you for generations after generations, it is unconstitutional for you not to non-cooperate and unconstitutional for you to co-operate with a government which has become so unjust as our government has become.

I am not anti-English; I am not anti-British; I am not anti any government; but I am anti-untruth – anti-humbug and anti-injustice …

---

[4] The English politician Edwin Montagu (1879–1924) served as Under-Secretary of State for India, 1910–14, and Secretary of State for India, 1917–22. In 1917–18, he researched and wrote a report on Indian constitutional reforms which formed the basis of the Government of India Act (1919), granting limited self-government.

[5] The English colonial administrator Frederic Thesiger, 3rd Baron Chelmsford later 1st Viscount Chelmsford (1868–1933) served as Viceroy of India, 1916–21.
[6] The Indian Muslim nationalist Shaukat Ali (1873–1938) founded the Khilafat movement with his brother Mohammad (1878–1931).
[7] Ceremonial rituals of sacrifice and worship.

I had hoped, at the Congress at Amritsar[8] – I am speaking God's truth before you – when I pleaded on bended knees before some of you for co-operation with the government. I had full hope that the British ministers – who are wise, as a rule – would placate the Mussulman sentiment; that they would do full justice in the matter of the Punjab atrocities. And therefore I said: Let us return goodwill to the hand of fellowship that has been extended to us, which I then believed was extended to us through the Royal Proclamation. It was on that account that I pleaded for co-operation.

But today, that faith having been obliterated by the acts of the British ministers, I am here to plead not for futile obstruction in the legislative council, but for real, substantial non-cooperation, which would paralyse the mightiest government on earth.

That is what I stand for today. Until we have wrung justice, and until we have wrung our self-respect from unwilling hands and from unwilling pens there can be no cooperation …

I deny being a visionary. I do not accept the claim of saintliness. I am of the earth, earthy, a common man as much as any one of you, probably much more than you are. I am prone to as many weaknesses as you are …

I have understood the secret of my own sacred Hinduism, I have learnt the lesson that non-cooperation is the duty not merely of the saint, but it is the duty of every ordinary citizen who – not knowing much, not caring to know much – wants to perform his ordinary household functions …

I am asking my countrymen in India to follow no other gospel than the gospel of self-sacrifice which precedes every battle.

Whether you belong to the school of violence or non-violence, you will still have to go through the fire of sacrifice and of discipline. May God grant you, may God grant our leaders, the wisdom, the courage and the true knowledge to lead the nation to its cherished goal. May God grant the people of India the right path, the true vision and the ability and the courage to follow this path, difficult and yet easy, of sacrifice. **,,**

[8] The annual session of the Indian National Congress was held at Amritsar in December 1919.

'Carry back to your towns, to your lands, to your houses, distant but near to my heart, the vigorous impression of this meeting. Keep the flame burning, because that which has not been may be, because if victory was maimed once, it does not follow that it can be maimed a second time!'

— *Benito Mussolini*

4

Benito Mussolini

Italian dictator

In 1919, Benito Amilcare Andrea Mussolini (1883–1945) founded the fascist movement, exploiting the widespread disillusionment felt by many Italians in the wake of World War II to promote an extreme nationalism. In 1922, Mussolini was invited by the Italian king, Victor Emmanuel III, to form a government and by 1929, through intimidation, patronage and propaganda, he had turned Italy into a totalitarian state. Ambitious to build an overseas empire, through the 1930s Mussolini increasingly allied his country with Nazi Germany and eventually led Italy to war against the Allies in 1939. Following the Allied landings in Sicily (1943), both the king and his own Fascist Council turned on him and in 1945 he was summarily executed while attempting to flee the country.

'We must win the peace'

25 June 1923, Rome, Italy

During his first year as prime minister, Mussolini was still strengthening his grasp on power. One key strand of his appeal was patriotism, and at a rally to mark the fifth anniversary of the Battle of the Piave, he gave this grandstanding speech in celebration of Italian martial success.

Italy had entered World War I in 1915 on the side of the UK and France, hoping to win territory from Austria–Hungary and Germany. A critical conflict occurred in June 1918, when Italian troops repulsed an attack by the Austro-Hungarian army across the river Piave. Four months later, the Italian army scored an even more decisive victory at the Battle of Vittorio Veneto. However, Italy received little in the peace treaties that followed the war; and it was partly out of resentment over this that Mussolini built his popularity.

Mussolini was a charismatic and inspiring public speaker, whose oratorical techniques – like his political policies – prefigured those of Adolf Hitler. Addressing a huge crowd at the Palazzo Venezia, he feigns reluctance to speak, before unleashing a typically rousing address.

Although he insists the Blackshirts' march on Rome 'buried the past', he alludes strongly to the city's ancient heritage as an invincible military power. His purpose is to enlist popular support and discourage dissent; and he excites the crowd into a denunciation of those who would 'maim victory', before rewarding them with a vision of Italy as a great and 'imperishable' power. The translation is by Baron Bernardo Quaranta di San Severino.

"Fellow soldiers: after your ranks, so well disciplined and of such fine bearing, have marched past His Majesty the King, the intangible symbol of the country; after the austere ceremony in its silent solemnity before the tomb of the Unknown Warrior – after this formidable display of sacred strength, words from me are absolutely superfluous, and I do not intend to make a speech. The march of today is a manifestation full of significance and warning. A whole people in arms has met today in spirit in the Eternal City.[1] It is a whole people who, above unavoidable party differences, finds itself strongly united when the safety of the common motherland is at stake.

On the occasion of the Etna eruption,[2] national solidarity was wonderfully manifested; from every town, every village, one might say from every hamlet, a fraternal heart-throb went out to the land stricken by calamity.

Today tens of thousands of soldiers, thousands of standards – with men coming to Rome from all parts of Italy and from the far-away colonies, from abroad – bear witness that the unity of the Italian nation is an accomplished and irrevocable fact.

After seven months of government, to talk to you, my comrades of the trenches, is the highest honour which could fall to my lot. And I do not say this in order to flatter you, nor to pay you a tribute which might seem formal on an occasion like this. I have the right to interpret the thoughts of this meeting, which gathers to listen to my words, as an expression of solidarity with the national government.

[Cries of assent.]

Let us not utter useless and fantastical words. Nobody attacks the sacred liberty of the Italian people. But I ask you: should there be liberty to maim victory?

[Cries of 'No! no!']

Should there be liberty to strike at the nation? Should there be liberty for those who have as their programme the overthrow of our national institutions?

[Cries of 'No! no!']

I repeat what I explicitly said before. I do not feel myself infallible, I feel myself a man like you. I do not repulse – I cannot – I shall not repulse any loyal and sincere collaboration.

Fellow soldiers: the task which weighs on my shoulders, but also on yours, is simply immense, and to it we shall be pledged for many years.

It is, therefore, necessary not to waste, but to treasure and utilize all the energies which could be turned to the good of our country.

Five years have passed since the Battle of the Piave, from that victory … It is necessary to proclaim, for you who listen to me, and also for those who read what I say, that the victory of the Piave was the deciding factor of the war. On the Piave the Austro-Hungarian Empire went to pieces, from the Piave started the flight on white wings of the victory of the people in arms.

---

[1] Rome.   [2] A major eruption of the Sicilian volcano had started earlier that month.

The government means to exalt the spiritual strength which rises out of the victory of a people in arms. It does not mean to disperse them, because it represents the sacred seed of the future. The more distant we get from those days, from that memorable victory, the more they seem to us wonderful, the more the victory appears enveloped in a halo of legend. In such a victory everybody would wish to have taken part!

We must win the peace! Too late somebody perceived that

> *... when the country is in danger, the duty of all citizens, from the highest to the lowest, is only one: to fight, to suffer and – if needs be – to die!*

We have won the war, we have demolished an empire which threatened our frontiers, stifled us and held us for ever under the extortion of armed menace. History has no end.

Comrades: the history of peoples is not measured by years, but by tens of years, by centuries. This manifestation of yours is an infallible sign of the vitality of the Italian people. The phrase 'we must win the peace' is not an empty one. It contains a profound truth. Peace is won by harmony, by work and by discipline. This is the new gospel which has been opened before the eyes of the new generations who have come out of the trenches; a gospel simple and straightforward, which takes into account all the elements, which utilizes all the energies, which does not lend itself to tyrannies of grotesque exclusivism, because it has one sole aim, a common aim: the greatness and the salvation of the nation!

Fellow soldiers: you have come to Rome, and it is natural – I dare to say, fated! Because Rome is always, as it will be tomorrow and in the centuries to come, the living heart of our race! It is the imperishable symbol of our vitality as a people. Who holds Rome, holds the nation.

The Blackshirts buried the past. I assure you, my fellow-soldiers, that my government, in spite of the manifest or hidden difficulties, will keep its pledges. It is the government of Vittorio Veneto.[3]

You feel it and you know it, and if you did not believe it, you would not be here assembled in this square.

Carry back to your towns, to your lands, to your houses, distant but near to my heart, the vigorous impression of this meeting. Keep the flame burning, because that which has not been may be, because if victory was maimed once, it does not follow that it can be maimed a second time!

[Loud cheers, repeated cries of, 'We swear it!']

I keep in mind your oath. I count upon you as I count upon all good Italians, but I count, above all, upon you, because you are of my generation, because you have come out from the bloody filth of the trenches, because you have lived and struggled and suffered in the face of death, because you have fulfilled your duty and have the right to vindicate that to which you are entitled, not only from the material but from the moral point of view.

---

[3] Mussolini refers to the battle between the Italian and Austro-Hungarian armies, October–November 1918. The Austro-Hungarian army collapsed following Italy's victory.

I tell you, I swear to you, that the time is past for ever when fighters returning from the trenches had to be ashamed of themselves; the time when, owing to the threatening attitudes of Communists, the officers received the cowardly advice to dress in plain clothes.

[Applause.]

All that is buried. You must not forget, and nobody forgets, that seven months ago 52,000 armed Blackshirts came to Rome to bury the past!

[Loud cheers.]

Soldiers, fellow soldiers: let us raise before our great unknown comrade the cry which sums up our faith. Long live the King! Long live Italy, victorious, impregnable, immortal!

[Loud cheers, with flags raised.] 〞

5

Franklin D Roosevelt

American statesman

Franklin Delano Roosevelt (1882–1945) came to power as US President during the Great Depression of 1929–39, which he met by launching his innovative New Deal programme. On the strength of his success in these reforms, Roosevelt was re-elected by a landslide in 1936, and secured a third term in 1940 and a fourth in 1944. During the late 1930s, he endeavoured to avoid involvement in the coming European conflict, but on the outbreak of World War II he modified the USA's neutrality in favour of the Allies. Eventually, the USA was brought fully into the conflict by Japan's attack on Pearl Harbor (December 1941). Roosevelt died three weeks before the Nazi surrender.

'The only thing we have to fear is fear itself'

4 March 1933, Washington, DC, USA

Franklin D Roosevelt's first inaugural address, delivered in the depths of the Great Depression, brought a much-needed message of hope. With over half the American workforce unemployed, farm prices at rock bottom and industry in disarray, the country was in despair. On accepting the nomination as Democratic candidate for the 1932 election, Roosevelt had promised a 'New Deal for the American people'. Now he was able to begin implementing policies that were little short of revolutionary in a country deeply mistrustful of socialism.

Roosevelt had been remarkably vague during the election campaign about how he planned to tackle the huge economic problems facing the nation. Now he set out his vision clearly and confidently, speaking both to the crowd gathered at the White House and to the country at large via radio broadcast, which was to become his favourite medium.

His tone is solemn, but displays the forthright style that was his trademark. All the major tenets of the New Deal are here, presented almost as a covenant between the government and the people. The speech is one of extraordinary optimism, portraying a bright future and evoking the still-potent national mythology of the pioneer spirit, without ever underestimating the impact of the Depression on ordinary citizens.

The immediate result was the so-called 'Hundred Days', in which an emergency session of Congress pushed through most of the necessary reforming legislation.

" I am certain that my fellow Americans expect that, on my induction into the presidency, I will address them with a candour and a decision which the present situation of our nation impels. This is pre-eminently the time to speak the truth, the whole truth, frankly and boldly. Nor need we shrink from honestly facing conditions in our country today. This great nation will endure as it has endured, will revive and will prosper.

So, first of all, let me assert my firm belief that the only thing we have to fear is fear itself – nameless, unreasoning, unjustified terror which paralyses needed efforts to convert retreat into advance. In every dark hour of our national life, a leadership of frankness and vigour has met with that understanding and support of the people themselves which is essential to victory. I am convinced that you will again give that support to leadership in these critical days.

In such a spirit, on my part and on yours, we face our common difficulties. They concern, thank God, only material things. Values have shrunken to fantastic levels; taxes have risen; our ability to pay has fallen; government of all kinds is faced by serious curtailment of income; the means of exchange are frozen in the currents of trade; the withered leaves of industrial enterprise lie on every side; farmers find no markets for their produce; the savings of many years in thousands of families are gone.

More important, a host of unemployed citizens face the grim problem of existence and an equally great number toil with little return. Only a foolish optimist can deny the dark realities of the moment.

Yet our distress comes from no failure of substance.

We are stricken by no plague of locusts. Compared with the perils which our forefathers conquered because they believed and were not afraid, we have still much to be thankful for. Nature still offers her bounty and human efforts have multiplied it. Plenty is at our doorstep, but a generous use of it languishes in the very sight of the supply. Primarily, this is because rulers of the exchange of mankind's goods have failed through their own stubbornness and their own incompetence, have admitted their failure and have abdicated. Practices of the unscrupulous money-changers stand indicted in the court of public opinion, rejected by the hearts and minds of men.

True they have tried, but their efforts have been cast in the pattern of an outworn tradition. Faced by failure of credit, they have proposed only the lending of more money. Stripped of the lure of profit by which to induce our people to follow their false leadership, they have resorted to exhortations, pleading tearfully for restored confidence. They know only the rules of a generation of self-seekers. They have no vision, and when there is no vision the people perish.

The money-changers have fled from their high seats in the temple of our civilization.[1] We may now restore that temple to the ancient truths. The measure of the restoration lies in the extent to which we apply social values more noble than mere monetary profit.

---

[1] A reference to Jesus' expulsion of money-changers from the temple of Jerusalem, an incident described in all four gospels of the New Testament, including Mark 11:15–18.

Happiness lies not in the mere possession of money; it lies in the joy of achievement, in the thrill of creative effort. The joy and moral stimulation of work no longer must be forgotten in the mad chase of evanescent profits.

These dark days will be worth all they cost us if they teach us that our true destiny is not to be ministered unto but to minister to ourselves and to our fellow men.

Recognition of the falsity of material wealth as the standard of success goes hand in hand with the abandonment of the false belief that public office and high political position are to be valued only by the standards of pride of place and personal profit...

and there must be an end to a conduct in banking and in business which too often has given to a sacred trust the likeness of callous and selfish wrongdoing. Small wonder that confidence languishes, for it thrives only on honesty, on honour, on the sacredness of obligations, on faithful protection, on unselfish performance; without them it cannot live. Restoration calls, however, not for changes in ethics alone. This nation asks for action, and action now.

Our greatest primary task is to put people to work. This is no unsolvable problem if we face it wisely and courageously. It can be accomplished in part by direct recruiting by the government itself, treating the task as we would treat the emergency of a war, but at the same time, through this employment, accomplishing greatly needed projects to stimulate and reorganize the use of our natural resources.

Hand in hand with this, we must frankly recognize the overbalance of population in our industrial centres and – by engaging on a national scale in a redistribution – endeavour to provide a better use of the land for those best fitted for the land. The task can be helped by definite efforts to raise the values of agricultural products and with this the power to purchase the output of our cities. It can be helped by preventing realistically the tragedy of the growing loss, through foreclosure, of our small homes and our farms. It can be helped by insistence that the federal, state, and local governments act forthwith on the demand that their cost be drastically reduced. It can be helped by the unifying of relief activities which today are often scattered, uneconomical and unequal. It can be helped by national planning for and supervision of all forms of transportation and of communications and other utilities which have a definitely public character. There are many ways in which it can be helped, but it can never be helped merely by talking about it. We must act and act quickly.

Finally, in our progress toward a resumption of work we require two safeguards against a return of the evils of the old order: there must be a strict supervision of all banking and credits and investments, so that there will be an end to speculation with other people's money; and there must be provision for an adequate but sound currency.

These are the lines of attack. I shall presently urge upon a new Congress, in special session, detailed measures for their fulfilment, and I shall seek the immediate assistance of the several states.

Through this programme of action, we address ourselves to putting our own national house in order and making income balance outgo.

Our international trade relations, though vastly important, are in point of time and necessity secondary to the establishment of a sound national economy. I favour as a practical policy the putting of first things first. I shall spare no effort to restore world trade by international economic readjustment, but the emergency at home cannot wait on that accomplishment.

The basic thought that guides these specific means of national recovery is not narrowly nationalistic. It is the insistence, as a first consideration, upon the interdependence of the various elements in and parts of the United States – a recognition of the old and permanently important manifestation of the American spirit of the pioneer. It is the way to recovery. It is the immediate way. It is the strongest assurance that the recovery will endure.

In the field of world policy I would dedicate this nation to the policy of the good neighbour – the neighbour who resolutely respects himself and, because he does so, respects the rights of others; the neighbour who respects his obligations and respects the sanctity of his agreements in and with a world of neighbours.

> *If I read the temper of our people correctly, we now realize as we have never realized before our interdependence on each other; that we cannot merely take but we must give as well...*

that if we are to go forward, we must move as a trained and loyal army, willing to sacrifice for the good of a common discipline, because without such discipline no progress is made, no leadership becomes effective. We are, I know, ready and willing to submit our lives and property to such discipline, because it makes possible a leadership which aims at a larger good. This I propose to offer, pledging that the larger purposes will bind upon us all as a sacred obligation with a unity of duty hitherto evoked only in time of armed strife.

With this pledge taken, I assume unhesitatingly the leadership of this great army of our people, dedicated to a disciplined attack upon our common problems.

Action in this image and to this end is feasible under the form of government which we have inherited from our ancestors. Our constitution is so simple and practical that it is possible always to meet extraordinary needs by changes in emphasis and arrangement without loss of essential form. That is why our constitutional system has proved itself the most superbly enduring political mechanism the modern world has produced. It has met every stress of vast expansion of territory, of foreign wars, of bitter internal strife, of world relations.

It is to be hoped that the normal balance of executive and legislative authority may be wholly adequate to meet the unprecedented task before us. But it may be that an unprecedented demand and need for undelayed action may call for temporary departure from that normal balance of public procedure.

I am prepared under my constitutional duty to recommend the measures that a stricken nation in the midst of a stricken world may require. These measures, or such other measures as the Congress may build out of its experience and wisdom, I shall seek, within my constitutional authority, to bring to speedy adoption.

But in the event that the Congress shall fail to take one of these two courses, and in the event that the national emergency is still critical, I shall not evade the clear course of duty that will then confront me. I shall ask the Congress for the one remaining instrument to meet the crisis – broad executive power to wage a war against the emergency, as great as the power that would be given to me if we were in fact invaded by a foreign foe.

For the trust reposed in me, I will return the courage and the devotion that befit the time. I can do no less.

We face the arduous days that lie before us in the warm courage of national unity; with the clear consciousness of seeking old and precious moral values; with the clean satisfaction that comes from the stern performance of duty by old and young alike. We aim at the assurance of a rounded and permanent national life.

We do not distrust the future of essential democracy.

The people of the United States have not failed. In their need they have registered a mandate that they want direct, vigorous action. They have asked for discipline and direction under leadership.

They have made me the present instrument of their wishes. In the spirit of the gift I take it.

In this dedication of a nation we humbly ask the blessing of God. May he protect each and every one of us. May he guide me in the days to come. **„**

'Long live the People's Front! Long live the alliance of all anti-fascists! Long live the people's republic!'

— La Pasionaria

6

La Pasionaria

Spanish journalist and politician

The daughter of a Basque miner, Isidora Dolores Gómez Ibárruri, known as La Pasionaria (1895–1989), was one of the founding members of the Spanish Communist Party in 1920. During the Civil War (1936–9) she became legendary for her passionate exhortations to the Spanish people to fight against the fascist forces, declaring: 'It is better to die on your feet than to live on your knees.'

'They shall not pass!'

19 July 1936, radio broadcast from Madrid, Spain

At dawn on 18 July 1936, Major General Francisco Franco – then occupying a command in the remote Canary Islands – released a manifesto in mainland Spain, declaring military rebellion against the leftist People's Front government. The uprising began that morning, and three years of bloody struggle followed.

La Pasionaria had her own reasons to loathe Franco: as the daughter of a miner, she had seen him put down the miner-led revolt of October 1934 in Asturias. She rightly saw Franco's rebellion as a calamity.

Already well known as a journalist, politician and public speaker – particularly popular among women – La Pasionaria quickly emerged as the mouthpiece of the Republican cause. This call to arms, broadcast by radio the day after Franco's manifesto, was one of many rousing speeches she made around this time, and her slogan 'They shall not pass!' became a rallying cry of the Spanish Civil War.

However, her supporters were doomed to failure. By 1 October, Franco had been declared head of state, although it was April 1939 before he was able to claim total victory.

"Workers, anti-fascists, and labouring people: rise as one man! Prepare to defend the republic, national freedom and the democratic liberties won by the people!

Everybody now knows from the communications of the government and of the People's Front[1] how serious the situation is. The workers, together with the troops which have remained loyal to the republic, are manfully and enthusiastically carrying on the struggle in Morocco and the Canary Islands.[2]

Under the slogan, 'Fascism shall not pass, the October butchers[3] shall not pass!'

Communists, socialists, anarchists and republicans, soldiers and all the forces loyal to the will of the people are routing the traitorous rebels, who have trampled in the mud and betrayed their vaunted military honour.

The whole country is shocked by the actions of these villains. They want with fire and sword to turn democratic Spain, the Spain of the people, into a hell of terrorism and torture. But they shall not pass!

All Spain has risen to the struggle. In Madrid the people have come out into the streets, lending strength to the government by their determination and fighting spirit, so that it may utterly exterminate the reactionary fascist rebels.

Young men and women: sound the alarm! Rise and join the battle!

Women, heroic women of the people: remember the heroism of the Austrian women![4] And you too fight side by side with your menfolk; together with them defend the bread and tranquillity of your children, whose lives are in danger!

Soldiers, sons of the people: stand steadfastly as one man on the side of the government, on the side of the working people, on the side of the People's Front, on the side of your fathers, brothers and comrades! March with them to victory! Fight for the Spain of 16 February![5]

Working people of all political trends!

The government has placed valuable means of defence into our hands in order that we may perform our duty with honour, in order that we may save Spain from the disgrace that would be brought upon her by a victory of the bloodthirsty October butchers. Not one of you must hesitate for a single moment, and tomorrow we shall be able to celebrate our victory.

Be prepared for action! Every worker, every anti-fascist, must regard himself as a mobilized soldier!

---

[1] The leftist coalition established in 1935, comprising liberals, socialists, communists and anarchists under the leadership of former prime minister Manuel Azaña y Díaz (1880–1940). He was elected president in 1936.
[2] The two Spanish colonies where Franco had established bases. At the time of this speech, Franco was assembling his troops in Morocco.
[3] La Pasionaria refers to Franco's brutal crushing of the revolution of October 1934.
[4] Women were active in resisting the Austrian fascist regime of 1934–8.
[5] The election won by the People's Front was held on 16 February 1936.

People of Catalonia, the Basque Country and Galicia, and all Spaniards: rise in the defence of the democratic republic, rise to consolidate the victory won by the people on 16 February! The Communist Party calls upon all of you to join the struggle. It calls upon all working people to take their place in the struggle in order completely to smash the enemies of the republic and of the freedom of the people.

Long live the People's Front!

Long live the alliance of all anti-fascists!

Long live the people's republic! "

'I lay down my burden'
– *Edward VIII*

7

Edward VIII

British monarch

Edward VIII, later HRH The Duke of Windsor (1894–1972), was the eldest son of George V (1865–1936). He succeeded his father in 1936, but abdicated less than 11 months later, prompted by general disapprobation and constitutional difficulties over his proposed marriage to the divorcee Mrs Wallis Simpson.

'*I lay down my burden*'

11 December 1936, Windsor, England

Edward was a very popular Prince of Wales in the 1920s and 1930s. His manner was charming and informal: impatient of tradition and ceremony, he hoped to modernize the British monarchy. He told his grandmother Queen Alexandra in 1914 that he would only marry someone he loved, and in the years following World War I he was attracted to many women, but none was thought suitable to marry the heir to the throne. In 1930 he met the American divorcee Wallis Simpson – who had already remarried – and became increasingly attached to her. The American newspapers publicized the relationship, but British papers did not.

When Edward succeeded to the throne on 20 January 1936, he was required to behave more formally. However, believing that the British people were beginning to accept the idea of remarriage after divorce, he planned to marry Mrs Simpson following her second divorce in October 1936. The incumbent prime minister, Stanley Baldwin, and church leaders felt strongly that a divorced woman was ineligible to be the wife and queen consort of the monarch because of his role as head of the Church of England. Edward then faced his famous romantic dilemma: he could remain king without marrying Mrs Simpson, or abdicate and marry her. He chose the latter course and made this broadcast to a stunned nation, which had been largely unaware of the situation.

Winston Churchill supported Edward at the time, but later said that his abdication had turned out for the best, since Edward's younger brother George VI was an ideal monarch and his wife, Queen Elizabeth, an ideal consort.

" At long last I am able to say a few words of my own. I have never wanted to withhold anything, but until now it has not been constitutionally possible for me to speak.

A few hours ago, I discharged my last duty as king and emperor, and now that I have been succeeded by my brother, the Duke of York,[1] my first words must be to declare my allegiance to him. This I do with all my heart.

You all know the reasons which have impelled me to renounce the Throne. But I want you to understand that in making up my mind I did not forget the country or the empire which, as Prince of Wales, and lately as king, I have for 25 years tried to serve.

But you must believe me when I tell you that I have found it impossible to carry the heavy burden of responsibility and to discharge my duties as king as I would wish to do without the help and support of the woman I love.

And I want you to know that the decision I have made has been mine and mine alone. This was a thing I had to judge entirely for myself. The other person most nearly concerned has tried up to the last to persuade me to take a different course. I have made this, the most serious decision of my life, only upon the single thought of what would in the end be best for all.

This decision has been made less difficult to me by the sure knowledge that my brother, with his long training in the public affairs of this country and with his fine qualities, will be able to take my place forthwith, without interruption or injury to the life and progress of the Empire. And he has one matchless blessing, enjoyed by so many of you and not bestowed on me – a happy home with his wife and children.

During these hard days, I have been comforted by Her Majesty my mother and by my family. The ministers of the crown, and in particular Mr Baldwin, the prime minister, have always treated me with full consideration. There has never been any constitutional difference between me and them and between me and Parliament. Bred in the constitutional tradition by my father, I should never have allowed any such issue to arise.

Ever since I was Prince of Wales, and later on when I occupied the Throne, I have been treated with the greatest kindness by all classes of the people, wherever I have lived or journeyed throughout the Empire. For that I am very grateful.

I now quit altogether public affairs, and I lay down my burden.

It may be some time before I return to my native land, but I shall always follow the fortunes of the British race and Empire with profound interest, and if at any time in the future I can be found of service to His Majesty in a private station I shall not fail.

And now we all have a new king. I wish him, and you, his people, happiness and prosperity with all my heart. God bless you all. God Save the King. "

---

[1] The British monarch George VI (1895–1952), younger brother of Edward, who reigned 1936–52.

'You can imagine what a bitter blow it is to me that all my long struggle to win peace has failed, yet I cannot believe that there is anything more, or anything different, that I could have done and that would have been more successful.'

— Neville Chamberlain

8

Neville Chamberlain

British statesman

Arthur Neville Chamberlain (1869–1940) became British prime minister in 1937. For the sake of peace, and with the country unprepared for war, in September 1938 he signed the Munich Agreement with German Chancellor Adolf Hitler, afterwards claiming to have found 'peace in our time'. Having meanwhile pressed on with rearmament, he declared war in 1939. Criticism of his war leadership accompanied initial military reverses, and in 1940 he yielded the premiership to Winston Churchill.

'This country is now at war with Germany'

3 September 1939, radio broadcast from London, England

Adolf Hitler had agreed a ten-year non-aggression pact with Poland in 1934, but early in 1939 he began laying claim to the 'Polish Corridor', which divided Germany from the Baltic and included the port of Gdánsk (known as Danzig to the Germans). Poland rejected this territorial claim and received guarantees of support from France and Britain. By early April, Hitler had formulated a plan for the invasion of Poland, and at the end of the month he renounced the Polish–German non-aggression pact. Meanwhile, diplomacy continued between Poland, Britain and France, which eventually led to military alliances being expanded and formalized. On 23 August, Chamberlain warned Hitler that Britain would stand by Poland, though the treaty was not signed until 25 August. Meanwhile, the Nazis were signing their own alliance with Russia, the Molotov–Ribbentrop Pact, which they would violate in due course.

When Germany finally invaded Poland on 1 September, the British people had little wish to go to war, but Chamberlain saw there was no alternative. Hitler's expansionist aspirations were now unmistakable, and the policies espoused by the Nazis had made Europe increasingly dangerous.

Britain, together with France, was obliged to declare war on Germany. In this famous radio broadcast to the British people, the Prime Minister outlines the events that had made this declaration unavoidable.

"This morning, the British ambassador in Berlin handed the German government a final note, stating that unless we heard from them by eleven o'clock that they were prepared at once to withdraw their troops from Poland, a state of war would exist between us.

I have to tell you now that no such undertaking has been received and that consequently this country is at war with Germany.

You can imagine what a bitter blow it is to me that all my long struggle to win peace has failed, yet I cannot believe that there is anything more, or anything different, that I could have done and that would have been more successful. Up to the very last, it would have been quite possible to arrange a peaceful and honourable settlement between Germany and Poland, but Hitler would not have it. He had evidently made up his mind to attack Poland whatever happened; and although he now says he put forward reasonable proposals which were rejected by the Poles, that is not a true statement. The proposals were never shown to the Poles, nor to us. And though they were announced in the German broadcast on Thursday night, Hitler did not wait to hear comments on them, but ordered his troops to cross the Polish frontier the next morning.

His action shows convincingly that there is no chance of expecting that this man will ever give up his practice of using force to gain his will.

He can only be stopped by force.

We and France are today, in fulfilment of our obligations, going to the aid of Poland, who is so bravely resisting this wicked and unprovoked attack on her people. We have a clear conscience. We have done all that any country could do to establish peace. The situation in which no word given by Germany's ruler could be trusted and no people or country could feel themselves safe has become intolerable. And now that we have resolved to finish it, I know that you will all play your part with calmness and courage.

When I have finished speaking, certain detailed announcements will be made on behalf of the government. Give these your closest attention. The government have made plans under which it will be possible to carry on the work of the nation in the days of stress and strain that may be ahead. But these plans need your help. You may be taking your part in the fighting services, or as a volunteer in one of the branches of civil defence. If so, you will report for duty in accordance with the instructions you have received. You may be engaged in work essential to the prosecution of war or for the maintenance of the life of the people – in factories, in transport, in public utility concerns, or in the supply of other necessaries of life. If so, it is of vital importance that you should carry on with your jobs.

Now may God bless you all. May he defend the right.

It is the evil things that we shall be fighting against – brute force, bad faith, injustice, oppression and persecution – and against them I am certain that the right will prevail."

'I have, myself, full confidence that if all do their duty ... we shall prove ourselves once again able to defend our island home, to ride out the storm of war and to outlive the menace of tyranny ...'

– *Winston Churchill*

9

Winston Churchill

British statesman and historian

Winston Leonard Spencer Churchill (1874–1965), an aristocratic Conservative MP who had served in a number of governmental positions including those of Home Secretary and Minister of Munitions, had warned of the rising Nazi threat in the mid-1930s. In 1940 Neville Chamberlain stepped down and Churchill became prime minister, seeing Britain through World War II, one of the most momentous periods in its history. Churchill quickly gained the loyalty of the British people and the confidence of the Allies. He was an accomplished orator, able to convince audiences that Britain would eventually prevail, even in the blackest moments.

'We shall fight on the beaches'

4 June 1940, London, England

The German attack on northern Europe began on 10 May 1940. It had been expected since the declaration of war by Britain and France on 3 September 1939, and during the intervening months Allied commanders had drawn up plans both defensive and offensive. When the attack began, German Panzer columns raced through Luxembourg, eastern Belgium and the Netherlands into northern France. Overwhelmed, Allied forces were forced to retreat, impeded by the surrender of the Belgian army. British and French forces fought to reach Dunkirk, where they were confined to a small area and faced annihilation after only two weeks' fighting. Churchill prepared to make a speech to the House explaining the prospect of defeat.

However, between 26 May and 2 June over 330,000 Allied troops were successfully evacuated from the beaches in what was called the 'Miracle of Dunkirk'. Although the troops had to abandon most of their equipment, their safe return to Britain averted a great catastrophe and there was national rejoicing.

Churchill's speech describes the heroic efforts of the Royal Navy and hundreds of merchant seamen in evacuating the Allied army, and the Royal Air Force for its success in defending the evacuation. But it also carries a powerful message of defiance, preparing listeners for difficult times ahead for Britain, warning that the struggle to overcome German aggression will not be easy, but assuring Britain of its ability to win through. The speech's eloquence moved many to tears – a response shared by the speaker himself.

" When a week ago today I asked the House to fix this afternoon as the occasion for a statement, I feared it would be my hard lot to announce the greatest military disaster in our long history … The whole root and core and brain of the British army – on which and around which we were to build and are to build the great British armies in the later years of the war – seemed about to perish upon the field or to be led into an ignominious and starving captivity.

That was the prospect a week ago. But another blow which might well have proved final was yet to fall upon us …

The surrender of the Belgian army compelled the British at the shortest notice to cover a flank to the sea more than 30 miles in length … It seemed impossible that any large number of Allied troops could reach the coast.

The enemy attacked on all sides with great strength and fierceness, and their main power, the power of their far more numerous air force, was thrown into the battle or else concentrated upon Dunkirk and the beaches. Pressing in upon the narrow exit, both from the east and from the west, the enemy began to fire with cannon upon the beaches by which alone the shipping could approach or depart. They sowed magnetic mines in the channels and seas; they sent repeated waves of hostile aircraft, sometimes more than 100-strong in one formation, to cast their bombs upon the single pier that remained, and upon the sand dunes upon which the troops had their eyes for shelter.

Their U-boats, one of which was sunk, and their motor launches took their toll of the vast traffic which now began. For four or five days, an intense struggle reigned. All their armoured divisions – or what was left of them – together with great masses of infantry and artillery, hurled themselves in vain upon the ever-narrowing, ever-contracting appendix within which the British and French armies fought.

Meanwhile, the Royal Navy, with the willing help of countless merchant seamen, strained every nerve to embark the British and Allied troops; 220 light warships and 650 other vessels were engaged. They had to operate upon the difficult coast, often in adverse weather, under an almost ceaseless hail of bombs and an increasing concentration of artillery fire. Nor were the seas, as I have said, themselves free from mines and torpedoes.

It was in conditions such as these that our men carried on, with little or no rest, for days and nights on end, making trip after trip across the dangerous waters, bringing with them always men whom they had rescued. The numbers they have brought back are the measure of their devotion and their courage. The hospital ships, which brought off many thousands of British and French wounded, being so plainly marked, were a special target for Nazi bombs; but the men and women on board them never faltered in their duty.

Meanwhile, the Royal Air Force, which had already been intervening in the battle, so far as its range would allow from home bases, now used part of its main metropolitan fighter strength and struck at the German bombers, and at the fighters which in large numbers protected them. This struggle was protracted and fierce.

Suddenly the scene has cleared, the crash and thunder has for the moment – but only for the moment – died away.

> *A miracle of deliverance, achieved by valour, by perseverance, by perfect discipline, by faultless service, by resource, by skill, by unconquerable fidelity, is manifest to us all …*

We must be very careful not to assign to this deliverance the attributes of a victory. Wars are not won by evacuations. But there was a victory inside this deliverance, which should be noted …

This was a great trial of strength between the British and German air forces.

Can you conceive a greater objective for the Germans in the air than to make evacuation from these beaches impossible, and to sink all these ships which were displayed, almost to the extent of thousands? Could there have been an objective of greater military importance and significance for the whole purpose of the war than this? They tried hard, and they were beaten back; they were frustrated in their task.

We got the army away; and they have paid fourfold for any losses which they have inflicted. Very large formations of German aeroplanes – and we know that they are a very brave race – have turned on several occasions from the attack of one-quarter of their number of the Royal Air Force, and have dispersed in different directions. Twelve aeroplanes have been hunted by two. One aeroplane was driven into the water and cast away, by the mere charge of a British aeroplane which had no more ammunition. All of our types – Hurricane, the Spitfire and the new Defiant – and all our pilots have been vindicated as superior to what they have at present to face …

There never had been, I suppose, in all the world, in all the history of war, such an opportunity for youth. The Knights of the Round Table, the Crusaders, all fall back into the past: not only distant but prosaic; these young men, going forth every morn to guard their native land and all that we stand for, holding in their hands these instruments of colossal and shattering power … deserve our gratitude, as do all of the brave men who, in so many ways and on so many occasions, are ready, and continue ready, to give life and all for their native land …

I return to the army. In the long series of very fierce battles, now on this front, now on that, fighting on three fronts at once … our losses in men have exceeded 30,000 killed, wounded and missing. I take occasion to express the sympathy of the House to all who have suffered bereavement or who are still anxious … But I will say this about the missing. We have had a large number of wounded come home safely to this country, but I would say about the missing that there may be very many reported missing who will come back home, some day, in one way or another …

Against this loss of over 30,000 men, we can set a far heavier loss certainly inflicted upon the enemy.

But our losses in material are enormous … The best of all we had to give had gone to the British Expeditionary Force, and although they had not the numbers of tanks and some articles of equipment which were desirable, they were a very well and finely equipped army. They had the first fruits of all that our industry had to give, and that is gone. And now here is this further delay. How long it will be, how long it will last, depends upon the exertions which we make in this island.

An effort the like of which has never been seen in our records is now being made. Work is proceeding everywhere, night and day, Sundays and weekdays. Capital and labour have cast aside their interests, rights and customs and put them into the common stock. Already the flow of munitions has leapt forward. There is no reason why we should not in a few months overtake the sudden and serious loss that has come upon us, without retarding the development of our general programme.

Nevertheless … the French army has been weakened, the Belgian army has been lost, a large part of those fortified lines upon which so much faith had been reposed is gone, many valuable mining districts and factories have passed into the enemy's possession, the whole of the Channel ports are in his hands, with all the tragic consequences that follow from that, and we must expect another blow to be struck almost immediately at us or at France. We are told that Herr Hitler has a plan for invading the British Isles …

We have, for the time being in this island, incomparably more powerful military forces than we have ever had at any moment in this war or the last. But this will not continue. We shall not be content with a defensive war. We have our duty to our Ally.[1] We have to reconstitute and build up the British Expeditionary Force once again, under its gallant commander-in-chief, Lord Gort. All this is in train; but in the interval we must put our defences in this island into such a high state of organization that the fewest possible numbers will be required to give effective security and that the largest possible potential of offensive effort may be realized.

On this we are now engaged …

Turning once again, and this time more generally, to the question of invasion, I would observe that there has never been a period in all these long centuries of which we boast when an absolute guarantee against invasion, still less against serious raids, could have been given to our people …

There was always the chance [of invasion], and it is that chance which has excited and befooled the imaginations of many Continental tyrants.

Many are the tales that are told. We are assured that novel methods will be adopted, and when we see the originality of malice, the ingenuity of aggression which our enemy displays, we may certainly prepare ourselves for every kind of novel stratagem and every kind of brutal and treacherous manoeuvre. I think that no idea is so outlandish that it should not

[1] Churchill refers to France, which was still attempting to repel the German invasion, though it would surrender three weeks later.

be considered and viewed with a searching – but at the same time, I hope, with a steady – eye. We must never forget the solid assurances of sea-power and those which belong to air power if it can be locally exercised.

I have, myself, full confidence that if all do their duty … we shall prove ourselves once again able to defend our island home, to ride out the storm of war and to outlive the menace of tyranny, if necessary for years, if necessary alone. At any rate, that is what we are going to try to do. That is the resolve of His Majesty's Government – every man of them. That is the will of Parliament and the nation …

Even though large tracts of Europe and many old and famous states have fallen or may fall into the grip of the Gestapo[2] and all the odious apparatus of Nazi rule, we shall not flag or fail.

We shall go on to the end, we shall fight in France, we shall fight on the seas and oceans, we shall fight with growing confidence and growing strength in the air, we shall defend our island, whatever the cost may be,

… we shall fight on the beaches, we shall fight on the landing grounds, we shall fight in the fields and in the streets, we shall fight in the hills; we shall never surrender …

And even if – which I do not for a moment believe – this island or a large part of it were subjugated and starving, then our empire beyond the seas, armed and guarded by the British fleet, would carry on the struggle, until in God's good time, the new world, with all its power and might, steps forth to the rescue and the liberation of the old. 🙰🙰

[2] Germany's Geheime Staatspolizei ('Secret State Police'), shortened to Gestapo, was known for its brutality.

'The Red Army, Red Navy and all citizens of the Soviet Union must defend every inch of Soviet soil, must fight to the last drop of blood for our towns and villages, must display the daring, initiative and mental alertness that are inherent in our people ...'

– *Joseph Stalin*

10

Joseph Stalin

Russian revolutionary and leader

After the October Revolution (1917), Joseph Stalin (1879–1953) was appointed Commissar for Nationalities and a member of the Politburo. With his appointment as General Secretary to the Central Committee in 1922, Stalin stealthily began to build up the power. After Lenin's death (1924) he assumed control and set about a reorganization of the USSR's resources with successive five-year plans. Stalin moved to 'discipline' those who opposed his will, bringing death by execution or famine to some 10 million peasants (1932–3). After his exclusion from the Munich Conference (1938), Stalin signed a non-aggression pact with Nazi Germany, which allowed him to prepare for the German invasion of 1941. Eventually, the Germans were defeated in a war of attrition. In the aftermath of World War II he inaugurated the 'Cold War' against all non-communist countries, while at home his ruthless purge of all opposition continued. He died in mysterious circumstances in 1953.

'The issue is one of life and death for the Soviet state'

3 July 1941, radio broadcast from Moscow, Russia

The USSR was ill-prepared for the German invasion of June 1941, code-named Operation Barbarossa after a 12th-century Holy Roman Emperor. Despite the non-aggression pact of 1939 – which included plans to divide up the countries of eastern Europe – Stalin had foreseen the possibility of German aggression, but did not expect it as soon as this.

The USSR's Red Army was well armed and plentiful in numbers – giving rise to some complacency – but its troops lacked training and communications equipment. Moreover, many of its most experienced officers and strategists had been killed or imprisoned during Stalin's ideological purges of 1936–8, and those who remained tended to tell him what he wanted to hear. Their German adversaries, meanwhile, were supremely well drilled and confident, having conquered much of Europe. The Luftwaffe – far better equipped than the Soviet air force – and Panzer tank divisions swiftly decimated Soviet positions.

This radio address, given less than two weeks after the invasion, was an effective morale-booster, employing familiar martial slogans such as 'Forward to victory!'. Its fiery rhetoric fuels faith in the Soviet forces, encourages civilians to participate in the fray and incites hatred for the invaders.

But it was not enough to forestall the rapid advance of German forces. By August 1941, they had reached the outskirts of Leningrad, which was under siege for 900 days. The Germans were eventually halted in November, after failing to take Moscow. A long and bitter struggle ensued, with heavy losses both to the combatants and to civilians.

"Comrades, citizens, brothers and sisters, men of our Army and Navy: my words are addressed to you, dear friends!

The perfidious attack by Hitlerite Germany on our fatherland, begun on 22 June, is continuing.

In spite of the heroic resistance of the Red Army, and although the enemy's finest divisions and finest air force units have already been smashed and have met their doom on the field of battle, the enemy continues to push forward, hurling fresh forces to the front …

How could it have happened that our glorious Red Army surrendered a number of our cities and districts to the fascist armies? Is it really true that the German-fascist troops are invincible, as the braggart fascist propagandists are ceaselessly blaring forth?

Of course not! History shows that there are no invincible armies and never have been. Napoleon's army was considered invincible, but it was beaten successively by the armies of Russia, England and Germany. Kaiser Wilhelm's German army in the period of the First Imperialist War was also considered invincible, but it was beaten several times by Russian and Anglo-French troops, and was finally smashed by the Anglo-French forces. The same must be said of Hitler's German-fascist army of today.

This army had not yet met with serious resistance on the continent of Europe. Only on our territory has it met with serious resistance. And if, as a result of this resistance, the finest divisions of Hitler's German-fascist army have been defeated by our Red Army, this means that it too can be smashed and will be smashed, as were the armies of Napoleon and Wilhelm …

It may be asked, how could the Soviet government have consented to conclude a non-aggression pact with such perfidious people, such fiends as Hitler and Ribbentrop?[1]

Was this not an error on the part of the Soviet government? Of course not!

Non-aggression pacts are pacts of peace between two states. It was such a pact that Germany proposed to us in 1939. Could the Soviet government have declined such a proposal? I think that not a single peace-loving state could decline a peace treaty with a neighbouring state, even though the latter were headed by such monsters and cannibals as Hitler and Ribbentrop. But that, of course, only on the one indispensable condition – that this peace treaty did not jeopardize, either directly or indirectly, the territorial integrity, independence and honour of the peace-loving state. As is well known, the non-aggression pact between Germany and the USSR was precisely such a pact …

What has fascist Germany gained and what has she lost by perfidiously tearing up the pact and attacking the USSR? She has gained a certain advantageous position for her troops for a short period of time, but she has lost politically by exposing herself in the eyes of the entire world as a bloodthirsty aggressor. There can be no doubt that this short-lived military gain

[1] The Nazi politician Joachim von Ribbentrop (1893–1946) served as German Foreign Minister, 1938–45. On 23 August 1939, he signed a non-aggression pact in Moscow with the Soviet Foreign Minister, Vyacheslav Molotov (1890–1986). This held until 22 June 1941, when Hitler launched Operation Barbarossa.

for Germany is only an episode, while the tremendous political gain of the USSR is a weighty and lasting factor that is bound to form the basis for the development of outstanding military successes of the Red Army in the war with fascist Germany.

That is why the whole of our valiant Red Army, the whole of our valiant Navy, all the falcons of our Air Force, all the peoples of our country, all the finest men and women of Europe, America and Asia, and, finally, all the finest men and women of Germany – denounce the treacherous acts of the German-fascists, sympathize with the Soviet government, approve of its conduct, and see that ours is a just cause, that the enemy will be defeated, and that we are bound to win …

The enemy is cruel and implacable.

He is out to seize our lands, watered by the sweat of our brows, to seize our grain and oil secured by the labour of our hands. He is out to restore the rule of the landlords, to restore Tsarism, to destroy the national culture and the existence as states of the Russians, Ukrainians, Byelorussians, Lithuanians, Latvians, Estonians, Uzbeks, Tatars, Moldavians, Georgians, Armenians, Azerbaijanians and the other free peoples of the Soviet Union, to Germanize them, to turn them into the slaves of German princes and barons.

Thus the issue is one of life and death for the Soviet state, of life and death for the peoples of the USSR;

… the issue is whether the peoples of the Soviet Union shall be free or fall into slavery.

The Soviet people must realize this and abandon all complacency; they must mobilize themselves and reorganize all their work on a new, war-time footing, where there can be no mercy to the enemy …

All our work must be immediately reorganized on a war footing; everything must be subordinated to the interests of the front and the task of organizing the destruction of the enemy.

The peoples of the Soviet Union now see that German fascism is untameable in its savage fury and hatred of our native country, which has ensured all its working people labour in freedom and prosperity. The peoples of the Soviet Union must risk against the enemy and defend their rights and their land.

The Red Army, Red Navy and all citizens of the Soviet Union must defend every inch of Soviet soil, must fight to the last drop of blood for our towns and villages, must display the daring, initiative and mental alertness that are inherent in our people …

In areas occupied by the enemy, guerrilla units, mounted and on foot, must be formed; sabotage groups must be organized to combat enemy units, to foment guerrilla warfare everywhere, blow up bridges and roads, damage telephone and telegraph lines, set fire to forests, stores and transports. In occupied regions conditions must be made unbearable for the enemy and all his accomplices. They must be hounded and annihilated at every step, and all their measures frustrated.

The war with fascist Germany cannot be considered an ordinary war.

It is not only a war between two armies, it is also a great war of the entire Soviet people against the German-fascist armies. The aim of this national patriotic war in defence of our country against the fascist oppressors is not only to eliminate the danger hanging over our country, but also to aid all the European peoples groaning under the yoke of German fascism …

Comrades, our forces are numberless. The overweening enemy will soon learn this to his cost. Side by side with the Red Army, many thousands of workers, collective farmers and intellectuals are rising to fight the enemy aggressor. The masses of our people will rise up in their millions. The working people of Moscow and Leningrad have already begun to form huge People's Guards in support of the Red Army. Such People's Guards must be raised in every city which is in danger of enemy invasion;

… all the working people must be roused to defend with their lives their freedom, their honour and their country in this patriotic war against German fascism.

In order to ensure the rapid mobilization of all the forces of the peoples of the USSR and to repulse the enemy who has treacherously attacked our country, a State Committee of Defence has been formed and the entire state authority has now been vested in it. The State Committee of Defence has entered on the performance of its functions and calls upon all our people to rally around the party of Lenin and Stalin and around the Soviet government, so as to render self-sacrificing support to the Red Army and Red Navy, to exterminate the enemy and secure victory.

All our forces for the support of our heroic Red Army and our glorious Red Navy! All the forces of the people for the destruction of the enemy! Forward to victory! **""**

11

Joseph Goebbels

German politician

Paul Joseph Goebbels (1897–1945) was an enthusiastic supporter of Adolf Hitler and joined the Nazi Party in 1924. With Hitler's accession to power, 'Jupp' was made head of the Ministry of Public Enlightenment and Propaganda. A bitter anti-Semite, he had a gift for mob oratory which made him a powerful exponent of the more radical aspects of the Nazi philosophy. He retained Hitler's confidence to the last. In the Berlin bunker where Hitler spent his final days, Goebbels and his wife, Magda, committed suicide after they had taken the lives of their six children.

'Let the storm break loose'

18 February 1943, Berlin, Germany

The opening stages of World War II had seen Germany triumphantly overrunning much of northern Europe. By November 1942, Germany had also made significant progress on the Eastern Front, driving deep into the Soviet Union. But Soviet resistance then forced German withdrawal, isolating the German Sixth Army at Stalingrad. By the end of January 1943, the Sixth Army had surrendered, while German forces in North Africa had retreated from the Allies. The tide of the war had turned.

As Hitler's chief propagandist, Goebbels knew it was vital that the German people did not weaken at the news of these reverses. On 18 February 1943, in front of film cameras and radio microphones, he addressed a specially selected audience of thousands, a cross-section of German society which included veterans of the Eastern Front. In the hour-long speech, of which this an edited section, Goebbels skilfully manipulated his audience to give enthusiastic vocal support to the concept of total war – the complete mobilization of the country's material and human resources. He employed the technique of posing dramatic questions to the audience, well aware that their responses would be broadcast to the world.

Goebbels said afterwards of his listeners, 'They applauded at just the right moments: it was the politically best-trained audience you can find in Germany.' Hitler's chief architect, Albert Speer, commented that, while Goebbels' delivery of the speech appeared highly emotional, it had been a calculated act. This translation is by Randall Bytwerk.

" You, my hearers, at this moment represent the whole nation. I wish to ask you ten questions that you will answer for the German people throughout the world – but especially for our enemies, who are listening to us on the radio.

[The crowd is at the peak of excitement. Each individual feels as if he is being spoken to personally. With full participation and enthusiasm, the crowd answers each question.]

The English maintain that the German people has lost faith in victory.

I ask you: Do you believe with the Führer and us in the final total victory of the German people? I ask you: Are you resolved to follow the Führer through thick and thin to victory, and are you willing to accept the heaviest personal burdens in the fight for victory?

Second: the English say that the German people are tired of fighting. I ask you: Are you ready to follow the Führer as the phalanx of the homeland, standing behind the fighting army, and to wage war with wild determination through all the turns of fate until victory is ours?

Third: the English maintain that the German people have no desire any longer to accept the government's growing demands for war work. I ask you: Are you and the German people willing to work, if the Führer orders, ten, twelve and if necessary fourteen hours a day and to give everything for victory?

Fourth: the English maintain that the German people are resisting the government's total war measures. They do not want total war, but capitulation!

[Shouts: 'Never! Never! Never!']

I ask you: Do you want total war?

If necessary,

... do you want a war more total and radical than anything that we can even imagine today?

Fifth: the English maintain that the German people have lost faith in the Führer. I ask you: is your confidence in the Führer greater, more faithful and unshakable than ever before? Are you absolutely and completely ready to follow him wherever he goes and do all that is necessary to bring the war to a victorious end?

[Thousands of voices join in shouting: 'Führer, command, we follow!' A wave of shouts of 'Heil!' flows through the hall.]

Sixth, I ask you: are you ready from now on to give your full strength to provide the Eastern Front with the men and munitions it needs to give Bolshevism the death blow?

Seventh, I ask you: do you take a holy oath to the front that the homeland stands firm behind them, and that you will give them everything they need to win the victory?

Eighth, I ask you: do you, especially you women, want the government to do all it can to encourage German women to put their full strength at work to support the war effort, and to release men for the front whenever possible, thereby helping the men at the front?

Ninth, I ask you: do you approve, if necessary, the most radical measures against a small group of shirkers and black-marketeers who pretend there is peace in the middle of war and use the need of the nation for their own selfish purposes? Do you agree that those who harm the war effort should lose their heads?

Tenth and lastly, I ask you: do you agree that above all in war, according to the National Socialist Party platform, the same rights and duties should apply to all, that the homeland should bear the heavy burdens of the war together, and that the burdens should be shared equally between high and low and rich and poor?

I have asked: you have given me your answers. You are part of the people, and your answers are those of the German people. You have told our enemies what they needed to hear so that they will have no false illusions or ideas.

Now, just as in the first hours of our rule and through the ten years that followed, we are bound firmly in brotherhood with the German people. The most powerful ally on earth, the people themselves, stand behind us and are determined to follow the Führer, come what may. They will accept the heaviest burdens to gain victory. What power on earth can hinder us from reaching our goal? Now we must and will succeed!

I stand before you not only as the spokesman of the government, but as the spokesman of the people … We are all children of our people, forged together by this critical hour of our national history. We promise you, we promise the front, we promise the Führer, that we will mould together the homeland into a force on which the Führer and his fighting soldiers can rely on absolutely and blindly. We pledge to do all in our life and work that is necessary for victory … With burning hearts and cool heads we will overcome the major problems of this phase of the war. We are on the way to eventual victory. That victory rests on our faith in the Führer.

This evening I once again remind the whole nation of its duty. The Führer expects us to do that which will throw all we have done in the past into the shadows. We do not want to fail him. As we are proud of him, he should be proud of us.

The great crises and upsets of national life show who the true men and women are. We have no right any longer to speak of the weaker sex, for both sexes are displaying the same determination and spiritual strength. The nation is ready for anything. The Führer has commanded, and we will follow him. In this hour of national reflection and contemplation, we believe firmly and unshakably in victory. We see it before us, we need only reach for it. We must resolve to subordinate everything to it. That is the duty of the hour. Let the slogan be: 'Now, people rise up and let the storm break loose!'

[Goebbels' final words were lost in a storm of applause.]

'We have the moral right, we had the duty to our people to do it, to kill this people who would kill us.'

– *Heinrich Himmler*

12

Heinrich Himmler

German politician and chief of police

Heinrich Luitpold Himmler (1900–45) joined the Nazi Party in 1925, and in 1929 Adolf Hitler made him head of the SS (Schutzstaffel, 'protection squadron'), which he developed from Hitler's personal bodyguard into a powerful party weapon. Inside Germany and later in Nazi-occupied countries, he developed the Gestapo (Geheime Staatspolizei, 'secret state police') and used this ruthless organization to unleash an unmatched political and anti-Semitic terror of espionage, wholesale detention, mass deportation, torture, execution and massacre. In July 1944, he was made commander-in-chief of the home forces and in April 1945 proposed an unconditional surrender to the Allies. Hitler immediately stripped him of power and issued orders for his arrest. Himmler disappeared but was captured by the British near Bremen. He committed suicide by swallowing a cyanide phial concealed in his mouth and thereby escaped trial for his central role in the murder of over seven million people.

'I am talking about ... the extermination of the Jewish people'

4 October 1943, Posen (Poznań), Poland

This horrifying speech illuminates the steady development of the Nazi genocide project. The official persecution of German Jews – and the establishment of concentration camps to house 'enemies of the state' – began soon after Hitler's appointment as chancellor in 1933. The Nazi Party itself was purged in 1934, and the Nuremberg Laws of September 1935 denied German citizenship to Jews and other 'non-Aryans'. On Kristallnacht ('night of crystals') in November 1938, Jewish businesses were ransacked, looted and burned. Concentration camps became extermination centres following the Wannsee Conference in January 1942, at which Nazi leaders discussed the destruction of all European Jews – the 'Final Solution to the Jewish Question'.

However, the enormity of this plan was daunting, practically as well as morally. In a three-hour speech to SS officers in Nazi-occupied Poland, Himmler demanded the suppression of squeamishness and mercy. He also emphasized the need for discipline and secrecy, thus implicating his deputies in the crime of the Holocaust. Yet, despite the clandestine circumstances, he had the meeting tape-recorded, even interrupting his speech to ensure that the recorder was working. The tapes later fell into the hands of the US military and were preserved as evidence of Nazi war crimes. This is a short extract from the transcript.

" I want to mention a very difficult subject before you, with complete candour. It should be discussed amongst us, yet nevertheless, we will never speak about it in public. Just as we did not hesitate in June[1] to carry out our duty as ordered, and stand comrades who had failed against the wall and shoot them – about which we have never spoken, and never will speak. That was, thank God, a kind of tact natural to us, a foregone conclusion of that tact, that we have never conversed about it amongst ourselves, never spoken about it. Everyone shuddered, and everyone was clear that the next time he would do the same thing again, if it were commanded and necessary.

I am talking about the evacuation of the Jews, the extermination of the Jewish people.

It is one of those things that is easily said. 'The Jewish people is being exterminated,' every party member will tell you. 'Perfectly clear: it's part of our plans. We're eliminating the Jews, exterminating them, a small matter.'

And then along they all come, all the 80 million upright Germans, and each one has his decent Jew. They say: 'All the others are swine, but here is a first-class Jew.' *[Some laughter.]* And none of them has seen it, has endured it. Most of you will know what it means when 100 bodies lie together, when 500 are there or when there are 1,000.

And to have seen this through and – with the exception of human weakness – to have remained decent, has made us hard and is a page of glory never mentioned and never to be mentioned.

Because we know how difficult things would be if today – in every city, during the bomb attacks, the burdens of war and the privations – we still had Jews as secret saboteurs, agitators and instigators.

We would probably be at the same stage as in 1916/17, if the Jews still resided in the body of the German people.

We have taken away the riches that they had, and I have given a strict order, which Obergruppenführer Pohl[2] has carried out. We have delivered these riches to the Reich, to the State. We have taken nothing from them for ourselves. A few, who have offended against this, will be [judged][3] in accordance with an order that I gave at the beginning: he who takes even one mark of this is a dead man.

A number of SS men have offended against this order. They are very few, and they will be dead men without mercy!

We have the moral right, we had the duty to our people to do it, to kill this people who would kill us.

---

[1] In the SS purge of 30 June–1 July 1934, known as 'The Night of the Long Knives', over 70 leading Nazis were murdered.
[2] The German naval officer Oswald Pohl (1892–1951) was an SS leader and a key player in the Holocaust. He survived the war and was eventually hanged for war crimes. During his trial testimony he claimed this was the first time he had been told officially that the 'Final Solution' meant the extermination of the Jews.
[3] The word was not spoken but implied.

We, however, do not have the right to enrich ourselves with even one fur, with one mark, with one cigarette, with one watch, with anything that we do not have.

Because we don't want, at the end of all this, to get sick and die from the same bacillus that we have exterminated.

I will never see it happen that even one bit of putrefaction comes in contact with us, or takes root in us. On the contrary, where it might try to take root, we will burn it out together. But altogether we can say: we have carried out this most difficult task for the love of our people. And we have suffered no defect within us, in our soul, or in our character. **"**

'Paris outraged! Paris broken!
Paris martyred! But Paris
liberated!'
– *Charles de Gaulle*

13

Charles de Gaulle

French military and political leader

At the time of the German invasion of France in 1940, Charles André Joseph Marie de Gaulle (1890–1970) was a general as well as Under-Secretary of War. Days before France signed an armistice with the German invaders he sought refuge in England to found the Free French Army. Though largely ignored by both Winston Churchill and Franklin D Roosevelt, he served as a focus for the resistance movement during the rest of the war. He returned to Paris in 1944 with the first liberation forces and became the country's first post-war leader. To many British and American politicians, de Gaulle epitomized Gallic obstinacy and self-interest; but while he could not match Churchill's brilliance in wartime, he may be regarded as a more influential and effective national leader in peacetime.

'Paris outraged! Paris broken! Paris martyred! But Paris liberated!'

25 August 1944, Paris, France

When de Gaulle made his triumphal return to Paris, France had been under German control for more than four years.

Following his escape to London in 1940, he had been sentenced to death for treason by the Vichy government, which was little more than a puppet regime of the Nazis; but he soon established himself as leader of the Free French Forces. In 1943, he moved his headquarters to the liberated French territory of Algeria.

In summer 1944, Allied forces landed in France (from the north in June; from the south in August), pushing back the German occupiers. As US troops closed in on Paris, the citizens went on strike and launched skirmishes against the occupying Germans. US forces under General Dwight D Eisenhower hesitated, aware that Adolf Hitler had ordered his troops to destroy the city rather than surrender it. Fearful of a massacre – and eager to pre-empt American military control of Paris – de Gaulle ordered the Free French Forces into Paris, and it was to them that the Germans surrendered on 24 August. This was a triumph for de Gaulle – who had flown in from Algiers that day – not least because US president Franklin D Roosevelt mistrusted him and had initially recognized the Vichy government.

The following day, de Gaulle addressed the expectant crowds from the Hôtel de Ville, announcing the liberation of the city and the restoration of French pride. In his speech, he plays successfully to the crowd's patriotism, personifying Paris as a heroic survivor, 'bleeding but resolute'.

On 28 August, he brought the provisional government home to Paris.

" Why try to resist the emotion which now seizes all of us, men and women alike, who are here at home, in a Paris standing tall, liberating herself, and able to do so with her own hands?

No! We shall not hide this profound and sacred emotion. These are overwhelming events in every one of our poor lives.

Paris! Paris outraged! Paris broken! Paris martyred! But Paris liberated! Liberated by herself, liberated by her people, supported by the armies of France, with the support and empowerment of all France,

... the France who fights back, the only France, the true France, the eternal France.

Well now! Since the enemy who held Paris has surrendered into our hands, France herself may return home to Paris.

She returns here, bleeding but resolute. She returns here enlightened by a great lesson, but more certain than ever of her obligations and her rights.

I shall speak first of her obligations, and I summarize them in full when I say that, for the moment, we must concern ourselves with obligations of war. The enemy is flagging but he is not yet beaten. He remains on our soil. We must not consider ourselves satisfied simply because, with the support of our beloved and esteemed allies, we have driven him from our home. We must invade his territory, for that is the victor's duty.

That is why the French advance party entered Paris with cannon fire. That is why the great French army of Italy has disembarked in the Midi,[1] and is making its way swiftly up the Rhône valley. That is why our brave, beloved forces of the interior will equip themselves with modern weapons. We must have revenge, retaliation, justice: that is why we shall continue to fight until the final day, until the day of complete and total victory.

All men here, and all who hear us throughout France, know that this duty of war demands national unity. Those others of us – we who shall have witnessed the greatest hours of our history – need desire nothing but to prove ourselves worthy of France right until the end.

Long live France! "

[1] A general term for the south of France.

14
Ho Chi Minh

Vietnamese statesman

Ho Chi Minh (1890–1969) founded the Viet Minh Independence League in 1941, directing successful military operations against the Japanese occupiers and later against the French. After declaring Vietnam's independence in 1945, he led the successful military operation against the French in the Indochina War (1946–54). After the partition of the country in 1954, he became prime minister (1954–5) and president (1954–69) of communist North Vietnam. Re-elected in 1960, he enlisted Chinese support in the war between North and South Vietnam and became a leading force in the conflict in the 1960s as it widened to draw in other countries, primarily the USA. Despite massive US military intervention in support of South Vietnam (1965–73), Ho Chi Minh's Viet Cong liberation front retained the initiative and forced a ceasefire in 1973, four years after the president's death.

'Vietnam has the right to be a free and independent country'

2 September 1945, Hanoi, Vietnam

Ho Chi Minh's opportunistic declaration of Vietnamese independence was a direct result of World War II. As part of Indochina, the country had been a valued French colony since 1868, but Japan invaded in 1940 and France was forced to recognize Japanese rule, in return for nominal sovereignty.

With American support, Ho's Viet Minh Independence League waged a guerrilla war against the Japanese occupiers. In March 1945, fearing an American invasion, the Japanese ousted France's nominal colonial rulers, installing the Vietnamese emperor Bao Dai (1913–97) as their puppet ruler. Five months later, Japan surrendered, Bao Dai abdicated, and the Viet Minh gained effective control over much of Vietnam.

On 2 September 1945, Japan signed the surrender agreement ending World War II. Ho seized his opportunity to declare Vietnam's independence, which he announced in this speech, given at Ba Dinh Square in Hanoi.

Ho Chi Minh begins by quoting from the American Declaration of Independence, of which he had been given a copy by his allies in US military intelligence. Denouncing the economic enslavement of Vietnam by France, he then proclaims the formation of the Democratic Republic of Vietnam.

" 'All men are created equal. They are endowed by their Creator with certain unalienable rights; among these are life, liberty, and the pursuit of happiness.'

This immortal statement was made in the Declaration of Independence of the United States of America in 1776. In a broader sense, this means: all the peoples on the earth are equal from birth; all the peoples have a right to live, to be happy and free.

The declaration of the French Revolution, made in 1791, on the rights of man and the citizen also states: 'All men are born free and with equal rights, and must always remain free and have equal rights.'[1] These are undeniable truths.

Nevertheless, for more than 80 years, the French imperialists, abusing the standard of liberty, equality, and fraternity, have violated our fatherland and oppressed our fellow citizens. They have acted contrary to the ideals of humanity and justice.

In the field of politics, they have deprived our people of every democratic liberty …

In the field of economics, they have fleeced us to the backbone, impoverished our people and devastated our land …

In the autumn of 1940, when the Japanese fascists violated Indochina's territory to establish new bases in their fight against the Allies, the French imperialists went down on their bended knees and handed over our country to them.

Thus, from that date, our people were subjected to the double yoke of the French and the Japanese. Their sufferings and miseries increased. The result was that, from the end of last year to the beginning of this year, from Quang Tri Province to the north of Vietnam, more than two million of our fellow citizens died from starvation.

On March 9 [1945], the French troops were disarmed by the Japanese. The French colonialists either fled or surrendered, showing that not only were they incapable of 'protecting' us, but that, in the span of five years, they had twice sold our country to the Japanese.

On several occasions before March 9, the Viet Minh League urged the French to ally themselves with it against the Japanese. Instead of agreeing to this proposal, the French colonialists so intensified their terrorist activities against the Viet Minh members, that before fleeing they massacred a great number of our political prisoners detained at Yen Bay and Cao Bang.

Notwithstanding all this, our fellow citizens have always manifested toward the French a tolerant and humane attitude. Even after the Japanese putsch of March 1945, the Viet Minh League helped many Frenchmen to cross the frontier, rescued some of them from Japanese jails, and protected French lives and property.

---

[1] Ho seems to refer to the Declaration of the Rights of Man and of the Citizen, which was approved by France's National Assembly in August 1789.

In the autumn of 1940, our country had in fact ceased to be a French colony and had become a Japanese possession.

After the Japanese had surrendered to the Allies, our whole people rose to regain our national sovereignty and to found the Democratic Republic of Vietnam. The truth is that we have wrested our independence from the Japanese and not from the French.

The French have fled, the Japanese have capitulated, Emperor Bao Dai has abdicated. Our people have broken the chains which for nearly a century have fettered them and have won independence for the fatherland. Our people at the same time have overthrown the monarchic regime that has reigned supreme for dozens of centuries. In its place has been established the present democratic republic.

For these reasons, we, members of the provisional government, representing the whole Vietnamese people, declare that from now on we break off all relations of a colonial character with France; we repeal all the international obligations that France has so far subscribed to on behalf of Vietnam, and we abolish all the special rights the French have unlawfully acquired in our fatherland.

The whole Vietnamese people, animated by a common purpose, are determined to fight to the bitter end against any attempt by the French colonialists to reconquer their country. We are convinced that the Allied nations, which at Teheran[2] and San Francisco[3] have acknowledged the principles of self-determination and equality of nations, will not refuse to acknowledge the independence of Vietnam.

A people who have courageously opposed French domination for more than 80 years, a people who have fought side by side with the Allies against the fascists during these last years, such a people must be free and independent.

For these reasons,

> *... we, members of the provisional government of the Democratic Republic of Vietnam, solemnly declare to the world that Vietnam has the right to be a free and independent country ...*

– and in fact it is so already. The entire Vietnamese people are determined to mobilize all their physical and mental strength, to sacrifice their lives and property in order to safeguard their independence and liberty. ""

---

[2] At the Teheran Conference (November–December 1943) the Allied leaders Churchill, Franklin D Roosevelt and Stalin had discussed, *inter alia*, the establishment of a post-war international organization.

[3] The San Francisco Conference or United Nations Conference on International Organization (April–June 1945) was the international meeting at which the United Nations Organization was established.

'They had a proud share in this feat of combat and development, one that will be immortalized in the ageless annals of Zion set free, that will be a monument to Jewish prowess in arms and in labour, the passport, now and always, to victory.'

– *David Ben-Gurion*

15

David Ben-Gurion

Israeli statesman

The Polish-born David Ben-Gurion originally David Gruen (1886–1973) emigrated to Palestine in 1906. A keen Zionist, he led the Mapai (Labour) Party from its formation in 1930 and after independence became prime minister of Israel (1948–53). During this period, he was responsible for the country's absorption of large numbers of refugees from Europe and Arab countries. He served as prime minister again from 1955 to 1963. He retired from politics in 1970 and spent the remainder of his life on a kibbutz.

'We dedicate today this Road of Valour'

12 December 1948, Ayalon, Israel

The roots of this speech can be traced back many centuries. The Jewish people believe that God promised them Canaan (or Palestine, the land between the Jordan and the Mediterranean) following their escape from Egypt. Despite a period of exile, they dominated the area until Roman times, when they were dispersed, and Palestine became home to Arabs. Following World War I, Britain administered Palestine under a League of Nations mandate (1922–47), during which time many Jews escaped from Nazi persecution to Palestine. Jews and Arabs lived together, but calls for a Jewish homeland provoked conflict with the majority Arab population.

In November 1947, the United Nations adopted a plan to partition Palestine into Jewish and Arab states, each comprising sections linked by extraterritorial roads. The Arabs rejected this scheme and war broke out. Roads linking Jewish settlements ran through Arab-controlled areas, enabling them to control access.

Operation Nachshon began in April 1948, with the aim of clearing a road to Jerusalem. After initial success, Jerusalem was again besieged. On 14 May, David Ben-Gurion announced Israel's independence; the following day the British mandate ended and Israel was invaded by her Arab neighbours. A route through the mountains to Jerusalem was forged on 9 June, and following further Israeli military successes, the country's borders were largely secured by the end of October.

On 11 December, UN Resolution 194 proposed a Conciliation Commission for the area, and the following day Ben-Gurion gave this rousing speech, dedicating the road to Jerusalem and celebrating the city's deliverance by Israeli troops.

On the road we open today is set the crown of our fight for the homeland and freedom.

Into its making went the most tragic heroism and the greatest grandeur of that fight, since the day we were called to face our many enemies and save Jerusalem.

This was the heart and soul of the War of Independence that has raged over the country now for more than a year. It was, it still is, a struggle in the eternal city[1] and round about it, and even more a struggle for the road to it. On mastery of the road hangs the city's fate.

Our Third Return[2] to Israel took a course opposite to the First and the Second.

We have come now not westering from the East, but from the Occident moving eastward; not from desert to sea, but from sea to desert. Of the three regions of the land – mountains, lowland and valley – we possessed the valley first. We took only little of the lowlands, and late. Of the mountains, we held almost nothing except for Jerusalem, which in every generation from every quarter drew Jews to it.

Within the last century, this magnetism has turned Jerusalem into a Jewish metropolis, with a great and growing Jewish majority. But it also meant that Jewish Jerusalem stood severed from the main centres of rural and urban settlement, for it was the coastal belt we held for the most part, and the valleys of Jezreel and Jordan, north of Lake Tiberias and south of it. In normal times, the threat to Jerusalem did not strike the eye. An hour's journey to Tel Aviv seemed of little concern, so long as it was safe.

How deadly was the danger soon appeared when the Arab states sought to encompass us. Many and bitter were the hurts our settlements endured in this War of Independence: the suffering of Jerusalem alone was sevenfold. Our enemy knew the mortal stroke he might with ease deliver was to seize and destroy this city of ours, distant from all concentrations of Jewish force and surrounded on all sides by a numerous, compact and daring Arab population in towns and villages whence every road led to Jerusalem.

The Jews had only one and almost its entire length traversed Arab areas, up hill and down dale, from Abu Kebir near Tel Aviv to Lifta at the gates of Jerusalem.

With strategic astuteness, the enemy deployed his strength from the start in the effort to sunder Jerusalem from Tel Aviv and the lowland, to halt all Jewish traffic to the city; and this while the Mandate was still in being, as long ago as December 1947.

The Mandate undertook to maintain freedom of movement on the road: its promises were not kept, and while yet British troops garrisoned Palestine, hunger and the sword were

---

[1] Jerusalem.
[2] In Jewish tradition, the First Return followed the Jews' period of captivity in Egypt in 1300 BC; the Second Return followed their period of exile in Babylon in 538 BC. The Third Return followed their period of dispersal by the Romans in AD 135.

menacing the Jewish capital. The state was still far off when we realized that, unless unaided we could blast a way through to Jerusalem and occupy a sufficient space on either side of this corridor, the city was doomed and our whole campaign might be lost.

With the incursion of Arab regulars right upon the Proclamation of the State,[3] the concentrated wrath of the enemy was vented upon Jerusalem, as it was in the days of the Prophet Ezekiel: 'For the king of Babylon standeth at the parting of the way, at the head of the two ways, to use divination; he shaketh the arrows to and fro, he inquireth of teraphim, he looketh in the liver. In his right hand is the lot Jerusalem, to set battering rams, to open the mouth for the slaughter, to lift up the voice with shouting, to set battering-rams against the gates, to cast up mounds, and to build forts.'[4]

In our days the king of Babylon[5] was joined by the king of the sons of Ammon,[6] but the army and champions of Israel, its builders and engineers, its warriors and workers, set the schemes of Babylon and Ammon at naught; they broke through to right and left, they thrust back the invaders and scattered them. Jerusalem was liberated and a broad, untroubled approach secured.

Thus, as April began, our War of Independence swung decisively from defence to attack. Operation Nachshon, to free the road, was launched with the capture of Arab Hulda, near where we stand today, and of Dir Muhsin, and culminated in the storming of Kastel, the great hill-fortress near Jerusalem, where Abdul Qader el Husseini,[7] perhaps the only real commander among the Arabs of Palestine, fell in action.

Jerusalem drew breath freely again, but not for long: reinforcements arrived from other Arab states, and it was beleaguered a second time. Upon it the enemy rained his fiercest blows indiscriminately, viciously, night and day without surcease. British guns, primed by British gunners, bombarded it. Our relief column was led by a gallant and honoured American Jew, Colonel David Michael Marcus.[8]

He was not fated, alas!, to enter the Jerusalem he came to free, and on the very eve of the first truce, he died in the Judean hills.

Here, in the Valley of Ayalon,[9] the Defence Army of Israel, only just taking form, made its first assault on the Arab lines at Latrun. In the van was the Seventh Brigade, newly mobilized, in the main of men landed a few days earlier from the detention camps of Cyprus.[10] Its units in a brave engagement penetrated the village and burned it down, but were forced back by massed artillery. A Palmach brigade,[11] with typical courage, renewed the assault, but it too had to withdraw, not unscathed. So the Arab Legion held the key still to Sha'ar Hagai,[12] the portal of the valley-way, and Jerusalem was in the toils.

[3] The proclamation of Israeli independence, made by Ben-Gurion on 14 May 1948.
[4] Ezekiel 21:21–2.
[5] An ancient city in Mesopotamia, south of modern Baghdad.
[6] Closely related to the Jews, but their traditional enemy.
[7] The Palestinian guerrilla Abdul Qader el-Husseini was mortally wounded fighting Israeli forces in Jerusalem, in April 1948. Following his death the Arab forces retreated.
[8] The Jewish–American soldier Brigadier General David Michael Marcus was a US Army officer who fought for Israel and led construction of the path (known as the

Burma Road) through the mountains to Jerusalem. He was accidentally killed by an Israeli sentry near Jerusalem, just hours before the ceasefire of 11 June 1948.
[9] A strategically important area of Israel (the scene of David's fight against Goliath, among many other battles) between Bet Guvrin and Latrun.
[10] The British authorities controlling Palestine had transported some illegal Jewish immigrants to detention camps in Cyprus.
[11] The first mobilized regiment of the Haganah – the Jewish underground militia.
[12] The Valley Gate, leading to Jerusalem.

It seemed as though we had been worsted at Latrun, yet the fighting there in actuality saved Jerusalem, even before the first truce gave it a brief respite, for we had compelled the enemy to shift a large part of his strength from the city to the valley. The shelling was more fitful and the citizens were heartened to hold out until the end. And more: the fighting gave us a new and open access from the coast through the foothills to Jerusalem.

At the end of May, the Eleventh Brigade took Beit Jiz[13] and Beit Susin[14] and the Palmach entered Zar'a,[15] birthplace of Samson.[16] These actions hewed out the line of shock and valour we call Burma Road,[17] on to deliverance and the salvation of Jerusalem. Afterwards, it was retraced along an easier and apter line, no longer to be makeshift in emergency but an established and enduring link, flanked by multiplying settlements that will unite to form a living bridge of men and husbandry from the principal zones of Jewish occupancy and power in the state to imperishable Jerusalem.

As we dedicate today this Road of Valour, this path of deliverance, let us remember in deepest thankfulness the soldiers and workers in their thousands who helped in its making ...

the battalions of infantry and the armoured cars, the artillery and the engineers who contrived it, the men who laid the pipeline, the men of Solel-Boneh,[18] from Jerusalem and Tel Aviv, the stout-hearted drivers.

They had a proud share in this feat of combat and development, one that will be immortalized in the ageless annals of Zion set free, that will be a monument to Jewish prowess in arms and in labour, the passport, now and always, to victory. "

---

[13] An Arab village.
[14] An Arab hamlet.
[15] A town west of Jerusalem, also known as Zora.
[16] Samson was a Hebrew judge and warrior who was betrayed to the Philistines by his lover Delilah. See Judges 16.

[17] The route built through the mountains which relieved the besieged city of Jerusalem on 9 June 1948 was called the Burma Road after the road built by the slave labour of Allied prisoners-of-war during World War II.
[18] A Histadrut public works and construction operation.

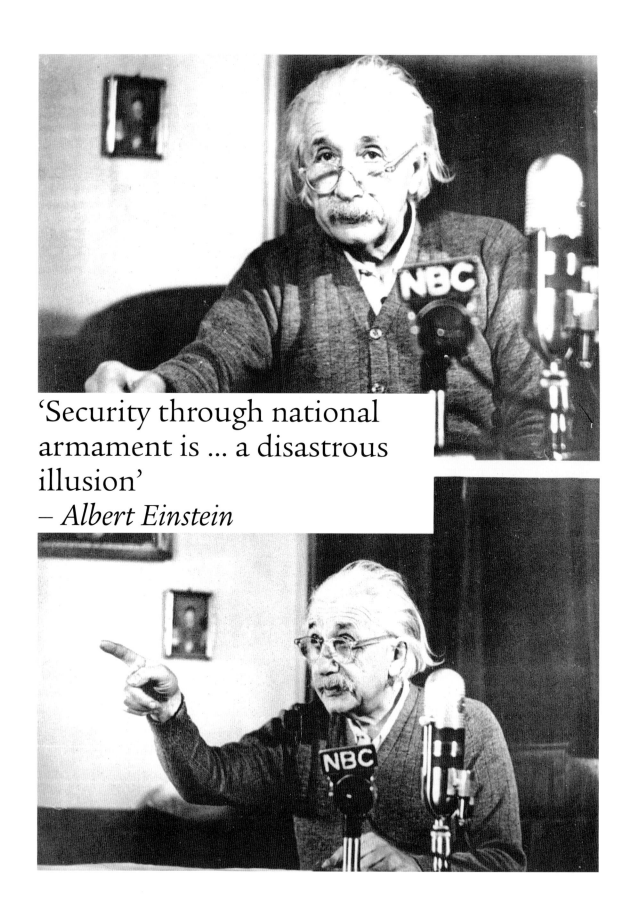

'Security through national armament is ... a disastrous illusion'
– *Albert Einstein*

16

Albert Einstein

German–Swiss–American scientist

Albert Einstein (1879–1955) achieved world fame through his special and general theories of relativity (1905 and 1916), and won the 1921 Nobel Prize in Physics. He ranks with Galileo Galilei and Sir Isaac Newton as one of the great contributors to the understanding of the universe, but by 1930 his best work was complete. After Adolf Hitler's rise to power, he left Germany and lectured at Princeton University, New Jersey, from 1934, becoming an American citizen and professor at Princeton in 1940. In 1939, he wrote to President Franklin D Roosevelt alerting him to the possibility of constructing an atomic bomb, thus helping to initiate the American effort to produce one. After World War II, however, Einstein urged international control of atomic weapons.

'Security through national armament is … a disastrous illusion'

19 February 1950, television broadcast from Princeton, New Jersey, USA

Between 1941 and 1962, Eleanor Roosevelt hosted various radio and television shows. These included a programme during which Einstein, then 71, discussed the issue of nuclear security.

Einstein had written his famous letter to her late husband, President Roosevelt, in August 1939. Recent research in France and America, it explained, meant 'it may become possible to set up a nuclear chain reaction in a large mass of uranium, by which vast amounts of power … would be generated'. The letter continued: 'This new phenomenon would also lead to the construction of bombs.' Einstein had recommended that the US government maintain permanent contact with the physicists working in that field, urged funding to facilitate progress and warned of evidence that German scientists were exploring the same area of research.

Einstein's letter had prompted Roosevelt to support American nuclear scientists. Their work, which became known as the Manhattan Project, led to development of the bombs that were dropped on Japan in August 1945. Einstein was appalled and later remarked, 'I could burn my fingers that I wrote that first letter to Roosevelt.' He spent much of his remaining ten years campaigning for international control of nuclear arms.

Though Einstein was a popular figure, with a playful public profile, his pacifism and socialism – the latter expressed in a famous essay of 1949 – led to his investigation by the Federal Bureau of Investigation. This did not discourage the liberal-minded Mrs Roosevelt from allowing him a platform for his views.

" I am grateful to you for the opportunity to express my conviction in this most important political question.

The idea of achieving security through national armament is, at the present state of military technique, a disastrous illusion. On the part of the United States, this illusion has been particularly fostered by the fact that this country succeeded first in producing an atomic bomb.

The belief seemed to prevail that in the end it were possible to achieve decisive military superiority.

In this way, any potential opponent would be intimidated, and security, so ardently desired by all of us, brought to us and all of humanity. The maxim which we have been following during these last five years has been, in short: security through superior military power, whatever the cost.

This mechanistic, technical-military psychological attitude had inevitable consequences. Every single act in foreign policy is governed exclusively by one viewpoint: how do we have to act in order to achieve utmost superiority over the opponent in case of war? Establishing military bases at all possible strategically important points on the globe. Arming and economic strengthening of potential allies.

Within the country: concentration of tremendous financial power in the hands of the military, militarization of the youth, close supervision of the loyalty of the citizens – in particular, of the civil servants – by a police force growing more conspicuous every day. Intimidation of people of independent political thinking.[1] Indoctrination of the public by radio, press, school. Growing restriction of the range of public information under the pressure of military secrecy.

The armament race between the USA and the USSR, originally supposed to be a preventive measure, assumes a hysterical character.

On both sides, the means to mass destruction are perfected with feverish haste, behind the respective walls of secrecy.

The H-bomb[2] appears on the public horizon as a probably attainable goal. Its accelerated development has been solemnly proclaimed by the President.[3]

If successful, radioactive poisoning of the atmosphere and hence annihilation of any life on Earth has been brought within the range of technical possibilities. The ghost-like character of this development lies in its apparently compulsory trend. Every step appears as the unavoidable consequence of the preceding one.

In the end, there beckons more and more clearly general annihilation.

---

[1] Einstein refers to the purge of alleged communists from American public life and institutions in the early 1950s, led by Senator Joseph McCarthy (1908–57).
[2] The hydrogen bomb, developed in the early 1950s, was a more sophisticated and devastating form of nuclear weapon, deriving its power from nuclear fusion.

[3] Harry S Truman.

Is there any way out of this impasse created by man himself? All of us, and particularly those who are responsible for the attitude of the US and the USSR, should realize that we may have vanquished an external enemy,[4] but have been incapable of getting rid of the mentality created by the war.

It is impossible to achieve peace as long as every single action is taken with a possible future conflict in view. The leading point of view of all political action should therefore be: What can we do to bring about a peaceful co-existence and even loyal co-operation of the nations?

The first problem is to do away with mutual fear and distrust.

Solemn renunciation of violence (not only with respect to means of mass destruction) is undoubtedly necessary.

Such renunciation, however, can only be effective if at the same time a supra-national judicial and executive body is set up, empowered to decide questions of immediate concern to the security of the nations. Even a declaration of the nations to collaborate loyally in the realization of such a 'restricted world government' would considerably reduce the imminent danger of war.

In the last analysis, every kind of peaceful co-operation among men is primarily based on mutual trust and only secondly on institutions such as courts of justice and police. This holds for nations as well as for individuals. And the basis of trust is loyal give and take. **,,**

[4] Einstein refers to the Axis powers of World War II, principally Germany, Japan and Italy.

'**Many abuses were made on Stalin's orders without reckoning with any norms of party and Soviet legality. Stalin was a very distrustful man, sickly suspicious ...**'

— Nikita Khrushchev

17

Nikita Khrushchev

Russian politician

A former shepherd boy and locksmith, Nikita Sergeyevich Khrushchev (1894–1971) joined the Bolshevik Party in 1918 and rose rapidly in the party organization. In 1953, on the death of Joseph Stalin, he became First Secretary of the All Union Party. Among the events of his administration were the 1956 Poznań riots, which he quelled, the Hungarian Uprising of 1956, which he crushed, and the failed attempt to install missiles in Cuba (1962). Khrushchev did much to enhance the ambitions and status of the USSR abroad but was nevertheless deposed in 1964.

'The cult of the individual and its harmful consequences'

25 February 1956, Moscow, Russia

Khrushchev's famous denouncement of Stalin was made in a closed, late-night session at the 20th Congress of the Communist Party of the Soviet Union, the first to be held since Stalin's death in 1953.

Just over a year earlier, the Shvernik Commission had been established under the leadership of Nikolai Shvernik, who had been nominal head of state during the Stalin era. Its remit was to investigate repression under Stalin, and in particular the 'Great Purge' of 1937–8, during which at least 1.5 million party members were arrested, many were tortured and some 680,000 were executed.

Though Shvernik's report was not made public, Khrushchev drew on its findings extensively while preparing this speech. In it, he focuses on several areas: Stalin's departures from the principles of Marxism–Leninism; his reliance on a terrifying police state; and his vanity: the 'cult of personality' was later used as a euphemistic umbrella term to refer to all Stalin's crimes.

The speech lasted over three hours: highlights are given here. Despite the secrecy, it soon leaked to other Eastern Bloc countries, paving the way for reconciliation with Marshal Josip Tito and his Yugoslavian communists in June.

Before long it reached the West – possibly with the tacit assent of the Soviet authorities – appearing in an American newspaper later the same year. It was not officially published in Russia until 1989. The West's relationship with Khrushchev was often troubled, but this speech is now seen as a turning point in the liberalization of eastern Europe.

" Russian Comrades … a lot has been said about the cult of the individual and about its harmful consequences.

After Stalin's death, the central committee of the party began to implement a policy of explaining concisely and consistently that it is impermissible and foreign to the spirit of Marxism–Leninism[1] to elevate one person, to transform him into a superman, possessing supernatural characteristics akin to those of a god. Such a man supposedly knows everything, sees everything, thinks for everyone, can do anything, is infallible in his behaviour.

Such a belief about a man – and specifically about Stalin – was cultivated among us for many years. The objective of the present report is not a thorough evaluation of Stalin's life and activity. Concerning Stalin's merits, an entirely sufficient number of books, pamphlets and studies had already been written in his lifetime. The role of Stalin in the preparation and execution of the socialist revolution, in the civil war and in the fight for the construction of socialism in our country is universally known. Everyone knows it well.

At present, we are concerned with a question which has immense importance for the party now and for the future – with how the cult of the person of Stalin has been gradually growing, the cult which became at a certain specific stage the source of a whole series of exceedingly serious and grave perversions of party principles, of party democracy, of revolutionary legality …

The great modesty of the genius of the revolution, Vladimir Ilich Lenin, is known. Lenin had always stressed the role of the people as the creator of history, the directing and organizational role of the party as a living and creative organism, and also the role of the central committee …

Always unyielding in matters of principle, Lenin never imposed by force his views upon his co-workers. He tried to convince; he patiently explained his opinions to others. Lenin always diligently observed that the norms of party life were realized, that the party statute was enforced, that the party congresses and the plenary sessions of the central committee took place at the proper intervals.

In addition to the great accomplishments of V I Lenin for the victory of the working class and of the working peasants, for the victory of our party and for the application of the ideas of scientific communism to life, his acute mind expressed itself also in this: that he detected in Stalin in time those negative characteristics which resulted later in grave consequences …

As later events have proven, Lenin's anxiety was justified. In the first period after Lenin's death Stalin still paid attention to his advice, but later he began to disregard the serious admonitions of Vladimir Ilich. When we analyse the practice of Stalin in regard to the direction of the party and of the country; when we pause to consider everything which Stalin perpetrated, we must be convinced that Lenin's fears were justified. The negative characteristics of Stalin, which in

[1] A socialist political philosophy based on the works of Karl Marx and Vladimir Ilich Lenin.

Lenin's time were only incipient, transformed themselves during the last years into a grave abuse of power by Stalin, which caused untold harm to our party …

Stalin acted not through persuasion, explanation, and patient co-operation with people, but by imposing his concepts and demanding absolute submission to his opinion …

Stalin originated the concept 'enemy of the people'. This term automatically rendered it unnecessary that the ideological errors of a man or men engaged in a controversy be proven; this term made possible the usage of the most cruel repression, violating all norms of revolutionary legality, against anyone who in any way disagreed with Stalin, against those who were only suspected of hostile intent, against those who had bad reputations.

This concept – 'enemy of the people' – actually eliminated the possibility of any kind of ideological fight or the making of one's views known on this or that issue, even those of a practical character. In the main, and in actuality, the only proof of guilt used, against all norms of current legal science, was the confession of the accused himself, and as subsequent probing proved, confessions were acquired through physical pressures against the accused.

This led to glaring violations of revolutionary legality, and to the fact that many entirely innocent persons, who in the past had defended the party line, became victims …

Everyone knows how irreconcilable Lenin was with the ideological enemies of Marxism, with those who deviated from the correct party line. At the same time, however, Lenin … advised that such people should be patiently educated, without the application of extreme methods … An entirely different relationship with people characterized Stalin.

Lenin's traits – patient work with people, stubborn and painstaking education of them, the ability to induce people to follow him without using compulsion, but rather through the ideological influence on them of the whole collective – were entirely foreign to Stalin. He discarded the Leninist method of convincing and educating; he abandoned the method of ideological struggle for that of administrative violence, mass repressions and terror …

Can it be said that Lenin did not decide to use even the most severe means against enemies of the Revolution when this was actually necessary? No; no one can say this. Vladimir Ilich demanded uncompromising dealings with the enemies of the Revolution and of the working class and when necessary resorted ruthlessly to such methods.

You will recall only V I Lenin's fight with the Socialist Revolutionary organizers of the anti-Soviet uprising,[2] with the counter-revolutionary kulaks in 1918 and with others, when Lenin without hesitation used the most extreme methods against the enemies. Lenin used such methods, however, only against actual class enemies and not against those who blunder,

[2] In July 1918, socialist revolutionaries had attempted a coup in Moscow, which was labelled the Anti-Soviet Uprising. Around the same time, Lenin had introduced repressive measures against peasant landowners (kulaks), who had been resisting the redistribution of their wealth and property.

who err, and whom it was possible to lead through ideological influence and even retain in the leadership …

Stalin, on the other hand, used extreme methods and mass repressions at a time when the Revolution was already victorious, when the Soviet state was strengthened, when the exploiting classes were already liquidated and socialist relations were rooted solidly in all phases of national economy; when our party was politically consolidated and had strengthened itself both numerically and ideologically …

Many abuses were made on Stalin's orders without reckoning with any norms of party and Soviet legality. Stalin was a very distrustful man, sickly suspicious …

The sickly suspicion created in him a general distrust even toward eminent party workers whom he had known for years. Everywhere and in everything he saw 'enemies', 'two-facers' and 'spies'. Possessing unlimited power, he indulged in great wilfulness and stifled people morally as well as physically. A situation was created where one could not express one's own volition …

Comrades: the cult of the individual acquired such monstrous size chiefly because Stalin himself, using all conceivable methods, supported the glorification of his own person. This is supported by numerous facts. One of the most characteristic examples of Stalin's self-glorification and of his lack of even elementary modesty is the edition of his *Short Biography*, which was published in 1948.[3]

This book is an expression of the most dissolute flattery, an example of making a man into a godhead, of transforming him into an infallible sage, 'the greatest leader, sublime strategist of all times and nations'.

We need not give here examples of the loathsome adulation filling this book. All we need to add is that they all were approved and edited by Stalin personally. Some of them were added in his own handwriting to the draft text of the book.

What did Stalin consider essential to write into this book? Did he want to cool the ardour of the flatterers who were composing his *Short Biography*? No! He marked the very places where he thought that the praise of his services was insufficient. Here are some examples characterizing Stalin's activity, added in Stalin's own hand …

'Although he performed his tasks as leader of the party and the people with consummate skill, and enjoyed the unreserved support of the entire Soviet people, Stalin never allowed his work to be marred by the slightest hint of vanity, conceit or self-adulation.'

Where and when could a leader so praise himself? Is this worthy of a leader of the Marxist–Leninist type? No. Precisely against this did Marx and Engels take such a strong position. This always was sharply condemned also by Vladimir Ilich Lenin.

[3] The first *Short Biography* was published in 1927, attributed to Stalin's secretary Ivan Tovstukha (1889–1935). A revised and expanded second edition appeared in 1948.

In the draft text of his book appeared the following sentence: 'Stalin is the Lenin of today.' This sentence appeared to Stalin to be too weak. Thus, in his own handwriting, he changed it to read: 'Stalin is the worthy continuer of Lenin's work, or, as it is said in our party, Stalin is the Lenin of today.' You see how well it is said, not by the nation but by Stalin himself …

Or let us take the matter of the Stalin Prizes.[4]

[Movement in the hall.]

Not even the Tsars created prizes which they named after themselves.

Stalin recognized as the best a text of the national anthem of the Soviet Union which contains not a word about the Communist Party; it contains, however, the following unprecedented praise of Stalin: 'Stalin brought us up in loyalty to the people. He inspired us to great toil and deeds'.

In these lines of the anthem, the whole educational, directional and inspirational activity of the great Leninist Party is ascribed to Stalin. This is, of course, a clear deviation from Marxism–Leninism, a clear debasing and belittling of the role of the party. We should add for your information that the presidium of the central committee has already passed a resolution concerning the composition of a new text of the anthem, which will reflect the role of the people and the role of the party.[5]

[Loud, prolonged applause.]

And was it without Stalin's knowledge that many of the largest enterprises and towns were named after him? Was it without his knowledge that Stalin monuments were erected in the whole country – these 'memorials to the living'? … Anyone who has visited the Stalingrad area must have seen the huge statue which is being built there, and that on a site which hardly any people frequent …

We should, in all seriousness, consider the question of the cult of the individual.

We cannot let this matter get out of the party, especially not to the press. It is for this reason that we are considering it here at a closed congress session. We should know the limits; we should not give ammunition to the enemy; we should not wash our dirty linen before their eyes …

Comrades: we must abolish the cult of the individual decisively, once and for all …

we must draw the proper conclusions concerning both ideological–theoretical and practical work. It is necessary for this purpose: first, in a Bolshevik manner to condemn and to eradicate the cult of the individual as alien to Marxism–Leninism and not consonant with the principles of party leadership and the norms of party life, and to fight inexorably all attempts at bringing back this practice in one form or another …

---

[4] Introduced in 1939, Stalin Prizes were intended as a Soviet equivalent to Nobel Prizes.

[5] Introduced in 1944, 'The Hymn of the Union of Soviet Socialist Republics' by Alexander V Alexandrov and Sergei V Mikhalkov was the USSR's official anthem until 1991.

Second, to continue systematically and consistently the work done by the party's central committee during the last years, a work characterized by minute observation in all party organizations, from the bottom to the top, of the Leninist principles of party leadership, characterized, above all, by the main principle of collective leadership …

Third, to restore completely the Leninist principles of Soviet Socialist democracy, expressed in the constitution of the Soviet Union, to fight wilfulness of individuals abusing their power. The evil caused by acts violating revolutionary socialist legality which have accumulated during a long time as a result of the negative influence of the cult of the individual has to be completely corrected.

Comrades: the 20th Congress of the Communist Party of the Soviet Union has manifested with a new strength the unshakeable unity of our party, its cohesiveness around the central committee, its resolute will to accomplish the great task of building communism.

[Tumultuous applause.]

And the fact that we present in all their ramifications the basic problems of overcoming the cult of the individual which is alien to Marxism–Leninism, as well as the problem of liquidating its burdensome consequences, is evidence of the great moral and political strength of our party.

[Prolonged applause.]

We are absolutely certain that our party, armed with the historical resolutions of the 20th Congress, will lead the Soviet people along the Leninist path to new successes, to new victories.

[Tumultuous, prolonged applause.]

Long live the victorious banner of our party – Leninism!

[Tumultuous, prolonged applause ending in standing ovation.] **”**

'This is a time for action'
– *Anthony Eden*

18

Anthony Eden

British statesman

Robert Anthony Eden later 1st Earl of Avon (1897–1977) served as the Conservative MP for Warwick and Leamington from 1923 to 1957, holding various governmental positions including that of Foreign Secretary. He succeeded Churchill as prime minister in 1955 and in 1956 he ordered British and French forces to occupy the Suez Canal Zone ahead of the invading Israeli army. His action was condemned by the United Nations and caused a bitter and prolonged controversy in Britain which did not subside when he ordered a withdrawal. In failing health, he abruptly resigned the premiership in 1957. Regarded as one of the Western world's most experienced statesmen, he aimed principally for world peace based on respect for law.

'This is a time for action'

2 November 1956, television and radio broadcast from London, England

This address to the British public was an attempt by Eden – by now prime minister – to justify military intervention in Egypt during the Suez Crisis. What makes the speech remarkable, however, is what he chose not to say. The crisis began when the Egyptian president, Gamal Abdel Nasser, nationalized the Suez Canal, previously controlled by British and French companies. Britain and France, fearful that Nasser might prevent oil shipments reaching Europe, made a secret agreement with Israel. Four days before Eden's address, Israeli troops invaded Egypt and took control of the Canal Zone.

Claiming no prior knowledge of the invasion, Eden announces plans to send British forces to police a ceasefire between the Israeli and Egyptian sides. In the process, of course, Britain would retake the Suez Canal. In conciliatory tones – designed to appease a country divided over the affair – he argues that intervention was necessary to prevent a 'forest fire' in the Middle East from spreading. He also reiterates the Labour leader Hugh Gaitskell's comparison of Nasser to Adolf Hitler and Benito Mussolini, an appeal to the patriotism of a Britain that had fought and won World War II in the previous decade. On 5 and 6 November, British and French forces began their occupation of the Canal Zone, but – in response to US diplomacy over the threat of Soviet intervention – they withdrew in December to let a UN peacekeeping force take over.

" Good evening. I know that you would wish me, as prime minister, to talk to you tonight on the problem which is in everybody's mind; and to tell you what has happened, what the government has done, and why it has done it …

First – the background.

For ten years there has been fighting and trouble and turmoil in the Middle East. Again and again passions have come to the boil. There have been raids and counter raids, and shooting and more shooting. Ever since the uneasy armistice of 1949 – Israel and the Arab states – Egypt has been insisting ever since then that she is still at war with Israel. Again and again the United Nations has tried to bring settlement and peace, but with the best will in the world it's failed. And all the time, Heaven knows, this country has worked tirelessly for agreement.

We've tried, for example, to prove our desire for friendship with Egypt. We made an agreement and withdrew from the Canal Zone. We made another agreement with Egypt about the Sudan. We hoped that these would lead to a new spirit in our relations with Egypt. Some people say we've gone much too far in conciliation; that we gave up too much; that we've been weak where we should have been strong.

Well, be that as it may, we've certainly gone to the limit in our efforts for friendship. All those friendly approaches have failed. It's no use blinking that fact. You've only to read the Egyptian government's own statement – what it intends to do. Its words – not mine. Let me give you two examples. The first refers to Israel. 'There will be no stability until this small but vile state is stifled.' A second example comes nearer home. 'We must not in any circumstances lose sight of our goal: to fight the British serpent and to expel it utterly from our lands' – and 'lands', of course, means the whole of the Middle East. That's been the Egyptian mood. The Egyptian threat – openly and publicly proclaimed.

But deeds speak even louder than words. We've seen the purchase of arms from behind the Iron Curtain;[1] and in early August – when Colonel Nasser seized the canal – Mr Gaitskell[2] called the threats to Israel 'clear notice of aggression to come'. He went on to say: 'It's all very familiar – it's exactly the same as we encountered from Mussolini and Hitler in those years before the war.' Strong words – but justified. No wonder Israel was worried.

Then, a few days ago, came the entry of Israeli troops into Egypt. Was that a dangerous situation? Was it likely to lead to a widespread flare-up in the Middle East? In the judgement of the government, it was. Was it likely to endanger widespread British and international interests? It was.

Well, it's possible to go on arguing who was the aggressor.

---

[1] The popularity of the phrase 'Iron Curtain' dates from 1946, when Winston Churchill used it in a speech in the USA to describe the parts of Europe under Soviet influence. However, its originator was the Nazi propagandist Joseph Goebbels, who used the phrase 'eiserner Vorhang' ('iron curtain') in a newspaper article in 1945.

[2] The English politician Hugh Gaitskell (1906–63) was leader of the Labour Party from 1955 until his death.

Was it Israel because she crossed the frontier? Or was it Egypt for what she'd done before? But that's not the real issue for us. If you see afar, the first question isn't how it started, but how to put it out. The hard and inescapable fact was that here was a situation likely to inflame the whole Middle East, with all that this would mean. That, in the government's view, was the fact of the situation – a grim, hard fact. A reality which no words could alter.

As a government we've had to wrestle with the problem of what action we should take, so have our French friends. The burden of that decision was tremendous, but inescapable. In the depths of our conviction we decided that here was the beginning of a forest fire, of immense danger to peace. We decided that we must act and act quickly.

What should we do? We put the matter to the Security Council. Should we have left it to them? Should we have been content to wait to see whether they would act? How long would this have taken? …

We acted swiftly, and reported to the Security Council, and I believe that before long it will become apparent to everybody that we acted rightly and wisely.

Our friends inside the Commonwealth and outside couldn't, in the very nature of things, be consulted in time. You just cannot have immediate action and extensive consultation as well. But our friends are coming … to see that we acted with courage and speed, to deal with a situation which just could not wait.

There are two things I would ask you not to forget. Never to forget.

> *We cannot allow – we could not allow – a conflict in the Middle East to spread; our survival as a nation depends on oil and nearly three-quarters of our oil comes from that part of the world.*

As a Labour Member of Parliament, speaking in support of the government, put it, 'to be without oil' – I quote him – 'to be without oil, is to see our industries grind to a standstill, and starvation overtake the people.' …

The other reflection is this. It's a personal one. All my life I've been a man of peace, working for peace, striving for peace, negotiating for peace. I've been a League of Nations man and a United Nations man, and I'm still the same man, with the same conviction, the same devotion to peace. I couldn't be other – even if I wished, but I'm utterly convinced that the action we have taken is right. …

There are times for courage, times for action. And this is one of them

In the interests of peace, I do hope we've learnt our lesson. Our passionate love of peace, our intense loathing of war have often held us back from using force, even at times when we knew in our heads, if not in our hearts, that its use was in the interests of peace. And I believe with all my heart, and head – for both are needed – that this is a time for action, effective and swift. Yes, even by the use of some force in order to prevent the forest fire from spreading; to prevent the horror and devastation of a larger war …

We learn that the Israeli forces have captured the Egyptian army in Sinai. We learn too, that [the] United Nations truce organization is trying to arrange contact between the two sides to establish terms of surrender. We hope that this organization will be able to arrange for all the captured Egyptians to return to Egypt. We shall certainly give them all the help we can in this.

It seems that Israel has succeeded in destroying the bases in Sinai and Gaza, in which Egyptian commando raiders were trained for attacks on Israel. Once British and French forces have occupied the key points on the canal, Her Majesty's government will ensure that the Israeli forces withdraw from Egyptian territory.

I've no doubt that is their intention, but they will not do so unless we are there to keep the peace, to give the necessary guarantees and prevent a repetition of these events.

So finally, my friends, what are we seeking to do? First and foremost, to stop the fighting, to separate the armies, and to make sure that there's no more fighting. We've stepped in because United Nations couldn't do so in time. If the United Nations will take over this police action we shall welcome it. Indeed we proposed that course to them. And police action means not only to end the fighting now, but also to bring a lasting peace to an area which for ten years has lived, or tried to live, under the constant threat of war.

Until there are United Nations forces there, ready to take over,

... we and the French must go on with the job, until the job is done.

All this could mean – let's hope and pray it does – that the outcome will be not only peace in the Middle East, but a strengthened United Nations, one with power to act as well as to talk – a real force for peace in the world.

Good night to you all. 🙰

'The dilemma of our age, with its infinite possibilities of self-destruction, is how to grow out of the world of armaments into a world of international security, based on law ...'

— *Dag Hammarskjöld*

19

Dag Hammarskjöld

Swedish statesman

Dag Hjalmar Agne Carl Hammarskjöld (1905–61) was Swedish Foreign Minister (1951–3) and became Secretary-General of the United Nations in 1953. Hammarskjöld, who once described himself as 'the curator of the secrets of 82 nations', played a leading part in the setting up of the UN Emergency Force in Sinai and Gaza in 1956, and worked for conciliation in the Middle East (1957–8). He died in an air crash near Ndola in Zambia in 1961 – some claim as the result of an assassination plot – and was awarded the Nobel Peace Prize posthumously in 1961.

'Without recognition of human rights we shall never have peace'

10 April 1957, New York City, USA

Dag Hammarskjöld's outstanding talent for diplomacy was put to the test during the final years of his life: indeed, if the conspiracy theories are true, it contributed to his early death. As Secretary-General of the United Nations, he had relatively little power, but as a negotiator he was calm, tactful and effective. Shortly before giving this speech, he had helped defuse the Suez Crisis in which British, French, Israeli and Egyptian forces went to war over control of the Suez Canal, and the USSR threatened to intervene. He had also created an emergency international force to maintain peace.

This address was given at the 50th anniversary celebrations of the American Jewish Committee. This had been a devastating half-century for Jews, yet had also seen the establishment of a Jewish homeland in Israel. However, Hammarskjöld refers only briefly to Jewish history, instead using his speech to explore some of the principles that informed his struggle for peace. Above all, he stresses the dependence of peace on a recognition of human rights, and the centrality of tolerance to the goals of his organization.

" Four years ago today, I was inducted into my present office, to which I had been catapulted without previous soundings, indeed, without any pre-warning. I felt that it was my duty to accept it, not because of any feeling of confidence in my personal capacity to overcome the difficulties which might arise, but because, under the conditions then prevailing, the one to whom the call had come seemed to me in duty bound to respond.

The situation that faced me at the very outset has proved not to be unique. It has been repeated several times in the past few years, most recently in relation to problems of the Middle East. The other day, returning from the latest visit to that area on a UN mission, I read a book by Arthur Waley[1] – certainly well known to many of you as one of the great interpreters of Chinese thought and literature, and as one of those great Jewish students of humane letters who have so splendidly enriched our cultural tradition. In his work, Waley quotes what an early Chinese historian had to say about the philosopher Sung Tzu[2] and his followers, some 350 years BC. To one who works in the United Nations, the quotation strikes a familiar note. It runs as follows:

Constantly rebuffed but never discouraged, they went round from state to state, helping people to settle their differences, arguing against wanton attack and pleading for the suppression of arms, that the age in which they lived might be saved from its state of continual war. To this end they interviewed princes and lectured the common people, nowhere meeting with any great success, but obstinately persisting in their task, till kings and commoners alike grew weary of listening to them. Yet undeterred they continued to force themselves on people's attention.

Is this a description of a quixotic group, whose efforts are doomed to failure? The wording, with its tone of frustration, may lead us to think so. However, I believe that this interpretation would be wrong. The historian tells us about a group engaged in a struggle he considers very much worthwhile and one which will have to go on until success is achieved …

We can learn from his attitude, both in our efforts to move towards peace and in our work for universal recognition of human rights.

We know that the question of peace and the question of human rights are closely related. Without recognition of human rights we shall never have peace, and it is only within the framework of peace that human rights can be fully developed.

In fact, the work for peace is basically a work for the most elementary of human rights: the right of everyone to security and to freedom from fear.

---

[1] The English Orientalist Arthur Waley (1889–1966) translated numerous Chinese and Japanese texts, as well as writing extensively on the Far East.

[2] The Chinese general and philosopher Sung Tzu (c.544–496 BC) is traditionally credited as the author of *Ping-fa* ('The Art of War'), a highly influential treatise on military tactics, but also on peacekeeping strategies.

We, therefore, recognize it as one of the first duties of a government to take measures in order to safeguard for its citizens this very right. But we also recognize it as an obligation for the emerging world community to assist governments in safeguarding this elementary human right without having to lock themselves in behind the wall of arms.

The dilemma of our age, with its infinite possibilities of self-destruction, is how to grow out of the world of armaments into a world of international security, based on law …

The effort may seem hopeless. It will prove hopeless unless we, all of us, show the persistence of Sung Tzu and his followers, and unless peoples and governments alike are willing to take smaller immediate risks in order to have a better chance to avoid the final disaster threatening us if we do not manage to turn the course of developments in a new direction.

The United Nations finds itself in a difficult stage of its development. It is still too weak to provide the security desired by all, while being strong enough and alive enough effectively to point out the direction in which the solution must be sought. In its present phase, the organization may look to many like a preacher who cannot impose the law he states or realize the gospel he interprets. It is understandable if those who have this impression turn away in distrust or with cynical criticism, forgetting that setbacks in efforts to implement an ideal do not prove that the ideal is wrong, and overlooking also that at the beginning of great changes in human society there must always be a stage of such frailty or seeming inconsistency.

It is easy to say that it is pointless to state the law if it cannot be enforced. However, to do so is to forget that if the law is the inescapable law of the future; it would be treason to the future not to state the law simply because of the difficulties of the present.

Indeed, how could it ever become a living reality if those who are responsible for its development were to succumb to the immediate difficulties arising when it is still a revolutionary element in the life of society?

The history of the Jewish people offers some of the most magnificent examples of how ideals and law may be brought to victory through courageous assertion of new universal principles, which the wise call folly when they are first introduced in a society shaped on a different pattern.

The thoughts I have tried to express apply to practically the whole field of United Nations activities, but in particular to the work of the organization for the implementation of the principles of the Charter in the fields of international security and disarmament and in the field of fundamental human rights. They apply likewise to the United Nations itself as an experiment in international organization.

But is not an experiment something tentative and passing?

And should not the United Nations be regarded as something definite and lasting?

I think it is important to be clear on this point. Certainly the experiences and achievements of the United Nations as it is today are helping us to build the future. …

The United Nations is, and should be, a living, evolving, experimental institution.

If it should ever cease to be so it should be revolutionized or swept aside for a new approach.

The growth of social institutions is always one where, step by step, the form which adequately meets the need is shaped through selection, or out of experience. Thus an effort that has not yielded all the results hoped for has not failed if it has provided positive experience on which a new approach can be based. An attempt which has proved the possibility of progress has served the cause of progress even if it has had to be renewed again and again, and in new forms or settings in order to yield full success. When we look back over the experiences in the United Nations over the past few months, we may differ amongst ourselves as to the wisdom of this or that particular stand and we may have doubts about the end result of this or that step. But I think we all can agree on the value and historical importance of certain developments.

First of all, it proved possible in an emergency to create for the first time a truly international force. This force, although modest in size and, for constitutional reasons, also modest in aim, broke new ground which inevitably will count in future efforts to preserve peace and promote justice …

… Deeply regrettable though the conflicts of views and interests were, it should not be forgotten that those who now feel they had to sacrifice for the maintenance of a principle, in a different situation may be the first to profit from the fact that the principle was maintained. As individuals we know that the law which restrains us likewise protects us. The same holds true in international life.

Some moments ago I referred to the fact that lasting peace is not possible without recognition of fundamental human rights and that human rights cannot reach their full development unless there is peace. The United Nations cannot lay down the law for the life within any national community. Those laws have to be established in accordance with the will of the people, as expressed in the forms indicated by their chosen constitution.

But just as the United Nations can promote peace, so it can, in joint deliberations, define the goals of human rights which should be the laws of the future in each nation. Whatever the distance between these goals and the everyday reality we meet all around the world, it is not vain thus to set the targets as they present themselves to the most mature political thinking of our age.

You have put 'the pursuit of equality at home and abroad' as a motto of your anniversary. Interpreted in a broad sense these words reflect a basic human right, equal in significance to the right to security and freedom from fear.

The underlying problems now making the Middle East such a troubled area lend special weight to the undertaking of the member nations in the Charter 'to practise tolerance'.

The words just quoted from the Charter are among those which link its text to a great ethical tradition. They are often overlooked, sometimes brushed aside as empty ornaments without political significance, sometimes honoured by lip-service. However, they represent an element without which the Charter and the system it creates would disintegrate. Both the work for peace and the work for human rights must be anchored in and inspired by a general approach which gives balance and substance to the results. Peace cannot be enforced for selfish reasons; equality cannot be imposed as an abstract concept. In fact, attempts to do so account for some of the darkest episodes in history.

The work for peace must be animated by tolerance and the work for human rights by respect for the individual.

A student of the growth of human rights through the ages will recognize its close relationship to the development of tolerance inspired by intellectual liberalism or, perhaps more often, by ethical concepts of religious origin.

Attempts are made to link the development of human rights exclusively to the liberal ideas which broke through to predominance in the Age of Enlightenment. However, to do so means tome to overlook the historical background of those ideas. It means also cutting our ties to a source of strength that we need in order to carry the work for human rights to fruition and to give to those rights, when established, their fitting spiritual content.

To some, the word 'tolerance' may sound strange in a time of 'Cold War' and of negotiations 'from positions from strength'; it may have an overtone of meekness or appeasement. And yet, have we reason to believe that what was true in the past is no longer true? It is not the weak but the strong who practice tolerance, and the strong do not weaken their position in showing tolerance. On the contrary, only through tolerance can they justify their strength. **））**

20

Harold Macmillan

British statesman

Maurice Harold Macmillan later 1st Earl of Stockton (1894–1986) stood successfully as Conservative MP for Stockton-on-Tees in 1924. Not always willing to conform to the party line, he remained a backbencher until 1940, after which he took on a succession of government posts. Defeated in the Labour landslide of 1945, he was returned later the same year for Bromley and held this seat until he retired in 1964. He was Minister of Housing (1951–4), Minister of Defence (1954–5), then Foreign Minister until the end of 1955, when he was appointed Chancellor of the Exchequer. On the resignation of Anthony Eden in 1957 he emerged, in R A Butler's words, as 'the best prime minister we have'. As an intellectual and an aristocrat, he was regarded with suspicion by many. Nevertheless, his economic expansionism at home, his resolution in foreign affairs, his integrity and his infectious optimism inspired confidence, and his popularity soared. In 1962, after some electoral setbacks, he carried out a drastic 'purge' of his government, involving seven Cabinet ministers. Further setbacks followed, including the Profumo scandal (1963), and ill health brought about his reluctant resignation in1963.

'Most of our people have never had it so good'

20 July 1957, Bedford, England

At this point in his career, Harold Macmillan's political fortunes were rising to their zenith. As Chancellor, he had been labelled 'Supermac' by the newspaper cartoonist Vicky, after presiding over a booming British economy. But his colonial policy, which facilitated independence in much of what remained of the British Empire, made him unpopular with the right of his party. So too did his 'One Nation Conservatism', whose economic and social philosophies more closely resembled the post-war social democratic policies of Clement Attlee than any former Tory platform.

But, whatever his issues with his party, Macmillan was popular with the country at large. Having inherited a thirteen-point deficit in the polls at his election to the party leadership, he would win the 1959 election with a seven-point lead.

However, this famous speech to the party faithful of Bedford was particularly taxing for Macmillan, partly because it addresses the end of Empire. What is so impressive about it is the quiet pragmatism that characterized his policy-making. He thrived by his well-known credo: 'If people want a sense of purpose they should get it from their archbishop. They should certainly not get it from their politicians.'

" Just over six months have passed since severe ill-health forced Sir Anthony Eden to lay down his burden. To all of us – his friends and colleagues – this was indeed a cruel blow. For he was endowed with two great qualities without which no politician, however able or however brilliant, can aspire to the name of statesman. These are courage and integrity. He had both, to a supreme degree …

It has fallen to me to be his successor; and I must tell you that I feel both encouraged and inspired by the loyalty and comradeship which have been shown to me during these six months …

This meeting, I must remind you, was originally planned to celebrate the jubilee of Bedfordshire's senior Member. Alan Lennox-Boyd[1] has served his constituency for an unbroken tenure of 25 years. Fortunately he is still quite a young man, and a man of immense vigour. He holds today one of the most arduous as well as one of the most important posts in the Cabinet. He has not spared himself. I do not suppose he has told you – but I will tell you – that since he became Colonial Secretary, only three years ago, he has travelled 80,000 miles – more than three times round the globe. He has won the admiration and respect of all the political leaders and indeed of all the people of our colonies. He has done something more – he has won their affection. Peoples of every race, religion and colour have come to look upon him as a friend.

This leads me to say something about changes and developments which have taken place in the Empire during recent years. I know there are some people who feel concerned at what is happening.

They even talk about the disintegration of the Empire. It is changing; but it is not disintegrating.

Colonial territories are taking steps everywhere towards self-government. But we should take pride in this, for it is we who have taught them; who have set them on the path. Our aim has always been to lead the colonial peoples along the road to self-government within the Commonwealth …

There is not a colony today which is not thinking of its future destiny. People are seeking new faiths and beliefs, trying to adjust themselves to the sudden impact of new thoughts, ideas and invention. But we must not be frightened by what is happening. For after all, it is of our own making.

Of all political forces, the new rise of nationalism is the most powerful, swift and elemental. It can be stubborn too. It can be led; but it cannot be driven. If we try to drive it backwards, we shall drive it to communism. Our task is to guide these forces with sympathy and

[1] Alan Lennox-Boyd later 1st Viscount Boyd of Merton (1904–83) became MP for Mid Bedfordshire in 1931, later serving as Minister for Transport and Aviation (1952–4) and Secretary of State for the Colonies (1954–9).

understanding. To this work nobody has given greater service than the Colonial Secretary. He is supported by the splendid officers of our fine colonial service.

In the long history of the past, the world has seen the rise and fall of great empires.

Let us take pride in this – that Britain is the only power which has, of its own volition, set about the task of giving full independence to all parts of its Empire as they become able to manage their own affairs.

This is not a sunset; it is the coming of a new dawn ...

Yet, despite all this, Great Britain is charged with 'imperialism' and 'colonialism'. So constant, indeed, have these attacks become that 'colonialism' has almost come to be the signature tune of the Moscow Radio and the 'Voice of the Arabs' in Cairo.

Let us contrast our own record with that of our communist accusers. Whilst 100 million people in Europe alone have, since the war, been fully absorbed into the communist bloc, more than five times that number in Asia and Africa have been helped to nationhood by governments of this country. Turn now to the last few months – four million citizens in Ghana have been built into a new free nation, while for ten million Hungarians freedom has been crushed by the Red Army …

The countries of the Commonwealth and of the colonial empire look to us for leadership in many fields.

First, defence. Here I am happy to tell you what a fine job the Member for Bedford, Mr Christopher Soames,[2] is doing in his new post. And by the way, your county of Bedford is really a very satisfactory county politically: all four Members support the government. Three of them are in the government – two in the Cabinet – and the fourth is an energetic and hard-working backbencher. No Mr Faint Hearts here, or among the thousands who send them to the House of Commons.

In defence I have continued the policy started by Mr Attlee and carried on by Sir Winston Churchill and Sir Anthony Eden, and now reaching its fruition. That is to say, we are making Britain an atomic and nuclear power. This is not the time for me to talk about defence in any detail. As you know, we are engaged upon a recasting of our defence services. It will be a long job, and a difficult one. And remember, on our success depends the end of conscription and the return to volunteer or regular forces …

For so long as I can remember, this country has been the traditional source of capital for the Commonwealth and the Empire. During the Victorian and Edwardian eras this reached immense figures. Indeed, it was to British capital that not only the Commonwealth and the colonies, but a great part of the world – including the United States – owed the foundations of their prosperity.

At the culminating point of this operation – that is, in the years immediately preceding the First War – Great Britain is believed to have exported some 7 per cent of her national income.

[2] Christopher Soames later Baron Soames (1920–87) was MP for Bedford, 1950–66, and in January 1957 had moved from a junior ministerial post at the Air Ministry to a similar post at the Admiralty.

Now, after two World Wars – and many other calls upon our resources which are absolutely essential if we are to keep ahead in the race and maintain our investing power – we cannot hope to do as much. But we are still doing pretty well …

Our problem today is how to do all the things that we want to do. We want to invest in the Commonwealth.

We want to improve conditions among the millions of people in Asia and Africa whose living standards are too low – and incidentally if we improve their conditions we shall improve the markets for our goods. We want to re-equip our factories and farms with the most up-to-date plant and machinery. We want to maintain and, if we can, improve our social services. And we must of course play our proper part in defence.

All these things together make up a heavy task, which we have succeeded in meeting over the last six years … Our general prospects are good. The balance of payments prospects are favourable – we look like earning a really worthwhile surplus this year …

These increased earnings come from the increasing production of most of our main industries – steel, coal, motorcars – a large part of the increase in output is going to exports or to investments. That is all to the good. Indeed, let's be frank about it: most of our people have never had it so good.

Go around the country, go to the industrial towns, go to the farms, and you will see a state of prosperity such as we have never had in my lifetime – nor indeed ever in the history of this country. What is beginning to worry some of us is, 'Is it too good to be true?' – or perhaps I should say, 'Is it too good to last?' For, amidst all this prosperity, there is one problem that has troubled us – in one way or another – ever since the war. It's the problem of rising prices.

Our constant concern today is – can prices be steadied while at the same time we maintain full employment in an expanding economy? Can we control inflation? This is the problem of our time.

It is true that prices have risen less since we took office. It is true that wages, and in the main salaries, have more than held their own in the race. Taking the nation as a whole, compared with six years ago, personal incomes are 40 per cent up, and though prices have risen they have only risen by 20 per cent. I read in the *Daily Mirror* this week a statement which said that the people were worried at 'too small wages chasing too big bills'. Whatever else is true, this isn't true. Wages have risen far beyond prices. But we must not, and we do not intend to allow these facts to blind us to the dangers …

Last year, when I was Chancellor, I described our position as brilliant but precarious. There must always be a risk, and it is surely the lesson in life not to take too much or press an advantage too far. If we do we may lose the greatest social and economic benefit that has come to us since the war – security.

The Conservative Party is not the party of any class or section. We govern in the interests of the whole nation …

and we cannot forget that some sections of the people have not shared in this general prosperity.[3] These are those who live on fixed incomes, including those who have retired from active work. We cannot, as a national party, see their interests sacrificed. The government have a clear duty in this matter, and we intend to discharge it …

In the long run, there is only one answer to the $64,000-dollar question[4] – to increase production. That's the answer. That is where the real hope lies. That is why the Chancellor of the Exchequer last April gave new incentives through lower taxation. That has been our policy ever since 1951 – in six out of seven budgets, the burden of taxation has been lowered. The nation today is paying £800 million a year less in taxes than it would be paying if the Socialist rates of 1951 had been maintained.

But you know, the government cannot do this all alone.

Of course, government action is needed and is being taken. But by itself it cannot solve the problem. This is a combined operation. We are all in it – government, industry, the general public. What we need is restraint and common sense – restraint in the demands we make, and common sense on how we spend our income. But the only form of restraint which can work in a free society is self-restraint …

This then is my theme, and this my message to you. An expanding Commonwealth, changing but taking new form, shedding old methods but reaching out to great new possibilities; Britain the centre of it, trusted by all and honoured as the natural leader. A material development of the Commonwealth to which Britain is making the largest contribution of any country in the world in money, and to which she can make increasing contributions in technical skill and experience.

Our own country buoyant, determined to maintain a high rate of investment, a high rate of savings and determined too to conquer the danger of inflation by rising activity.

So, midway through this year 1957, we are masters of our own fate. It lies in our own hands; with wisdom, good sense, good feeling and comradeship, we can achieve our purpose. I have no doubt at all what the outcome will be. **”**

---

[3] Macmillan's 'One Nation Conservatism' promoted connection and harmony between different social classes – particularly between the aristocracy and the working class.

[4] *The $64,000 Question* was a US television game show which screened 1955–8. The phrase entered popular parlance on both sides of the Atlantic.

21

Patrice Lumumba

Congolese politician

Patrice Hemery Lumumba (1925–61) helped form the Mouvement national congolais (MNC) in 1958 to challenge Belgian rule and, when Congo became an independent republic, became its first prime minister (1960). He sought a unified Congo and opposed the secession of Katanga Province under Moise Tshombe. Less than three months after coming to power, he was arrested by his own army, handed over to the Katangese, brutalized and eventually murdered in January 1961. His name, however, remains significant as the embodiment of African nationalism and as an opponent of Balkanization manipulated by ex-colonial countries and their allies.

'An honest, loyal, strong, popular government'

23 June 1960, Léopoldville (now Kinshasa), Congo

This speech represents a brief dawn of optimism in the stormy history of Congolese politics. Lumumba gave this exhilarated address to the Congolese Chamber a week before independence was officially declared. It was preceded by the announcement of the Cabinet, in which Lumumba held the twin posts of prime minister and Minister of National Defence.

In his speech, translated here by H R Lane, Lumumba commends the government to the Chamber and expresses his desire to establish law and order. He also attempts to position the country as truly independent, aligned to neither the USA nor the USSR, though he does acknowledge the need for Belgian support.

" Mr President, dear colleagues, ladies and gentlemen: the crisis that threatened to endanger the future of our young nation has fortunately been resolved, thanks to the Congolese wisdom that all the elected representatives have shown in the face of the danger that confronted us. You have been the first to demonstrate to everyone that is our duty to bring about union and solidarity …

Today, in victory, in triumph, we are still united and unanimous: our entire nation rejoices at this.

Gentlemen: the government that you are about to vote on is an honest, loyal, strong, popular government, which represents the entire nation, having been chosen by you to serve the interests of our homeland. All the members of my team and I formally pledge that this government will remain a government of the people, by the people and for the people.[1]

Strengthened by this popular support, the government will endeavour to keep the nation's territory and its unity intact and protect it from attack from any quarter.

The vastness of the territory and its great diversity make certain steps necessary, however. The government views this situation realistically. We must be able to modify the administrative divisions of the old regime by legal means so that each citizen may find happiness among his fellows.

This government will endeavour to establish the rule of law and order everywhere in the country, without hesitating; but as it goes about this task, it will always respect the inalienable rights of man and the citizen as a sacred good.

This government will consider its first duty to be that of leading the popular masses along the path to social justice, wellbeing and progress, carefully avoiding adventures that might lead to catastrophes that we wish to spare our people. We want nothing to do with new forms of dictatorship.

This government will endeavour to maintain friendly relations with all foreign countries, but it will not succumb to the temptations of joining one or another of the blocs that have now divided the world between them, as it might so easily do; it will also not hesitate to espouse a noble and just cause on the international plane, and in Africa in particular.

Gentlemen: in the name of the government of the Congo, in the name of the Congolese people and also in the certainty that I am speaking for all the members of this parliament, I now address our Belgian friends in particular, and have this to say to them: in the last three-quarters of a century, you have created an enormous handiwork in this country. It was not always immune to criticism, certainly, but now that the outrages perpetrated during the elections are at an end, we must recognize that it constitutes the unshakable foundation on which we are going to build our nation together …

---

[1] Lumumba quotes from Abraham Lincoln's Gettysburg Address of 19 November 1863.

We will need the help of Belgians and of all men of goodwill more than ever; we will do our utmost to ensure that the co-operation that will begin tomorrow will be of benefit to all. The religious missions will be assured of being able to continue their apostolate, thanks to the freedom of opinion and the religious freedom that our constitution will guarantee. The members of the former colonial administration have now turned their powers of government over to the Congolese, but their counsel and their experience will remain the surest guarantee of sound government.

Lastly, you will understand why I wish to conclude my remarks with an expression of the overwhelming emotion I feel. The members of the first government of the Congo are faced with a grave task, and they are well aware of how complex it is. We are face to face with an immense country, with extraordinary potentialities. We have at our side a young, resolute, intelligent people capable of being the equal of other nations.

We are privileged to be beginning our national life at the same time as other countries in Africa.

This huge continent is awakening and looking toward a better future.

The Congolese people will fulfil its destiny through unity and solidarity.

Gentlemen: whether or not this destiny is a happy one and one truly worthy of our people will depend on each one of us, on our work each day of our lives. I am proud to see the Congo, our homeland, take its place in the ranks of free peoples.

May I ask you, dear brothers, on this solemn day on which the Congo is achieving its total independence, on which a democratic government is taking over, on which justice is being established, on which each of us will henceforth enjoy total personal freedom, on which the sun has suddenly come out in this country to dissipate the long darkness of the colonial regime, to raise your voices with me:

Long live the independent Congo!

Long live the united Congo!

Long live freedom!

'We are at the end of an era, and not only here in Cuba. No matter what is hoped or said to the contrary, the form of capitalism we have known, in which we were raised, and under which we have suffered, is being defeated all over the world.'

— Ernesto 'Che' Guevara

22

Ernesto 'Che' Guevara

Argentinian revolutionary leader

Ernesto Guevara de la Serna nicknamed Che (1928–67) graduated in medicine at the University of Buenos Aires (1953). He travelled widely in South America, then joined Fidel Castro's revolutionary movement in Mexico (1955), and played an important part in the Cuban Revolution (1956–9). He was awarded Cuban citizenship in 1959 and held several government posts under Castro. An activist of revolution elsewhere, including Africa, he left Cuba in 1965 to become a guerrilla leader in South America, and was captured and executed by government troops in Bolivia while trying to foment a revolt. He became an icon for left-wing youth in the 1960s.

'To be a revolutionary you have first to have a revolution'

19 August 1960, Havana, Cuba

The repressive policies and economic struggles that marked Castro's long regime in Cuba have diminished his folk-hero status. No such problem for his right-hand man Che Guevara, whose good looks and youthful death (aged 39) created an enduring romantic image.

But Che – whose nickname is an Argentinian greeting – was more than simply a handsome pin-up. While training as a doctor, he developed a keen understanding of politics, economics and Marxist ideology; he later became an expert guerrilla strategist. He was famously described by the French philosopher and writer Jean-Paul Sartre as 'the most complete human being of our time'.

During the revolution led by Castro, Guevara spent two years living in Cuba's Sierra Maestra mountains, and helped lead the peasant army to victory, overthrowing the despotic regime of General Fulgencio Batista. After Castro's installation as prime minister, Cuba underwent rapid socio-economic change, forging an alliance with the USSR in defiance of American sanctions. Guevara spearheaded revolutionary reforms, often leading by example, and won enormous affection from the Cuban people.

This speech, translated by Beth Kurti, was given to medical professionals at the Confederation of Cuban Workers. In it, Guevara harks back to his professional roots but relates all work to egalitarian principles.

He was a fiery speaker, who invariably wore green fatigues and black beret – even when addressing the United Nations in 1964 – and constantly smoked cigars despite severe asthma. Witnesses describe the 'charisma' and 'moral sense' of his speeches. Though his relationship with Castro ultimately soured, he is still considered a national hero in Cuba.

" Almost everyone knows that years ago I began my career as a doctor. And when I began as a doctor, when I began to study medicine, the majority of the concepts I have today, as a revolutionary, were absent from my store of ideals …

After graduation … I began to travel throughout America,[1] and I became acquainted with all of it …

I came into close contact with poverty, hunger, and disease; with the inability to treat a child because of lack of money; with the stupefaction provoked by continual hunger and punishment … And I began to realize at that time that there were things that were almost as important to me as becoming a famous scientist or making a significant contribution to medical science: I wanted to help those people. …

… I realized a fundamental thing. For one to be a revolutionary doctor or to be a revolutionary at all, there must first be a revolution. Isolated individual endeavour, for all its purity of ideals, is of no use, and the desire to sacrifice an entire lifetime to the noblest of ideals serves no purpose if one works alone, solitarily, in some corner of America, fighting against adverse governments and social conditions which prevent progress.

To create a revolution, one must have what there is in Cuba – the mobilization of a whole people …

who learn by the use of arms and the exercise of militant unity to understand the value of arms and the value of this unity.

And now we have come to the nucleus of the problem we have before us at this time. Today one finally has the right and event he duty to be, above all things, a revolutionary doctor, that is to say a man who utilizes the technical knowledge of his profession in the service of the revolution and the people. But now old questions reappear: How does one actually carry out a work of social welfare? How does one unite individual endeavour with the needs of society?

… In Cuba a new type of man is being created,[2] whom we cannot fully appreciate here in the capital, but who is found in every corner of the country. Those of you who went to the Sierra Maestra on 26 July[3] must have seen two completely unknown things. Firstly, an army with hoes and pickaxes, an army whose greatest pride is to parade in the patriotic festivals of Oriente[4] with hoes and axes raised, while their military comrades march with rifles.

But you must have seen something even more important. You must have seen children whose physical constitutions appeared to be those of eight-or nine-year-olds, yet almost all of whom are 13 or 14 …

---

[1] Guevara refers to Latin America, much of which he explored by motorbike with his friend Alberto Granado (1922–11).
[2] Central to Guevara's political philosophy was the creation of El Hombre Nuevo ('The New Man'), a Cuban communist who would be motivated by a spirit of collectivism and expect moral rather than material rewards. He strove to exemplify this ascetic doctrine with his own conduct.

[3] Castro's first attempt to overthrow Batista was on 26 July 1953, On the same date in 1959, Castro returned to office as prime minister, after briefly resigning, effectively ousting President Manuel Urritia six months after his appointment. Cubans now celebrate 26 July as a national holiday.
[4] Until 1976, an eastern province of Cuba, the location of the Sierra Maestra.

In this tiny Cuba, with its four or five television channels and hundreds of radio stations, with all the advances of modern science, when those children arrived at school for the first time at night and saw the electric light bulbs, they exclaimed that the stars were very low that night. And those children, some of whom you must have seen, are learning in collective schools skills ranging from reading to trades, and even the very difficult science of becoming revolutionaries.

Those are the new humans being born in Cuba. They are being born in isolated areas, in different parts of the Sierra Maestra, and also in the cooperatives and work centres.

All this has to do with the theme of our talk today, the integration of the physician or any other medical worker, into the revolutionary movement … The principle upon which the fight against disease should be based is the creation of a robust body; but not the creation of a robust body by the artistic work of a doctor upon a weak organism; rather, the creation of a robust body with the work of the whole collectivity, upon the entire social collectivity.

Some day, therefore, medicine will have to convert itself into a science that serves to prevent disease and orients the public toward carrying out its medical duties. Medicine should only intervene in cases of extreme urgency, to perform surgery or something else which lies outside the skills of the people of the new society we are creating …

But for this task of organization, as for all the revolutionary tasks, fundamentally it is the individual who is needed …

We are at the end of an era, and not only herein Cuba. No matter what is hoped or said to the contrary, the form of capitalism we have known, in which we were raised, and under which we have suffered, is being defeated all over the world … Such a profound social change demands equally profound changes in the mental structure of the people …

One way of getting to the heart of the medical question is not only to visit and become acquainted with the people who make up the cooperatives and work centres, but to find out what diseases they have, what their sufferings are, what have been their chronic miseries for years, and what has been the inheritance of centuries of repression and total submission. The doctor, the medical worker, must go to the core of his new work, which is the man within the mass, the man within the collectivity.

Always, no matter what happens in the world, the doctor is extremely close to his patient and knows the innermost depths of his psyche. Because he is the one who attacks pain and mitigates it, he performs an invaluable labour of much responsibility in society.

A few months ago, here in Havana, it happened that a group of newly graduated doctors did not want to go into the country's rural areas, and demanded remuneration before they would agree to go. From the point of view of the past it is the most logical thing in the world for this to occur; at least, so it seems to me, for I can understand it perfectly. The situation brings back to me the memory of what I was and what I thought a few years ago … the gladiator who rebels, the solitary fighter who wants to assure a better future, better conditions, and to make valid the need people have of him.

But what would have happened if – instead of these boys, whose families generally were able to pay for their years of study – others of less fortunate means had just finished their schooling and were beginning the exercise of their profession? …

What would have happened, simply, is that the peasants would have run, immediately and with unreserved enthusiasm, to help their brothers.

They would have requested the most difficult and responsible jobs in order to demonstrate that the years of study they had received had not been given in vain. What would have happened is what will happen in six or seven years, when the new students, children of workers and peasant, receive professional degrees of all kinds …

None of us – none of the first group which arrived in the *Granma*,[5] who settled in the Sierra Maestra and learned to respect the peasant and the worker living with him – had a peasant or working-class background. Naturally, there were those who had had to work, who had known certain privations in childhood; but hunger, what is called real hunger, was something none of us had experienced. But we began to know it in the two long years in the Sierra Maestra. And then many things became very clear …

We understood perfectly that the life of a single human being is worth a million times more than all the property of the richest man on earth.

And we learned it; we, who were not of the working class nor of the peasant class. And are we now going to tell the four winds, we who were the privileged ones, that the rest of the people in Cuba cannot learn it also?

Yes, they can learn it: the Revolution today demands that they learn it, demands that it be well understood that far more important than a good remuneration is the pride of serving one's neighbour; that much more definitive and much more lasting than all the gold that one can accumulate is the gratitude of a people. And each doctor, within the circle of his activities, can and must accumulate that valuable treasure, the gratitude of the people …

We shall see that diseases need not always be treated as they are in big-city hospitals. We shall see that the doctor has to be a farmer also and plant new foods and sow, by example, the desire to consume new foods, to diversify the Cuban nutritional structure, which is so limited, so poor, in one of the richest countries in the world, agriculturally and potentially. The first thing we will have to do is not to go to the people to offer them our wisdom.

We must go, rather, to demonstrate that we are going to learn with the people, that together we are going to carry out that great and beautiful common experiment: the construction of a new Cuba …

I was telling you that to be a revolutionary you have first to have a revolution. We already have it. Next, you have to know the people with whom you are going to work …

[5] The small, overloaded vessel on which Castro, Guevara and 80 others set sail from Mexico on 25 November 1956, to begin the revolution in Cuba.

… The new armies which are being formed to defend the country must be armies with different tactics. The doctor will have an enormous importance within the plan of the new army. He must continue being a doctor, which is one of the most beautiful tasks there is and one of the most important in war … In time of danger they should go immediately to solve the problems of the poor people of Cuba. But the militias offer also an opportunity to live together, joined and made equal by a uniform, with men of all the social classes of Cuba.

If we medical workers – and permit me to use once again a title which I had forgotten some time ago – are successful, if we use this new weapon of solidarity, if we know the goals, know the enemy, and know the direction we have to take, then all that is left for us to know is the part of the way to be covered each day. And that part no one can show us; that part is the private journey of each individual. Now that we have all the elements for our march toward the future, let us remember the advice of Martí:[6] 'The best way of telling is doing.'

Let us march, then, toward Cuba's future. "

[6] The Cuban journalist and poet José Martí (1853–95) became the figurehead of the independence movement. He was one of the leaders of the Second War of Independence against Spain, but was killed during his first battle. He is still celebrated as a Cuban national hero, almost as ubiquitously as Che himself.

'Ich bin ein Berliner'
– *John F Kennedy*

23

John F Kennedy

American statesman

John Fitzgerald Kennedy (1917–63) was elected to the US House of Representatives as a Democrat from Massachusetts in 1946, won a Senate seat in 1952 and the next year married Jacqueline Lee Bouvier (1929–94). He won the presidential nomination in 1960 and became the first Catholic and, at 43, the youngest person to be elected president. He introduced a legislative programme, the 'New Frontier', which aimed to extend civil rights and to provide funding for education, medical care for the elderly and the space programme, though much of it stalled in Congress. He faced a series of foreign policy crises, including the unsuccessful invasion of Fidel Castro's Cuba at the Bay of Pigs (April 1961), the building of the Berlin Wall (August 1961) and the Cuban Missile Crisis (October 1962). On 22 November 1963, he was assassinated by rifle fire while being driven in an open car through Dallas, Texas. Although the legislative achievements of his brief administration were modest, his martyrdom enabled his successor and vice president, Lyndon B Johnson, to promote the social reforms of the 'Great Society' as his legacy.

'Ich bin ein Berliner'

26 June 1963, West Berlin, West Germany

Kennedy left the USA in June 1963 for a goodwill tour of five nations in western Europe. West Germany was the first of these countries and Berlin – situated in East Germany but divided into east and west halves by the recently built wall – was his most eagerly anticipated destination.

East Germany had erected the wall in August 1961 to prevent skilled workers escaping to the more prosperous West Germany and threatening the viability of its economy. The concrete structure, replete with watchtowers, gun positions and mines, was over 4.5 metres (15 feet) high in parts and ran for some 160 kilometres (100 miles) around the perimeter of West Berlin.

A crowd of 120,000 cheering Berliners gathered to hear Kennedy speak on the steps of the Schöneberger Rathaus, West Berlin's city hall, near the wall itself. His speech later caused wry smiles since, in some parts of Germany (although not Berlin), *ein Berliner* is a type of doughnut. Amusement was the last thing on the audience's mind, however: they regarded Kennedy's address as a major morale boost and a message of defiance to their communist neighbours.

“ I am proud to come to this city as the guest of your distinguished Mayor,[1] who has symbolized throughout the world the fighting spirit of West Berlin. And I am proud to visit the Federal Republic with your distinguished Chancellor,[2] who for so many years has committed Germany to democracy and freedom and progress, and to come here in the company of my fellow American, General Clay,[3] who has been in this city during its great moments of crisis and will come again if ever needed.

Two thousand years ago the proudest boast was 'civis Romanus sum'.[4] Today, in the world of freedom, the proudest boast is 'Ich bin ein Berliner'. I appreciate my interpreter translating my German!

There are many people in the world who really don't understand, or say they don't, what is the great issue between the free world and the communist world. Let them come to Berlin. There are some who say that communism is the wave of the future. Let them come to Berlin. And there are some who say, in Europe and elsewhere, we can work with the communists. Let them come to Berlin. And there are even a few who say that it is true that communism is an evil system, but it permits us to make economic progress.

Lass' sie nach Berlin kommen. Let them come to Berlin.

Freedom has many difficulties and democracy is not perfect, but we have never had to put a wall up to keep our people in, to prevent them from leaving us. I want to say, on behalf of my countrymen, who live many miles away on the other side of the Atlantic, who are far distant from you, that they take the greatest pride that they have been able to share with you, even from a distance, the story of the last 18 years.

I know of no town, no city, that has been besieged for 18 years that still lives with the vitality and the force, and the hope and the determination of the city of West Berlin.

While the Wall is the most obvious and vivid demonstration of the failures of the communist system, for all the world to see, we take no satisfaction in it, for it is, as your Mayor has said, an offence not only against history but an offence against humanity, separating families, dividing husbands and wives and brothers and sisters, and dividing a people who wish to be joined together.

What is true of this city is true of Germany:

... real, lasting peace in Europe can never be assured as long as one German out of four is denied the elementary right of free men, and that is to make a free choice.

---

[1] The German statesman Willy Brandt (1913–92) served as Mayor of Berlin, 1957–66, and later Chancellor of the Federal Republic of Germany, 1969–74.
[2] The German statesman Konrad Adenauer (1876–1967) served as Chancellor of the Federal Republic of Germany, 1949–63.
[3] The US soldier General Lucius D Clay (1897–1978) was the director of civilian affairs in Germany after World War II.
[4] Latin: 'I am a Roman citizen.'

In 18 years of peace and good faith, this generation of Germans has earned the right to be free, including the right to unite their families and their nation in lasting peace, with goodwill to all people. You live in a defended island of freedom, but your life is part of the main.

So let me ask you, as I close, to lift your eyes beyond the dangers of today, to the hopes of tomorrow, beyond the freedom merely of this city of Berlin, or your country of Germany, to the advance of freedom everywhere, beyond the Wall to the day of peace with justice, beyond yourselves and ourselves to all mankind.

Freedom is indivisible, and when one man is enslaved, all are not free. When all are free, then we can look forward to that day when this city will be joined as one and this country and this great continent of Europe in a peaceful and hopeful globe. When that day finally comes, as it will, the people of West Berlin can take sober satisfaction in the fact that they were in the frontlines for almost two decades.

All free men, wherever they may live, are citizens of Berlin ...

and, therefore, as a free man, I take pride in the words: 'Ich bin ein Berliner.' ''

'I have a dream'
– *Martin Luther King*

24

Martin Luther King

American clergyman and civil rights leader

Shortly after Martin Luther King, Jr (1929–68) became pastor of the Dexter Avenue Baptist Church in Montgomery, Alabama, Rosa Parks (1913–2005) was arrested for refusing to give up her seat on a bus to a white passenger. This sparked the Montgomery bus boycott (1955–6), and King came to national prominence as its eloquent and courageous leader. In 1957, he founded the Southern Christian Leadership Conference, which organized civil rights activities throughout the country. A brilliant orator, King galvanized the movement and in 1963 led the March on Washington, where he delivered the famous 'I have a dream' speech. Inspired by the example of Mahatma Gandhi, he espoused a philosophy of non-violence and passive resistance. King's efforts were instrumental in securing passage of the Civil Rights Act of 1964 and the Voting Rights Act of 1965. He was assassinated in Memphis, Tennessee, while on a civil rights mission.

'I have a dream'

28 August 1963, Washington, DC, USA

One of the most moving, inspirational and famous of all 20th-century speeches, this address was the high point of the March on Washington for Jobs and Freedom. The brainchild of the black leader Philip Randolph (1889–1979), it was the result of co-operation between, among others, the National Association for the Advancement of Colored People, the Congress of Racial Equality and King's own Southern Christian Leadership Conference. The organizers hoped that the march would speed the passage of President John F Kennedy's Civil Rights Bill into law.

King gave his speech – which was broadcast on television and published in newspapers – from the steps of the Lincoln Memorial to about 250,000 people, a fifth of whom were white. The first half, on which he had been working until 4am the night before, is sprinkled with biblical and political allusions – to Lincoln's Emancipation Proclamation and the Declaration of Independence among other texts – to build the case for African–American freedom and equality. The second part, incredibly, was improvised: King made the brilliant decision that relaying his dream of multi-racial harmony would connect with his audience at the deepest level.

"I am happy to join with you today in what will go down in history as the greatest demonstration for freedom in the history of our nation.

[Cheers and applause.]

Five score years ago, a great American, in whose symbolic shadow we stand today,[1] signed the Emancipation Proclamation. This momentous decree came as a great beacon light of hope to millions of negro slaves who had been seared in the flames of withering injustice. It came as a joyous daybreak, to end the long night of their captivity.

But one hundred years later, the negro still is not free

One hundred years later, the life of the negro is still sadly crippled by the manacles of segregation and the chains of discrimination. One hundred years later, the negro lives on a lonely island of poverty in the midst of a vast ocean of material prosperity.

[Applause.]

One hundred years later, the negro is still languished in the corners of American society and finds himself an exile in his own land. And so we've come here today to dramatize a shameful condition.

In a sense we've come to our nation's capital to cash a cheque. When the architects of our republic wrote the magnificent words of the Constitution and the Declaration of Independence, they were signing a promissory note to which every American was to fall heir. This note was a promise that all men – yes, black men as well as white men – would be guaranteed the unalienable rights of life, liberty and the pursuit of happiness.

It is obvious today that America has defaulted on this promissory note, insofar as her citizens of colour are concerned. Instead of honouring this sacred obligation, America has given the negro people a bad cheque, a cheque which has come back marked 'insufficient funds'.

[Cheers and applause.]

But we refuse to believe that the bank of justice is bankrupt. We refuse to believe that there are insufficient funds in the great vaults of opportunity of this nation. And so we've come to cash this cheque, a cheque that will give us, upon demand, the riches of freedom and the security of justice.

[Cheers and applause.]

We have also come to this hallowed spot to remind America of the fierce urgency of now.

This is no time to engage in the luxury of cooling off or to take the tranquillizing drug of gradualism. *[Cheers and applause.]* Now is the time to make real the promises of democracy. Now is the time to rise from the dark and desolate valley of segregation to the sunlit path of racial justice. Now is the time to lift our nation from the quicksands of racial injustice to the solid rock of brotherhood. Now is the time to make justice a reality for all of God's children.

[1] King refers to Abraham Lincoln.

It would be fatal for the nation to overlook the urgency of the moment. This sweltering summer of the negro's legitimate discontent will not pass until there is an invigorating autumn of freedom and equality. Nineteen sixty-three is not an end, but a beginning. Those who hoped that the negro needed to blow off steam and will now be content will have a rude awakening if the nation returns to business as usual.

[Cheers and applause.]

There will be neither rest nor tranquillity in America until the negro is granted his citizenship rights. The whirlwinds of revolt will continue to shake the foundations of our nation until the bright day of justice emerges.

But that is something that I must say to my people, who stand on the warm threshold which leads into the palace of justice. In the process of gaining our rightful place, we must not be guilty of wrongful deeds. Let us not seek to satisfy our thirst for freedom by drinking from the cup of bitterness and hatred.

[Cheers and applause.]

We must forever conduct our struggle on the highest plane of dignity and discipline. We must not allow our creative protest to degenerate into physical violence.

Again and again, we must rise to the majestic heights of meeting physical force with soul force.

The marvellous new militancy which has engulfed the negro community must not lead us to a distrust of all white people, for many of our white brothers, as evidenced by their presence here today, have come to realize that their destiny is tied up with our destiny. *[Cheers and applause.]* And they have come to realize that their freedom is inextricably bound to our freedom. We cannot walk alone.

And as we walk, we must make the pledge that we shall always march ahead. We cannot turn back. There are those who are asking the devotees of civil rights, 'When will you be satisfied?' We can never be satisfied as long as the negro is the victim of the unspeakable horrors of police brutality. We can never be satisfied as long as our bodies, heavy with the fatigue of travel, cannot gain lodging in the motels of the highways and the hotels of the cities.

[Cheers and applause.]

We cannot be satisfied as long as a negro in Mississippi cannot vote and a negro in New York believes he has nothing for which to vote. No, no we are not satisfied and

... we will not be satisfied until justice rolls down like waters and righteousness like a mighty stream.[2]

I am not unmindful that some of you have come here out of great trials and tribulations. Some of you have come fresh from narrow jail cells. Some of you have come from areas where your quest for freedom left you battered by the storms of persecution and staggered

---

[2] See Amos 5:24.

by the winds of police brutality. You have been the veterans of creative suffering. Continue to work with the faith that unearned suffering is redemptive.

Go back to Mississippi, go back to Alabama, go back to South Carolina, go back to Georgia, go back to Louisiana, go back to the slums and ghettos of our northern cities, knowing that somehow this situation can and will be changed. Let us not wallow in the valley of despair. I say to you today my friends – [cheers and applause] so even though we face the difficulties of today and tomorrow, I still have a dream. It is a dream deeply rooted in the American dream.

I have a dream that one day this nation will rise up and live out the true meaning of its creed: 'We hold these truths to be self-evident, that all men are created equal.'

[Cheers and applause.]

I have a dream that one day on the red hills of Georgia the sons of former slaves and the sons of former slave-owners will be able to sit down together at the table of brotherhood. I have a dream that one day even the state of Mississippi, a state sweltering with the heat of injustice, sweltering with the heat of oppression, will be transformed into an oasis of freedom and justice. I have a dream that my four little children will one day live in a nation where they will not be judged by the colour of their skin but by the content of their character. I have a dream today.

[Cheers and applause.]

I have a dream that one day, down in Alabama, with its vicious racists, with its Governor having his lips dripping with the words of interposition and nullification[3] – one day right there in Alabama little black boys and black girls will be able to join hands with little white boys and white girls as sisters and brothers. I have a dream today.

[Cheers and applause.]

I have a dream that one day every valley shall be exalted, and every hill and mountain shall be made low; the rough places will be made plain, and the crooked places will be made straight, and the glory of the Lord shall be revealed and all flesh shall see it together.[4]

This is our hope.

This is the faith that I go back to the South with. With this faith, we will be able to hew out of the mountain of despair a stone of hope. With this faith, we will be able to transform the jangling discords of our nation into a beautiful symphony of brotherhood. With this faith we will be able to work together, to pray together, to struggle together, to go to jail together, to stand up for freedom together, knowing that we will be free one day.

[Applause.]

This will be the day, this will be the day when all of God's children will be able to sing with new meaning:

'My country 'tis of thee, Sweet land of liberty, Of thee I sing: Land where my fathers died, Land of the pilgrims' pride, From every mountainside, Let freedom ring!'[5]

[3] The US politician John M Patterson served as Governor of Alabama 1958–63. His period in office was marked by opposition to the Civil Rights Movement.
[4] See Isaiah 40:4–5.
[5] The hymn 'America (My Country, 'Tis of Thee)', sung to the tune of 'God Save the Queen'.

And if America is to be a great nation, this must become true. And so let freedom ring from the prodigious hilltops of New Hampshire. Let freedom ring from the mighty mountains of New York. Let freedom ring from the heightening Alleghenies of Pennsylvania. Let freedom ring from the snow-capped Rockies of Colorado. Let freedom ring from the curvaceous slopes of California. But not only that; let freedom ring from Stone Mountain of Georgia. Let freedom ring from Lookout Mountain of Tennessee. Let freedom ring from every hill and molehill of Mississippi.

From every mountainside let freedom ring.

[Cheers and applause.]

And when this happens, when we allow freedom to ring, when we let it ring from every village and every hamlet, from every state and every city, we will be able to speed up that day when all of God's children – black men and white men, Jews and gentiles, Protestants and Catholics – will be able to join hands and sing in the words of the old negro spiritual: 'Free at last! Free at last! Thank God Almighty, we are free at last!'

[Tumultuous cheers and applause.] 🙿🙿

'Uncle Sam's hands are dripping with blood, dripping with the blood of the black man in this country. He's the earth's number-one hypocrite.'

— *Malcolm X*

25

Malcolm X

American civil rights leader

While serving a prison sentence for burglary in his early twenties, Malcolm X originally Malcolm Little, later el-Hajj Malik el-Shabazz (1925–65), came under the influence of Elijah Muhammad (1897–1975), leader of the Nation of Islam movement. He embraced Islam, changed his name and, after his release in 1952, became Muhammad's chief disciple; he greatly expanded the organization's following and became the most effective spokesman for Black Power. In 1964, having been suspended from the Nation of Islam, Malcolm founded the Organization for Afro-American Unity, dedicated to the alliance of American blacks and other non-white peoples. Malcolm's extreme stance and the inflammatory nature of his oratory appealed to many blacks in the northern urban ghettos, but had been met with criticism by moderate civil rights leaders. In February 1965, Malcolm died after being shot 15 times at Audubon Ballroom in Harlem, New York City.

'*The ballot or the bullet*'

3 April 1964, Cleveland, Ohio, USA

This powerful speech is a response to the sweeping events of its time – as Malcolm X says here, 1964 'threatens to be the most explosive year America has ever witnessed'. In the run-up to the presidential elections in November, there was an urgent desire among African–Americans for President Lyndon B Johnson to secure passage of the civil rights legislation proposed by President John F Kennedy before he was assassinated. This was partly expressed in the increasing refusal of many black people to accept the programme of non-violent protest endorsed by Martin Luther King.

Also in 1964 came Malcolm's own break from the Nation of Islam and a shift in his stance, in recognition that the struggle for equality was moving from the political to the economic sphere.

Malcolm urges assertion over compromise; in place of King's dream of multi-racial harmony, he describes a 'nightmare' of segregation and mistreatment – the only response to which, he urges, must be black unity and black action. Malcolm borrowed the phrase 'the ballot or the bullet' from the 19th-century abolitionist leader Frederick Douglass, but its roots go to the heart of American history, and the anti-colonial war of liberation from England.

" Mr Moderator, Brother Lomax,[1] brothers and sisters, friends and enemies: I just can't believe everyone in here is a friend, and I don't want to leave anybody out. The question tonight, as I understand it, is 'The Negro Revolt, and Where Do We Go from Here?' or 'What Next?' In my little humble way of understanding it, it points toward either the ballot or the bullet …

… I'm not here tonight to discuss my religion. I'm not here to try and change your religion. I'm not here to argue or discuss anything that we differ about, because it's time for us to submerge our differences and realize that it is best for us to first see that we have the same problem, a common problem, a problem that will make you catch hell whether you're a Baptist, or a Methodist, or a Muslim, or a nationalist. Whether you're educated or illiterate, whether you live on the boulevard or in the alley, you're going to catch hell just like I am. We're all in the same boat and we all are going to catch the same hell from the same man. He just happens to be a white man …

All of us have suffered here, in this country, political oppression at the hands of the white man. …

Now in speaking like this, it doesn't mean that we're anti-white, but it does mean we're anti-exploitation, we're anti-degradation, we're anti-oppression. And if the white man doesn't want us to be anti-him, let him stop oppressing and exploiting and degrading us …

If we have differences, let us differ in the closet. When we come out in front, let us not have anything to argue about until we get finished arguing with the man. If the late President Kennedy could get together with Khrushchev and exchange some wheat,[2] we certainly have more in common with each other than Kennedy and Khrushchev had with each other.

If we don't do something real soon, I think you'll have to agree that we're going to be forced either to use the ballot or the bullet. It's one or the other in 1964. It isn't that time is running out – time has run out!

Nineteen sixty-four threatens to be the most explosive year America has ever witnessed.

The most explosive year. Why? It's a political year. It's the year when all of the white politicians will be back in the so-called negro community, jiving you and me for some votes. The year when all of the white political crooks will be right back in your and my community with their false promises, building up our hopes for a let-down, with their trickery and their treachery, with their false promises which they don't intend to keep. As they nourish these dissatisfactions, it can only lead to one thing, an explosion; and now we have the type of black man on the scene in America today – I'm sorry, Brother Lomax – who just doesn't intend to turn the other cheek any longer …

---

[1] The US academic and writer Louis Lomax (1922–70).   [2] In June 1963, Kennedy arranged to sell $250 million of surplus wheat to the Soviet Union to alleviate a food shortage.

I'm not a politician, not even a student of politics; in fact, I'm not a student of much of anything. I'm not a Democrat. I'm not a Republican, and I don't even consider myself an American. If you and I were Americans, there'd be no problem. Those honkies[3] that just got off the boat, they're already Americans; Polacks[4] are already Americans; the Italian refugees are already Americans. Everything that came out of Europe, every blue-eyed thing, is already an American. And as long as you and I have been over here, we aren't Americans yet.

Well, I am one who doesn't believe in deluding myself. I'm not going to sit at your table and watch you eat, with nothing on my plate, and call myself a diner. Sitting at the table doesn't make you a diner, unless you eat some of what's on that plate. Being here in America doesn't make you an American. Being born here in America doesn't make you an American. Why, if birth made you American, you wouldn't need any legislation; you wouldn't need any amendments to the Constitution; you wouldn't be faced with civil rights filibustering in Washington, DC, right now. They don't have to pass civil rights legislation to make a Polack an American.

No, I'm not an American. I'm one of the 22 million black people who are the victims of Americanism.

One of the 22 million black people who are the victims of democracy, nothing but disguised hypocrisy …

These 22 million victims are waking up. Their eyes are coming open. They're beginning to see what they used to only look at. They're becoming politically mature …

… With Kennedy and Nixon when they ran for president, it was so close they had to count all over again.[5] Well, what does this mean? It means that when white people are evenly divided, and black people have a bloc of votes of their own: it is left up to them to determine who's going to sit in the White House and who's going to be in the dog house.

It was the black man's vote that put the present administration in Washington, DC. Your vote, your dumb vote, your ignorant vote, your wasted vote put in an administration in Washington, DC, that has seen fit to pass every kind of legislation imaginable, saving you until last, then filibustering on top of that.

And your and my leaders have the audacity to run around clapping their hands and talk about how much progress we're making. And what a good president we have. If he wasn't good in Texas, he sure can't be good in Washington, DC …[6]

And these negro leaders have the audacity to go and have some coffee in the White House with a Texan, a southern cracker – that's all he is – and then come out and tell you and me that he's going to be better for us because, since he's from the South, he knows how to deal with the Southerners. What kind of logic is that? Let Eastland[7] be president, he's from the South too. He should be better able to deal with them than Johnson.

---

[3] A pejorative term for white people.
[4] A pejorative term for Polish immigrants.
[5] In the presidential election of 1960, Nixon received marginally more of the popular vote than Kennedy but, under the electoral college system, Kennedy won by a clear margin. Recounts were held in 11 states.

[6] Following Kennedy's assassination, he was succeeded by Vice President Lyndon B Johnson, a Texan, who in fact introduced reforms to tackle poverty. He also hired the first African-American White House secretary, Gerri Whittington (1931–93), who became a celebrity as a result.

In this present administration, they have in the House of Representatives 257 Democrats to only 177 Republicans. They control two-thirds of the House vote. Why can't they pass something that will help you and me? In the Senate, there are 67 senators who are of the Democratic Party. Only 33 of them are Republicans. Why, the Democrats have got the government sewed up, and you're the one who sewed it up for them.

And what have they given you for it? Four years in office, and just now getting around to some civil rights legislation … They get all the negro vote, and after they get it, the negro gets nothing in return. All they did when they got to Washington was give a few big negroes big jobs. Those big negroes didn't need big jobs; they already had jobs. That's camouflage, that's trickery, that's treachery, window-dressing …

That's why, in 1964, it's time now for you and me to become more politically mature and realize what the ballot is for; what we're supposed to get when we cast a ballot; and that if we don't cast a ballot, it's going to end up in a situation where we're going to have to cast a bullet. It's either a ballot or a bullet …

You don't need to go to the employer alone, it is the government itself, the government of America, that is responsible for the oppression and exploitation and degradation of black people in this country. And you should drop it in their lap. This government has failed the negro. This so-called democracy has failed the negro. And all these white liberals have definitely failed the negro …

You take the people who are in this audience right now. They're poor. We're all poor as individuals. Our weekly salary individually amounts to hardly anything. But if you take the salary of everyone in here collectively, it'll fill up a whole lot of baskets. It's a lot of wealth. If you can collect the wages of just these people right here for a year, you'll be rich – richer than rich. When you look at it like that, think how rich Uncle Sam had to become, not with this handful, but millions of black people. Your and my mother and father, who didn't work an eight-hour shift, but worked from 'can't see' in the morning until 'can't see' at night, and worked for nothing, making the white man rich, making Uncle Sam rich. This is our investment. This is our contribution, our blood.

Not only did we give of our free labour, we gave of our blood. Every time he had a call to arms, we were the first ones in uniform. We died on every battlefield the white man had. We have made a greater sacrifice than anybody who's standing up in America today. We have made a greater contribution and have collected less …

I might stop right here to point out one thing. Whenever you're going after something that belongs to you, anyone who's depriving you of the right to have it is a criminal. Understand that. Whenever you are going after something that is yours, you are within your legal rights to lay claim to it. And anyone who puts forth any effort to deprive you of that which is yours is breaking the law, is a criminal. And this was pointed out by the Supreme Court decision. It outlawed segregation.

7 The US politician James O Eastland (1904–86) served as Democratic Senator from Mississippi, 1941 and 1943–1978. He was notorious for his unashamed racist and anti-Semitic views and his opposition to the Civil Rights Movement.

Which means segregation is against the law.

Which means a segregationist is breaking the law. A segregationist is a criminal. You can't label him as anything other than that. And when you demonstrate against segregation, the law is on your side. The Supreme Court is on your side.

Now, who is it that opposes you in carrying out the law? The police department itself. With police dogs and clubs. Whenever you demonstrate against segregation, whether it is segregated education, segregated housing, or anything else, the law is on your side, and anyone who stands in the way is not the law any longer. They are breaking the law; they are not representatives of the law.

Any time you demonstrate against segregation and a man has the audacity to put a police dog on you, kill that dog, kill him, I'm telling you, kill that dog. I say it, if they put me in jail tomorrow, kill that dog. Then you'll put a stop to it. Now, if these white people in here don't want to see that kind of action, get down and tell the mayor to tell the police department to pull the dogs in. That's all you have to do. If you don't do it, someone else will.

If you don't take this kind of stand, your little children will grow up and look at you and think 'shame'. If you don't take an uncompromising stand, I don't mean go out and get violent; but at the same time you should never be non-violent unless you run into some non-violence. I'm non-violent with those who are non-violent with me. But when you drop that violence on me, then you've made me go insane, and I'm not responsible for what I do. And that's the way every negro should get.

Any time you know you're within the law, within your legal rights, within your moral rights, in accord with justice, then die for what you believe in. But don't die alone. Let your dying be reciprocal.

This is what is meant by equality. What's good for the goose is good for the gander …

Uncle Sam's hands are dripping with blood, dripping with the blood of the black man in this country.

He's the earth's number-one hypocrite. He has the audacity – yes, he has – imagine him posing as the leader of the free world. The free world! And you over here singing 'We Shall Overcome'. Expand the civil rights struggle to the level of human rights. Take it into the United Nations, where our African brothers can throw their weight on our side, where our Asian brothers can throw their weight on our side, where our Latin-American brothers can throw their weight on our side, and where 800 million Chinamen are sitting there waiting to throw their weight on our side.

Let the world know how bloody his hands are. Let the world know the hypocrisy that's practised over here. Let it be the ballot or the bullet. Let him know that it must be the ballot or the bullet. **"**

'Perhaps it is the least understood fact of American political life: the enormous buried violence of women in this country today.'

— *Betty Friedan*

26

Betty Friedan

American feminist and writer

Elizabeth Naomi Friedan née Goldstein (1921–2006) was founder and first president of the National Association for Women (1966), and headed the National Women's Strike for Equality (1970). Her best-selling book *The Feminine Mystique* (1963) analysed the role of women in American society and articulated their frustrations.

'Hostility between the sexes has never been worse'

January 1969, Chicago, Illinois, USA

The socio-political ferment spreading throughout the USA during the 1960s saw an explosion of feminist activity. In *The Feminine Mystique*, Friedan had described 'the problem that has no name': the discontent of an articulate group of university-educated women sublimating their own intellectual, economic and emotional lives to live vicariously through their husbands and children.

This was also a time of post-war conservatism, when abortion was illegal and reliable contraception was not readily available, even to married women. At the first national conference on abortion law, which laid the foundation for the National Association for the Repeal of Abortion Laws, Friedan gave this address, which she entitled, 'A Woman's Civil Right'.

Her closely argued speech is forceful but not hectoring, advancing the hypothesis that a sexual revolution, leading to absolute equality between men and women, was impossible unless women were able to control their own reproductive lives. Integral to this was a 'woman's right to choose' – a phrase she may have coined.

Friedan later attempted to have women's right to control their own fertility enshrined in the Constitution. Proposed in 1971, the Equal Rights Amendment would have ended discrimination based on gender. It was approved by both houses of Congress, but failed to be ratified by three-quarters of the states and was thus narrowly defeated.

" This is the first decent conference that's ever been held on abortion, because this is the first conference in which women's voices are being heard and heard strongly …

Only one voice needs to be heard on the question of whether a woman will or will not bear a child, and that is the voice of the woman herself …

her own conscience, her own conscious choice. Then, and only then, will women move out of their definition as sex objects to personhood and self-determination …

Yesterday, an obscene thing happened in the city of New York. A Committee of the State Legislature held hearings on the question of abortion. Women like me asked to testify. We were told that testimony was by invitation only. Only one woman was invited to testify on the question of abortion in the state of New York – a Catholic nun.

The only other voices were those of men. It is obscene that men, whether they be legislators or priests or even benevolent abortion reformers, should be the only ones heard on the question of women's bodies and there productive process, on what happens to the people that actually bear the children in this society.

The right of woman to control her reproductive process must be established as a basic, inalienable, civil right, not to be denied or abridged by the state – just as the right of individual and religious conscience is considered an inalienable private right in both American tradition and in the American constitution.

This is how we must address all questions governing abortion, access to birth control, and contraceptive devices. Don't talk to me about abortion reform. Abortion reform is something dreamed up by men, maybe good-hearted men, but they can only think from their male point of view … What right have they to say? What right has any man to say to any woman – you must bear this child? What right has any state to say? This is a woman's right, not a technical question needing the sanction of the state, or to be debated in terms of technicalities – they are all irrelevant.

This question can only be confronted in terms of the basic personhood and dignity of woman, which is violated for ever if she does not have the right to control her own reproductive process.

It is quite remarkable what has happened in the little more than a year during which some of us have begun to talk about abortion in these terms … New York State was having a constitutional convention and Larry Lader[1] invited me to the meeting of all the different groups … who were working on abortion reform.

---

[1] The US campaigner Lawrence 'Larry' Lader (1920–2006) wrote the book *Abortion* (1966) and co-founded the National Association for the Repeal of Abortion Laws in 1969.

I said, we're going into the New York State constitutional convention demanding a Bill of Rights for women, and we are going to demand that it be written into the Constitution that the right of a woman to control her reproductive process must be established as a civil right, a right not to be denied or abridged by the state. Most of the people at that table, people working on abortion reform, were men. They looked at me in absolute horror, as if I was out of my mind …

If I were easily intimidated, I would have slunk out. But I said, well, you may be right but as far as we are concerned, this is the only way that abortion is worth talking about; we're going to demand it and let's see what happens. As I left, a couple of the women who were sitting quietly at the table came up and said, 'We'd like to help.' Then, lo and behold, I began to hear ministers and ADA[2] and ACLU[3] and others begin to voice the same position, in terms of woman's basic right …

Women, even though they're almost too visible as sex objects in this country, are invisible people.

As the negro was the invisible man, so women are the invisible people who have a share in the decisions of the mainstream of government, of politics, of the church – who don't just cook the church supper, but preach the sermon; who don't just look up the ZIP codes[4] and address the envelopes, but make the political decisions; who don't just do the housework of industry, but make some of the executive decisions. Women, above all, who say what their own lives and personalities are going to be, and no longer listen to or even permit male experts to define what 'feminine' is or isn't.

The essence of the denigration of women is our definition as sex object … Am I saying that women must be liberated from sex? No. I am saying that sex will only be liberated to be a human dialogue, sex will only cease to be a sniggering, dirty joke and an obsession in this society, when women become active self-determining people, liberated to a creativity beyond motherhood, to a full human creativity.

Am I saying that women must be liberated from motherhood? No. I am saying that motherhood will only be a joyous and responsible human act when women are free to make, with full conscious choice and full human responsibility, the decisions to become mothers. Then, and only then, will they be able to embrace motherhood without conflict, when they will be able to define themselves not just as somebody's mother, not just as servants of children, not just as breeding receptacles, but as people for whom motherhood is a freely chosen part of life … Then, and only then, will motherhood cease to be a curse and a chain for men and for children.

The hostility between the sexes has never been worse. The image of women in avant-garde plays, novels and movies, and behind the family situation comedies on television is that mothers are man-devouring, cannibalistic monsters, or else Lolitas,[5] sex objects – and objects

---

[2] Americans for Democratic Action, founded in 1947 to promote a liberal political agenda.
[3] The American Civil Liberties Union, founded in 1920 to campaign for civil rights.
[4] The Zone Improvement Plan introduced ZIP codes throughout the USA in 1963 to improve the efficiency of the postal service.

[5] The original Lolita appears in a novel of that name (1955) by the Russian-born US novelist Vladimir Nabokov (1899–1977). A 12-year-old girl who elopes with her middle-aged stepfather, the character has become a byword for male fantasies about the sexual availability of pubescent girls.

not even of heterosexual impulse, but of sado-masochism. That impulse – the punishment of women – is much more of a factor in the abortion question than anybody ever admits.

Motherhood is a bane almost by definition, or at least partly so, as long as women are forced to be mothers – and only mothers – against their will.

Like a cancer cell living its life through another cell, women today are forced to live too much through their children and husbands …

Perhaps it is the least understood fact of American political life: the enormous buried violence of women in this country today. Like all oppressed people, women have been taking their violence out on their own bodies, in all the maladies with which they plague the MDs and the psychoanalysts. Inadvertently, and in subtle and insidious ways, they have been taking their violence out, too, on their children and on their husbands, and sometimes they're not so subtle …

Am I saying that women have to be liberated from men? That men are the enemy? No. I am saying the

> ### *… men will only be truly liberated to love women and to be fully themselves when women are liberated to have a full say in the decisions of their lives and their society.*

Until that happens, men are going to bear the guilty burden of the passive destiny they have forced upon women, the suppressed resentment, the sterility of love when it is not between two fully active, joyous people, but has in it the element of exploitation …

Men have enormous capacities in them that they have to repress and fear in order to live up to the obsolete, brutal, bear-killing, Ernest Hemingway,[6] crew-cut Prussian, napalm-all-the-children-in-Vietnam, bang-bang-you're-dead image of masculinity. Men are not allowed to admit that they sometimes are afraid. They are not allowed to express their own sensitivity, their own need to be passive sometimes and not always active. Men are not allowed to cry. So they are only half-human, as women are only half-human, until we can go this next step forward. All the burdens and responsibilities that men are supposed to shoulder alone makes them, I think, resent women's pedestal, much as that pedestal may be a burden for women.

This is the real sexual revolution. Not the cheap headlines in the papers about at what age boys and girls go to bed with each other and whether they do it with or without the benefit of marriage. That's the least of it. The real sexual revolution is the emergence of women from passivity, from the point where they are the easiest victims for all the seductions, the waste, the worshipping of false gods in our affluent society, to full self-determination and full dignity. And it is the emergence of men from the stage where they are inadvertent brutes and masters to sensitive, complete humanity …

---

[6] The US novelist Ernest Hemingway (1899–1961) was famous for his machismo and enthusiasm for hunting.

If we are finally allowed to become full people, not only will children be born and brought up with more love and responsibility than today, but we will break out of the confines of that sterile little suburban family to relate to each other in terms of all the possible dimensions of our personalities – male and female, as comrades, as colleagues, as friends, as lovers …

It's crucial, therefore, that we see this question of abortion as more than a quantitative move, more than a politically expedient move.

Abortion repeal is not a question of political expediency. It is part of something greater. It is historic that we are addressing ourselves this weekend to perhaps its first national confrontation by women and men …

In this confrontation, we are making an important milestone in this marvellous revolution that began long before any of us here were born and which still has a long way to go. As the pioneers from Mary Wollstonecraft[7] to Margaret Sanger[8] gave us the consciousness that brought us from our several directions here, so we here – in changing the very terms of the debate on abortion to assert woman's right to choose and to define the terms of our lives ourselves – move women further to full human dignity. Today, we moved history forward … 🙶

[7] The English writer Mary Wollstonecraft (1759–97) was a pioneer of women's rights and her work, which includes *Thoughts on the Education of Daughters* (1787) and *A Vindication of the Rights of Woman* (1792), is now considered a precursor of feminism.

[8] The US birth-control activist Margaret Sanger née Higgins (1879–1966) founded the American Birth Control League in 1921.

27

Edward Heath

British statesman

Edward Richard George Heath also called Ted Heath, later Sir Edward Heath (1916–2005), entered Parliament in 1950, one of R A Butler's 'One Nation' new Tory intellectuals. Elected leader of the Conservative Party in July 1965, he led the opposition until, on winning the 1970 general election, he became prime minister. At the beginning of 1973, the UK finally became a member of the European Community, which Heath considered his crowning achievement. After a long confrontation with the miners' union in 1973, the Conservatives narrowly lost the general election of February 1974, the loss being confirmed by another election in October 1974. In 1975, he was replaced as leader by Margaret Thatcher.

'A Europe which is free, democratic, safe and happy'

2 January 1973, London, England

Britain's entry into the European Community on 1 January 1973 was a personal triumph for Edward Heath. When his predecessor Harold Macmillan realized the mistake Britain had made in refusing to join the European Economic Community in 1957, Heath headed the negotiating team that applied for membership in 1961, only to be vetoed by France. He never lost sight of his ambition, however, and when the House of Commons voted by a majority of 112 to go into Europe in October 1971, he celebrated by playing Bach on the organ. Yet EC membership was and continued to be a deeply divisive issue: the Commons passed the second reading of the European Communities Bill in February 1972 by only eight votes.

Eleven months after the second reading of the European Communities Bill, Heath was once again in jubilatory mood, demonstrated by this speech given at a dinner at Hampton Court held by the British Council of the European Movement. Unlike future Conservative and Labour leaders, he had no qualms over the political and social, as well as economic, aims of the European Community, 'whose scope will gradually extend until it covers virtually the whole field of collective human endeavour'.

Divergent attitudes towards Europe continued to be a feature of future Conservative governments and in 2016 a referendum was held to determine whether or not the UK should remain in the European Union (as it is now called). The result – unforeseen by most commentators – was a vote to leave, Some saw Heath as a charmless, awkward communicator, but this address demonstrates both his sense of idealism and his optimism.

" Mr Chairman: I am delighted to be able to respond to a toast, moved with such eloquence by a European[1] who has brought to this cause a personal conviction, determination and compassion which we deeply admire. It is fitting that he should be with us here tonight, as we celebrate British entry into the Community …

Many have worked with him for this result, but we recognize with gratitude his own personal contribution which has been so considerable …

Twenty-five years ago, at the first gathering of the European Movement[2] at The Hague, Sir Winston Churchill looked forward to the day when, 'men and women of every country will think as much of being European as of belonging to their native land and wherever they go in this wide domain will truly feel, "Here I am at home".'

Tonight as we meet on the eve of the 'Fanfare for Europe' festival to mark British entry into the Community, we are one step nearer to making Churchill's dream a reality.

It is appropriate that here to celebrate this great event there should be not only a distinguished gathering of British people but also a large number of our fellow Europeans. We welcome you all – diplomatic representatives of other Community countries, presidents of the Community's institutions and distinguished elder statesmen of the Community, the 'Fathers of Europe'.

The enlargement of the Community has finally come about in this, the 25th anniversary year of the European Movement. This movement has provided much of the impetus towards European unity, and I would like to pay tribute to its work over these years.

The European Movement has brought together people from very different political, social and professional backgrounds, who are united in their belief that Britain's future should be one of partnership with our European neighbours.

In particular I would like to thank the British Council of the European Movement for their work in preparing the way for British entry into the Community.

The meaning of our accomplished membership of the Community for the British people themselves is, and is rightly, a preoccupation of many in this country. I would like to pay tribute to all those journalists and others responsible for the public media who have done so much in the last few days to ensure, by their contributions in the press, radio and elsewhere, that the real meaning of membership is understood.

We meet tonight in a palace conceived and built by Cardinal Wolsey,[3] a statesman who wrestled with the problems of Europe at a time when nationalism was in the ascendant throughout Europe. Wolsey sought to further the interests of his church, his country and his master – but at the same time he tried to keep in check the national rivalries which threatened to destroy the medieval ideal of a Europe which was essentially one.

---

[1] The Dutch agricultural technocrat Sicco Mansholt (1908–95) served as President of the European Commission, 1972–3.
[2] A lobbying association established in 1948 to work towards the unification of Europe. Churchill was among its founders.

[3] The English churchman and politician Cardinal Thomas Wolsey (c.1475–1530) was Henry VIII's chief minister between 1515 and 1529.

The forces of division proved too strong. Wolsey lost his position, he lost this palace, he was lucky not to lose his head. Europe entered on four centuries of bitter rivalry, each phase of which reached its climax in a destructive war.

Now, in 1973, we can fairly claim that since the end of the last war there has been another sea change in the history of Europe. For

… since 1945 the story of Europe has been essentially one of reconciliation instead of rivalry. In that story the founding of the European Community was one milestone.

The enlargement yesterday of that Community from six to nine members was another milestone of equal importance …

We have been accustomed during these years to hear the Community described as the Common Market. I hope that this is a habit which we can now abandon. Certainly the unified market is a fact of enormous significance. But it is only the first step in a journey which will carry us well beyond questions of tariffs and trade. For what we are building is a Community whose scope will gradually extend until it covers virtually the whole field of collective human endeavour.

I believe that the real significance of last autumn's summit meeting was precisely this. We were able to agree on the guidelines for this progress towards a wider Community.

We were able to show how, in one field after another, we could come together as neighbours to achieve by co-operation the many aims which we share and which we could not hope to realize in isolation. One of our most important decisions at that meeting was that we should work urgently towards building a European foreign policy. I believe that this is not a luxury for our Community but a clear necessity.

It is a necessity if we consider our relations with the United States. I think that all of us here tonight recognize the part which the United States has played in making possible the creation of this new Community. I am not thinking mainly of the economic help given to Europe after the war, massive and timely though this was. I am thinking rather of the consistent policy of successive administrations who have held that it was a fundamental interest of the United States that Europe should unite – an interest which outweighed the increased competition and the occasional disagreements with American policy which a united Europe was bound to involve.

In this field we can see most clearly how artificial is the distinction between foreign policy and economic policy. Our aim in Europe must be to build up our own strength, and our own Community of purpose, across the whole field of policy. Our aim must be that Europe can emerge as a valid partner of the United States in strengthening the prospects for peace and prosperity across the world …

A common policy is equally necessary in our dealings with the Soviet Union and with eastern Europe. We can see clearly enough that the whole relationship between eastern and western Europe is now once again in a state of flux. We welcome the progress which has already been made by the federal German government in working out a better relationship with its neighbours. We know that in the course of 1973 there will be further important decisions to be taken.

Our aim can be simply defined. It is to enable both western and eastern Europe to make progress without being held back by mutual suspicions or the threat of war. I am sure that we shall only succeed in this purpose if we in western Europe speak with a common voice and act with a common energy. Members of the Community, with their uniquely successful experience of the policies of reconciliation, have an important contribution to make to a better relationship with eastern Europe.

> ## *For we want to build, as our ultimate objective, a Europe which is not only prosperous – but a Europe which is free, democratic, safe and happy …*

The political task which faces us is as ambitious as any yet undertaken by a group of nations acting together. And it embraces every aspect of our responsibilities as governments and as leaders of democratic political societies. That task requires us to fulfil the needs and ambitions of our citizens.

We are, all of us throughout the Community, increasingly concerned to put right the defects and injustice of modern society.

As industry advances to the greater prosperity we expect, it has imposed new burdens on us all. Only in the last few years have we become fully aware of the effects of industrial activity on this scale: the ruin of the landscape, the pollution of the atmosphere, the poisoning of rivers and estuaries … To stop this we must act together …

There is another expectation, yet more difficult to fulfil. Throughout the nations of western Europe, and particularly among our young citizens, we have all noticed – and applauded – the growing demand that the richer nations should work more effectively to help the less developed countries, in their struggle to create conditions of life compatible with human dignity and self-respect …

The prizes to be gained by common action are very great. There is the prize of peace. There is the prize of prosperity. There is the prize of building in Europe a society which will correspond more closely to the hopes of the peoples whom we represent. These have been the aims which have inspired the founders of the European Movement. Today we can see that they are no longer far-off dreams. They are prizes which now lie within our grasp. We must show the imagination and the strength of purpose to make them our own. **,,**

'In any organization, the man at the top must bear the responsibility. That responsibility, therefore, belongs here in this office. I accept it.'

— Richard M Nixon

28

Richard M Nixon

American politician

After practising as a lawyer, Richard Milhous Nixon (1913–94) served in the US Navy (1942–6), then ran for Congress as a Republican in California. His fearless outspokenness and tactical brilliance boosted his political career, and he was a prominent member of the House Committee on Un-American Activities. He became the Republican presidential candidate in 1960, losing narrowly to John F Kennedy, but went on to win the presidential election in 1968 by a small margin. In 1972, he was re-elected with a large majority. In June 1972, there was a burglary at the Democratic National Committee's headquarters in the Watergate building, Washington, in which Nixon's re-election team was swiftly implicated. During the official investigation which followed, Nixon lost credibility. On 9 August 1974, after several leading members of his government had been found guilty of involvement in the Watergate scandal, he resigned, thus averting the threat of impeachment.

'There can be no whitewash at the White House'

30 April 1973, broadcast from Washington, DC, USA

The Watergate scandal began on 17 June 1972, when police arrested five men who had broken into the headquarters of the Democratic Party at the Watergate building in Washington, DC. They were soon linked to the Republican Party's Committee for the Re-election of the President.

Nixon may have had no prior knowledge of the break-in – whose perpetrators had broken in three weeks earlier to install bugging devices – but quickly realized it could undermine his re-election chances. He therefore ordered the FBI to halt its investigations, paid hush money to the five burglars and instructed his special counsel, John Dean, to conceal any involvement by the administration.

By early 1973, however, the conspiracy of concealment was unravelling. The *Washington Post* had already broken news of the scandal, and in February a special Senate committee was set up to investigate the affair. In televised hearings, Dean accused Nixon of involvement in the cover-up. Nixon responded by firing Dean; three other aides swiftly resigned.

In this speech, broadcast from the Oval Office of the White House at 9pm, he announced these resignations and proclaimed his innocence. Nixon made a show of leadership, accepting responsibility for mistakes even if they were not of his making, and looking beyond the scandal to the 'great goals' of peace, opportunity, decency and civility. Later, he would be forced to resign over the affair.

❝ Good evening. I want to talk to you tonight from my heart on a subject of deep concern to every American.

In recent months, members of my administration and officials of the Committee for the Re-election of the President – including some of my closest friends and most trusted aides – have been charged with involvement in what has come to be known as the Watergate affair. These include charges of illegal activity during and preceding the 1972 presidential election and charges that responsible officials participated in efforts to cover up that illegal activity.

The inevitable result of these charges has been to raise serious questions about the integrity of the White House itself.

Tonight I wish to address those questions.

Last June 17, while I was in Florida trying to get a few days' rest after my visit to Moscow,[1] I first learned from news reports of the Watergate break-in. I was appalled at this senseless, illegal action, and I was shocked to learn that employees of the re-election committee were apparently among those guilty. I immediately ordered an investigation by appropriate government authorities. On September 15, as you will recall, indictments were brought against seven defendants in the case.

As the investigations went forward, I repeatedly asked those conducting the investigation whether there was any reason to believe that members of my administration were in any way involved. I received repeated assurances that there were not …

Until March of this year, I remained convinced that the denials were true and that the charges of involvement by members of the White House staff were false. The comments I made during this period, and the comments made by my press secretary in my behalf, were based on the information provided to us at the time we made those comments. However, new information then came to me which persuaded me that there was a real possibility that some of these charges were true, and suggesting further that there had been an effort to conceal the facts both from the public, from you, and from me.

As a result, on March 21, I personally assumed the responsibility for co-ordinating intensive new inquiries into the matter, and I personally ordered those conducting the investigations to get all the facts and to report them directly to me, right here in this office.

I again ordered that all persons in the government or at the re-election committee should co-operate fully with the FBI, the prosecutors, and the grand jury. I also ordered that anyone who refused to co-operate in telling the truth would be asked to resign from government service. And, with ground rules adopted that would preserve the basic constitutional separation of powers between the Congress and the presidency, I directed that members of the White House staff should appear and testify voluntarily under oath before the Senate committee which was investigating Watergate.

---

[1] In May 1972, Nixon visited Moscow to sign arms limitation treaties with the USSR.

I was determined that we should get to the bottom of the matter, and that the truth should be fully brought out – no matter who was involved …

Whatever may appear to have been the case before, whatever improper activities may yet be discovered in connection with this whole sordid affair, I want the American people, I want you to know beyond the shadow of a doubt that during my term as president, justice will be pursued fairly, fully, and impartially, no matter who is involved.

This office is a sacred trust and I am determined to be worthy of that trust.

Looking back at the history of this case, two questions arise. How could it have happened? Who is to blame?

Political commentators have correctly observed that during my 27 years in politics I have always previously insisted on running my own campaigns for office.

But 1972 presented a very different situation. In both domestic and foreign policy, 1972 was a year of crucially important decisions, of intense negotiations, of vital new directions, particularly in working toward the goal which has been my overriding concern throughout my political career – the goal of bringing peace to America, peace to the world.

That is why I decided, as the 1972 campaign approached, that the presidency should come first and politics second. To the maximum extent possible, therefore, I sought to delegate campaign operations, to remove the day-to-day campaign decisions from the president's office and from the White House. I also, as you recall, severely limited the number of my own campaign appearances.

Who, then, is to blame for what happened in this case?

For specific criminal actions by specific individuals, those who committed those actions must, of course, bear the liability and pay the penalty.

For the fact that alleged improper actions took place within the White House or within my campaign organization, the easiest course would be for me to blame those to whom I delegated the responsibility to run the campaign. But that would be a cowardly thing to do.

I will not place the blame on subordinates – on people whose zeal exceeded their judgement and who may have done wrong in a cause they deeply believed to be right.

In any organization, the man at the top must bear the responsibility. That responsibility, therefore, belongs here in this office. I accept it. And I pledge to you tonight, from this office, that I will do everything in my power to ensure that the guilty are brought to justice and that such abuses are purged from our political processes in the years to come, long after I have left this office.

Some people, quite properly appalled at the abuses that occurred, will say that Watergate demonstrates the bankruptcy of the American political system. I believe precisely the opposite is true. Watergate represented a series of illegal acts and bad judgements by a number of individuals. It was the system that has brought the facts to light and that will bring those guilty to justice – a system that in this case has included a determined grand jury, honest prosecutors, a courageous judge, John Sirica,[2] and a vigorous free press.[3]

It is essential now that we place our faith in that system – and especially in the judicial system. It is essential that we let the judicial process go forward, respecting those safeguards that are established to protect the innocent as well as to convict the guilty. It is essential that in reacting to the excesses of others, we not fall into excesses ourselves. It is also essential that we not be so distracted by events such as this that we neglect the vital work before us, before this nation, before America, at a time of critical importance to America and the world.

Since March, when I first learned that the Watergate affair might in fact be far more serious than I had been led to believe, it has claimed far too much of my time and my attention. Whatever may now transpire in the case, whatever the actions of the grand jury, whatever the outcome of any eventual trials, I must now turn my full attention – and I shall do so – once again to the larger duties of this office. I owe it to this great office that I hold, and I owe it to you – to my country … There is vital work to be done toward our goal of a lasting structure of peace in the world – work that cannot wait, work that I must do …

When I think of this office – of what it means – I think of all the things that I want to accomplish for this nation, of all the things I want to accomplish for you.

On Christmas Eve, during my terrible personal ordeal of the renewed bombing of North Vietnam[4] – which after 12 years of war finally helped to bring America peace with honour – I sat down just before midnight. I wrote out some of my goals for my second term as president. Let me read them to you.

'To make it possible for our children, and for our children's children, to live in a world of peace.

'To make this country be more than ever a land of opportunity – of equal opportunity, full opportunity for every American.

'To provide jobs for all who can work, and generous help for those who cannot work.

'To establish a climate of decency and civility, in which each person respects the feelings and the dignity and the God-given rights of his neighbour.

'To make this a land in which each person can dare to dream, can live his dreams – not in fear, but in hope – proud of his community, proud of his country, proud of what America has meant to himself and to the world.'

---

[2] The US lawyer John Sirica (1904–92) was the Chief Judge of the District Court for the District of Columbia. He presided over the burglars' trial, and later demanded that Nixon turn over his recordings of White House conversations.
[3] Nixon alludes to the investigative reporting of the *Washington Post* journalists Bob Woodward (1943–) and Carl Bernstein (1944–), who received leaked information about the scandal from a source known then only as 'Deep Throat'. In 2005, his identity was revealed as W Mark Felt (1913–2008), a senior FBI official during the early 1970s.

These are great goals. I believe we can, we must work for them. We can achieve them. But we cannot achieve these goals unless we dedicate ourselves to another goal.

We must maintain the integrity of the White House, and that integrity must be real, not transparent. There can be no whitewash at the White House.

We must reform our political process, ridding it not only of the violations of the law but also of the ugly mob-violence and other inexcusable campaign tactics that have been too often practised and too readily accepted in the past, including those that may have been a response by one side to the excesses or expected excesses of the other side. Two wrongs do not make a right.

I have been in public life for more than a quarter of a century. Like any other calling, politics has good people and bad people. And let me tell you, the great majority in politics – in the Congress, in the federal government, in the state government – are good people. I know that it can be very easy, under the intensive pressures of a campaign, for even well-intentioned people to fall into shady tactics, to rationalize this on the grounds that what is at stake is of such importance to the nation that the end justifies the means. And both of our great parties have been guilty of such tactics in the past.

In recent years, however, the campaign excesses that have occurred on all sides have provided a sobering demonstration of how far this false doctrine can take us.

The lesson is clear: America, in its political campaigns, must not again fall into the trap of letting the end, however great that end is, justify the means.

I urge the leaders of both political parties, I urge citizens, all of you, everywhere, to join in working toward a new set of standards, new rules and procedures to ensure that future elections will be as nearly free of such abuses as they possibly can be made. This is my goal. I ask you to join in making it America's goal. ""

---

[4] On 18 December 1972, Nixon ordered a new bombing campaign against North Vietnam, code-named Operation Linebacker Two. It lasted for 12 days and resulted in the deaths of up to 1,600 North Vietnamese and 90 US airmen.

'I have come bearing an olive branch
and a freedom fighter's gun'
– *Yasser Arafat*

29

Yasser Arafat

Palestinian resistance leader and politician

Yasser Arafat real name Mohammed Abed Ar'ouf (1929–2004) co-founded the Al Fatah resistance group in 1956. By 1969, Arafat's Al Fatah group had gained control of the Palestinian Liberation Organization (PLO; founded in 1964), and he became its acknowledged (though not universally popular) leader. The organization was formally recognized by the United Nations in 1974. Under Arafat's leadership, the PLO's original aim – to create a secular state over the whole of former Palestine – was modified to one of establishing an independent state within the territory. In 1993, Arafat and the Israeli prime minister Yitzhak Rabin negotiated a peace agreement in the USA (signed in Cairo in 1994), under which Israel withdrew from Jericho and the Gaza Strip.

Arafat returned as head of a Palestinian state (1994) and in 1995 he negotiated a Israeli withdrawal from the West Bank. Peace, however, proved increasingly fragile and by 2003 Arafat was widely considered unable to control Arab militancy. He died in November 2004 of an illness whose nature was disputed.

'*I have come bearing an olive branch and a freedom fighter's gun*'

13 November 1974, New York City, USA

Yasser Arafat was the first representative of a non-governmental organization to be invited to address the General Assembly of the United Nations. He appeared at their New York headquarters wearing a *kaffiyeh* headscarf, with his gun-belt strapped around his waist. Although it is unlikely that there was a weapon in the holster, the timing was remarkable. In 1972, the Black September Organization – believed to be linked to the PLO – had murdered 11 Israeli athletes at the Munich Summer Olympics.

In this speech, Arafat blames the troubles of the Middle East on imperialism and Zionism. These, he says, conspired in the partition of Palestinian land following the Balfour Declaration (1917), by which the British foreign secretary Arthur Balfour expressed British support for the establishment of a Jewish homeland in Palestine. Arafat seeks to legitimize the PLO as freedom fighters by reiterating the themes of just cause and legitimate struggle, and reminds his listeners that many of them achieved independence through similar colonial wars. His repetition of the word 'exile' also has echoes in the Jewish history of exile and diaspora. Arafat ends his speech with a veiled threat of further violence.

Despite this, he received a standing ovation from most of the audience. A year later, Resolution 3237 granted the PLO observer status at the UN. It was the first non-governmental body to be recognized in this way.

" Mr President: I thank you for having invited the Palestinian Liberation Organization to participate in this plenary session of the United Nations General Assembly. This is a very important occasion …

Our world aspires to peace, justice, equality and freedom. It wishes that oppressed nations, at present bent under the weight of imperialism, might gain their freedom and their right to self-determination. It hopes to place the relations between nations on a basis of equality, peaceful coexistence, mutual respect for each other's internal affairs, secure national sovereignty, independence and territorial unity on the basis of justice and mutual benefit …

Great numbers of peoples, including those of Zimbabwe, Namibia, South Africa and Palestine, among many others, are still victims of oppression and violence … It is imperative that the international community should support these peoples in their struggles, in the furtherance of their rightful causes, in the attainment of their right to self-determination …

[But] despite abiding world crises, despite even the gloomy powers of backwardness and disastrous wrong, we live in a time of glorious change.

An old world order is crumbling before our eyes, as imperialism, colonialism, neo-colonialism and racism, the chief form of which is Zionism, ineluctably perish.

We are privileged to be able to witness a great wave of history bearing peoples forward into a new world which they have created. In that world just causes will triumph. Of that we are confident.

The question of Palestine belongs to this perspective of emergence and struggle … Present at this very moment in our midst are those who, while they occupy our homes, as their cattle graze in our pastures, and as their hands pluck the fruit of our trees, claim at the same time that we are disembodied spirits, fictions without presence, without traditions or future …

For there are amongst you – and here I refer to the United States of America and others like it – those who supply our enemy freely with planes and bombs and with every variety of murderous weapon. They take hostile positions against us, deliberately distorting the true essence of the problem. All this is done not only at our expense, but at the expense of the American people, and of the friendship we continue to hope can be cemented between us and this great people, whose history of struggle for the sake of freedom we honour and salute.

I cannot now forgo this opportunity to appeal from this rostrum directly to the American people, asking it to give its support to our heroic and fighting people. I ask it wholeheartedly to endorse right and justice, to recall George Washington[1] to mind, heroic Washington whose purpose was his nation's freedom and independence; Abraham Lincoln,[2]

---

[1] George Washington (1732–99) was the first president of the USA, serving 1789–97.   [2] Abraham Lincoln (1809–65) was the 16th president of the USA, serving 1861–5. He is widely considered one of the most important former presidents, who oversaw the abolition of slavery and improved federal union.

champion of the destitute and the wretched; also Woodrow Wilson,[3] whose doctrine of Fourteen Points remains subscribed to and venerated by our people …

As our discussion of the question of Palestine focuses upon historical roots, we do so because we believe that any question now exercising the world's concern must be viewed radically, in the true root sense of that word, if a real solution is ever to be grasped … The roots of the Palestinian question reach back into the closing years of the 19th century, in other words, to that period which we call the era of colonialism and settlement, as we know it today. This is precisely the period during which Zionism as a scheme was born; its aim was the conquest of Palestine by European immigrants, just as settlers colonized, and indeed raided, most of Africa …

Just as colonialism and its demagogues dignified their conquests, their plunder and limitless attacks upon the natives of Africa with appeals to a 'civilizing and modernizing' mission, so too did waves of Zionist immigrants disguise their purposes as they conquered Palestine …

Zionist theology was utilized against our Palestinian people: the purpose was not only the establishment of Western-style settler colonialism but also the severing of Jews from their various homelands and subsequently their estrangement from their nations. Zionism is an ideology that is imperialist, colonialist, racist; it is profoundly reactionary and discriminatory; it is united with anti-Semitism in its retrograde tenets and is, when all is said and done, another side of the same base coin. For when what is proposed is that adherents of the Jewish faith, regardless of their national residence, should neither owe allegiance to their national residence nor live on equal footing with its other, non-Jewish citizens – when that is proposed we hear anti-Semitism being proposed.

So the Zionist movement allied itself directly with world colonialism in a common raid on our land. Allow me now to present a selection of historical truths about this alliance.

The Jewish invasion of Palestine began in 1881. Before the first large wave of immigrants started arriving, Palestine had a population of half a million; most of the population was either Muslim or Christian, and only 20,000 were Jewish. Every segment of the population enjoyed the religious tolerance characteristic of our civilization. Palestine was then a verdant land, inhabited mainly by an Arab people in the course of building its life and dynamically enriching its indigenous culture.

Between 1882 and 1917 the Zionist movement settled approximately 50,000 European Jews in our homeland. To do that it resorted to trickery and deceit in order to implant them in our midst. Its success in getting Britain to issue the Balfour Declaration[4] once again demonstrated the alliance between Zionism and imperialism. Furthermore, by promising to the Zionist movement what was not hers to give, Britain showed how oppressive was the rule of imperialism.

---

[3] Woodrow Wilson (1856–1924) was the 28th president of the USA, serving 1913–21. In January 1918, he set out his 'Fourteen Points, a programme for world peace'.

[4] Arthur Balfour's famous 'Declaration' was a letter of 1917, in which he stated that 'His Majesty's government view with favour the establishment in Palestine of a national home for the Jewish people'.

As it was constituted then, the League of Nations abandoned our Arab people, and Wilson's pledges and promises came to nought. In the guise of a mandate, British imperialism was cruelly and directly imposed upon us, to enable the Zionist invaders to consolidate their gains in our homeland …

By 1947 the number of Jews had reached 600,000; they owned about 6 per cent of Palestinian arable land. The figure should be compared with the population of Palestine, which at that time was 1,250,000.

As a result of the collusion between the mandatory power and the Zionist movement and with the support of some countries, this General Assembly early in its history approved a recommendation to partition our Palestinian homeland … When we rejected that decision, our position corresponded to that of the natural mother who refused to permit King Solomon to cut her son in two when the unnatural mother claimed the child for herself and agreed to his dismemberment.

Furthermore, even though the partition resolution granted the colonialist settlers 54 per cent of the land of Palestine, their dissatisfaction with the decision prompted them to wage a war of terror against the civilian Arab population … They built their own settlements and colonies on the ruins of our farms and our groves.

The roots of the Palestine question lie here. Its causes do not stem from any conflict between two religions or two nationalisms. Neither is it a border conflict between neighbouring states. It is the cause of a people deprived of its homeland, dispersed and uprooted, and living mostly in exile and in refugee camps.

With support from imperialist and colonialist Powers, [Israel] managed to get itself accepted as a United Nations member. It further succeeded in getting the Palestine question deleted from the agenda of the United Nations and in deceiving world public opinion by presenting our cause as a problem of refugees in need either of charity from do-gooders, or settlement in a land not theirs.

Not satisfied with all this, the racist entity, founded on the imperialist-colonialist concept, turned itself into a base of imperialism and into an arsenal of weapons.

This enabled it to assume its role of subjugating the Arab people and of committing aggression against them, in order to satisfy its ambitions for further expansion on Palestinian and other Arab lands. In addition to the many instances of aggression committed by this entity against the Arab States, it has launched two large-scale wars, in 1956 and 1967, thus endangering world peace and security.

As a result of Zionist aggression in June 1967, the enemy occupied Egyptian Sinai as far as the Suez Canal. The enemy occupied Syria's Golan Heights, in addition to all Palestinian land west of the Jordan. All these developments have led to the creation in our area of what has come to be known as the 'Middle East problem'. The situation has been rendered more serious by the enemy's persistence in maintaining its unlawful occupation and in further consolidating it, thus establishing a beachhead for world imperialism's thrust against our Arab nation …

The fourth war broke out in October 1973, bringing home to the Zionist enemy the bankruptcy of its policy of occupation, expansion and its reliance on the concept of military might. Despite all this, the leaders of the Zionist entity are far from having learned any lesson from their experience. They are making preparations for the fifth war, resorting once more to the language of military superiority, aggression, terrorism, subjugation and, finally, always to war in their dealings with the Arabs …

As a son of Jerusalem, I treasure for myself and my people beautiful memories and vivid images of the religious brotherhood that was the hallmark of our holy city before it succumbed to catastrophe … Our revolution has not been motivated by racial or religious factors. Its target has never been the Jew as a person, but racist Zionism and undisguised aggression. In this sense, ours is also a revolution for the Jew as a human being as well. We are struggling so that Jews, Christians and Muslims may live in equality, enjoying the same rights and assuming the same duties, free from racial or religious discrimination.

We do distinguish between Judaism and Zionism. While we maintain our opposition to the colonialist Zionist movement, we respect the Jewish faith. Today, almost one century after the rise of the Zionist movement, we wish to warn of its increasing danger to the Jews of the world, to our Arab people and to world peace and security …

Those who call us terrorists wish to prevent world public opinion from discovering the truth about us and from seeing the justice on our faces …

The difference between the revolutionary and the terrorist lies in the reason for which each fights. For

… whoever stands by a just cause and fights for the freedom and liberation of his land from the invaders, the settlers and the colonialists cannot possibly be called terrorist …

This is actually a just and proper struggle, consecrated by the United Nations Charter and by the Universal Declaration of Human Rights. As to those who fight against the just causes, those who wage war to occupy, colonize and oppress other people, those are the terrorists …

Their terrorism fed on hatred and this hatred was even directed against the olive tree in my country, which has been a proud symbol and which reminded them of the indigenous inhabitants of the land, a living reminder that the land is Palestinian – thus they sought to destroy it … Their terrorism even reached our sacred places in our beloved and peaceful Jerusalem. They have endeavoured to de-Arabize it and make it lose its Muslim and Christian character by evicting its inhabitants and annexing it …

Need one remind this assembly of the numerous resolutions adopted by it condemning Israeli aggressions committed against Arab countries, Israeli violations of human rights and the articles of the Geneva Conventions, as well as the resolutions pertaining to the annexation of the city of Jerusalem and its restoration to its former status? The only description for these acts is that they are acts of barbarism and terrorism. And yet, the

Zionist racists and colonialists have the temerity to describe the just struggle of our people as terror. Could there be a more flagrant distortion of truth than this?

… I am a rebel and freedom is my cause. I know well that many of you present here today once stood in exactly the same resistance position as I now occupy and from which I must fight. You once had to convert dreams into reality by your struggle … Why therefore should I not dream and hope? For is not revolution the making real of dreams and hopes? So let us work together that my dream may be fulfilled, that I may return with my people out of exile, there in Palestine to live with this Jewish freedom-fighter and his partners, with this Arab priest and his brothers, in one democratic state where Christian, Jew and Muslim live in justice, equality, fraternity and progress. Is this not a noble dream? … In my formal capacity as Chairman of the Palestine Liberation Organization and leader of the Palestinian revolution, I appeal to you to accompany our people in its struggle to attain its right to self-determination …

> ### *Today I have come bearing an olive branch and a freedom fighter's gun.*

Do not let the olive branch fall from my hand. I repeat: do not let the olive branch fall from my hand. **"**

'The lady's not for turning'
– *Margaret Thatcher*

30

Margaret Thatcher

British politician

Margaret Hilda Thatcher née Roberts, later Baroness Thatcher (1925–2013), was elected MP for Finchley in 1959 and joined the Shadow Cabinet in 1967. In Edward Heath's government (1970–74) she served as Secretary of State for Education and Science. She was elected leader of the Conservative Party in 1975 and became prime minister in May 1979. In her first administration, she reduced inflation, but unemployment rose. Her popularity was boosted by the recapture of the Falkland Islands following the Argentinian invasion of 1982 and she was reelected in June 1983. During her second term, she placed greater emphasis on the market economy. The economy continued to grow during her second administration, but her tough stance was unpopular in several quarters. She was returned for a third term in 1987. On the international stage, she established a close friendship with US president Ronald Reagan, won the admiration of Soviet president Mikhail Gorbachev, and was credited with helping end the Cold War. After 1989, her leadership of the party was challenged and in November 1990 she resigned. Much of her economic legacy became common ground between the British political parties after Tony Blair became Labour leader in 1994.

'The lady's not for turning'

10 October 1980, Brighton, England

Margaret Thatcher's keynote speech to the 1980 Conservative Party conference, the middle section of which is reproduced here, was a rousing statement of defiance against critics outside and within the party who had attacked her government's counter-inflationary policies, blaming them for the growth in unemployment. While she acknowledged the 'human tragedy' of Britain's two million unemployed, she insisted that low inflation offered the only real hope of long-term prosperity. Additional measures, she hinted, were curbing the wastefulness of local authorities and nationalized utilities – measures which Thatcher would increasingly effect during her 11 years in office, limiting the powers of local authorities and privatizing the utility companies.

The most famous line of the speech – and one of the most memorable of her career – was a direct riposte to commentators who were predicting that Thatcher would be forced to make a 'U-turn' on her economic policy, just as Edward Heath's government had been in 1972. However, an equally telling moment – in terms of the national mood and the prime minister's mettle – occurred earlier in the speech, when protesters burst into the conference hall, shouting 'Tories out! We want jobs!'. Thatcher responded, to thunderous applause, 'Never mind, it's wet outside. I expect they wanted to come in. You can't blame them; it's always better where the Tories are.'

" The level of unemployment in our country today is a human tragedy. Let me make it clear beyond doubt: I am profoundly concerned about unemployment. Human dignity and self-respect are undermined when men and women are condemned to idleness. The waste of a country's most precious assets – the talent and energy of its people – makes it the bounden duty of government to seek a real and lasting cure.

If I could press a button and genuinely solve the unemployment problem, do you think that I would not press that button this instant?

Does anyone imagine that there is the smallest political gain in letting this unemployment continue, or that there is some obscure economic religion which demands this unemployment as part of its ritual? This government are pursuing the only policy which gives any hope of bringing our people back to real and lasting employment …

I know that there is another real worry affecting many of our people.

Although they accept that our policies are right, they feel deeply that the burden of carrying them out is falling much more heavily on the private than on the public sector. They say that the public sector is enjoying advantages but the private sector is taking the knocks and at the same time maintaining those in the public sector with better pay and pensions than they enjoy.

I must tell you that I share this concern and understand the resentment. That is why I and my colleagues say that to add to public spending takes away the very money and resources that industry needs to stay in business let alone to expand. Higher public spending, far from curing unemployment, can be the very vehicle that loses jobs and causes bankruptcies in trade and commerce. That is why we warned local authorities that since rates are frequently the biggest tax that industry now faces, increases in them can cripple local businesses. Councils must, therefore, learn to cut costs in the same way that companies have to.[1]

That is why I stress that if those who work in public authorities take for themselves large pay increases they leave less to be spent on equipment and new buildings. That in turn deprives the private sector of the orders it needs, especially some of those industries in the hard-pressed regions. Those in the public sector have a duty to those in the private sector not to take out so much in pay that they cause others unemployment. That is why we point out that every time high wage settlements in nationalized monopolies lead to higher charges for telephones, electricity, coal and water, they can drive companies out of business and cost other people their jobs.

If spending money like water was the answer to our country's problems, we would have no problems now.

If ever a nation has spent, spent, spent and spent again, ours has. Today that dream is over. All of that money has got us nowhere but it still has to come from somewhere.

---

[1] 'Rate-capping', which limited local councils' entitlement to levy property tax – or 'rates' – became a contentious issue during Thatcher's first administration.

Those who urge us to relax the squeeze, to spend yet more money indiscriminately in the belief that it will help the unemployed and the small businessman, are not being kind or compassionate or caring. They are not the friends of the unemployed or the small business. They are asking us to do again the very thing that caused the problems in the first place. We have made this point repeatedly.

I am accused of lecturing or preaching about this. I suppose it is a critic's way of saying, 'Well, we know it is true, but we have to carp at something.' I do not care about that. But I do care about the future of free enterprise, the jobs and exports it provides and the independence it brings to our people. Independence? Yes, but let us be clear what we mean by that. Independence does not mean contracting out of all relationships with others. A nation can be free but it will not stay free for long if it has no friends and no alliances. Above all, it will not stay free if it cannot pay its own way in the world. By the same token, an individual needs to be part of a community and to feel that he is part of it. There is more to this than the chance to earn a living for himself and his family, essential though that is.

Of course, our vision and our aims go far beyond the complex arguments of economics, but unless we get the economy right we shall deny our people the opportunity to share that vision and to see beyond the narrow horizons of economic necessity.

Without a healthy economy we cannot have a healthy society. Without a healthy society the economy will not stay healthy for long.

But it is not the state that creates a healthy society. When the state grows too powerful, people feel that they count for less and less.

> ### *The state drains society, not only of its wealth but of initiative, of energy, the will to improve and innovate as well as to preserve what is best.*

Our aim is to let people feel that they count for more and more. If we cannot trust the deepest instincts of our people we should not be in politics at all. Some aspects of our present society really do offend those instincts.

Decent people do want to do a proper job at work, not to be restrained or intimidated from giving value for money. They believe that honesty should be respected, not derided. They see crime and violence as a threat, not just to society but to their own orderly way of life. They want to be allowed to bring up their children in these beliefs, without the fear that their efforts will be daily frustrated in the name of progress or free expression. Indeed, that is what family life is all about.

There is not a generation gap in a happy and united family.

People yearn to be able to rely on some generally accepted standards. Without them you have not got a society at all, you have purposeless anarchy. A healthy society is not created by its institutions, either. Great schools and universities do not make a great nation, any more than great armies do. Only a great nation can create and involve great institutions – of learning, of healing, of scientific advance. And a great nation is the voluntary creation of its people – a people composed of men and women whose pride in themselves is founded on the knowledge of what they can give to a community of which they in turn can be proud.

If our people feel that they are part of a great nation and they are prepared to will the means to keep it great, a great nation we shall be, and shall remain. So, what can stop us from achieving this? What then stands in our way? The prospect of another winter of discontent?[2] I suppose it might.

But I prefer to believe that certain lessons have been learnt from experience, that we are coming, slowly, painfully, to an autumn of understanding. And I hope that it will be followed by a winter of common sense. If it is not, we shall not be diverted from our course.

To those waiting with bated breath for that favourite media catchphrase, the 'U-turn', I have only one thing to say. 'You turn if you want to. The lady's not for turning.'[3] 🙶

---

[2] In the winter of 1978–9, James Callaghan's Labour government faced a series of public sector strikes, leaving the country at various times without postal, firefighting or rubbish collection services. This period, which led to Labour's defeat in the 1979 general election, became known as the 'winter of discontent', a phrase drawn from the opening line of *Richard III* (c.1592) by William Shakespeare.
[3] This line plays on the title of the verse play *The Lady's Not for Burning* (1949) by the English dramatist Christopher Fry (1907–2005).

'I believe that communism is another sad, bizarre chapter in human history whose last pages even now are being written. I believe this because the source of our strength in the quest for human freedom is not material, but spiritual.'

— Ronald Reagan

31

Ronald Reagan

American politician

A successful Hollywood actor, Ronald Wilson Reagan (1911–2004) became interested in politics when serving as president of the Screen Actors' Guild (1947–52) and moved increasingly towards Republicanism, particularly following his marriage in 1952 to the affluent actress Nancy Davis (1921–2016). He joined the Republican Party in 1962 and in 1966 was elected governor of California, a post he held until 1972. In 1980, after two previous attempts, he captured the party's presidential nomination and convincingly defeated President Jimmy Carter (1924–). He survived an attempted assassination in 1981 and secured re-election by a record margin in 1984. His programme of tax cuts and deficit financing brought about rapid economic upturn between 1983 and 1986, while on the international stage he became a convert to détente, holding four summit meetings with Soviet leader Mikhail Gorbachev and signing a treaty for the scrapping of intermediate nuclear forces. Dubbed 'the great communicator' for his accomplished handling of the media, Reagan had a unique, populist rapport with 'mainstream America' and left office an immensely popular figure.

'The aggressive impulses of an evil empire'

8 March 1983, Orlando, Florida, USA

Among Reagan's priorities when he came to power was the restoration of the USA's military and moral pre-eminence; to this end, he authorized vast increases in defence spending and pursued a conservative social agenda.

This speech, made at the annual convention of the National Association of Evangelicals, is a clear reflection of Reagan's main aims: the first half (omitted here) dealt with the importance of Christianity in American life and discussed sexual morality and abortion; the second half dismisses calls for the USA to freeze its nuclear arsenal, and famously describes the Soviet Union as an 'evil empire'.

The speech, and this phrase in particular, divided opinion around the world. The Soviet authorities were incensed – an official response stated that Reagan's administration could 'think only in terms of confrontation and bellicose, lunatic anti-communism'. Others, however, thought that by introducing the notion of 'evil' into the Cold War, Reagan had claimed the moral high ground and gained new confidence for the USA.

Years later, Reagan said of his speech, 'It was portrayed as some kind of know-nothing, arch-conservative statement … [but] the Soviet system has purposely starved, murdered and brutalized its own people … Is the system that allowed this not evil?'

" During my first press conference as president, in answer to a direct question, I pointed out that, as good Marxist–Leninists, the Soviet leaders have openly and publicly declared that the only morality they recognize is that which will further their cause, which is world revolution. I think I should point out I was only quoting Lenin, their guiding spirit, who said in 1920 that they repudiate all morality that proceeds from supernatural ideas – that's their name for religion – or ideas that are outside class conceptions. Morality is entirely subordinate to the interests of class war. And everything is moral that is necessary for the annihilation of the old, exploiting social order and for uniting the proletariat.

Well, I think the refusal of many influential people to accept this elementary fact of Soviet doctrine illustrates an historical reluctance to see totalitarian powers for what they are. We saw this phenomenon in the 1930s. We see it too often today.

This doesn't mean we should isolate ourselves and refuse to seek an understanding with them. I intend to do everything I can to persuade them of our peaceful intent, to remind them that it was the West that refused to use its nuclear monopoly in the '40s and '50s for territorial gain, and which now proposes a 50 per cent cut in strategic ballistic missiles and the elimination of an entire class of land-based, intermediate-range nuclear missiles.

At the same time, however, they must be made to understand we will never compromise our principles and standards.

... We will never give away our freedom. We will never abandon our belief in God.

And we will never stop searching for a genuine peace. But we can assure none of these things America stands for through the so-called nuclear freeze solutions proposed by some.

The truth is that a freeze now would be a very dangerous fraud, for that is merely the illusion of peace. The reality is that we must find peace through strength.

I would agree to a freeze if only we could freeze the Soviets' global desires. A freeze at current levels of weapons would remove any incentive for the Soviets to negotiate seriously in Geneva[1] and virtually end our chances to achieve the major arms reductions which we have proposed. Instead, they would achieve their objectives through the freeze …

A number of years ago, I heard a young father, a very prominent young man in the entertainment world, addressing a tremendous gathering in California. It was during the time of the Cold War, and communism and our own way of life were very much on people's minds. And he was speaking to that subject. And suddenly, though, I heard him saying, 'I love my little girls more than anything.'

[1] In 1983, negotiations between the USSR and the USA for the reduction of intermediate-range nuclear weapons were held in Geneva, Switzerland. The Soviets walked out of these discussions on 23 November of that year.

And I said to myself, 'Oh, no, don't. You can't – don't say that.' But I had underestimated him.

He went on: 'I would rather see my little girls die now, still believing in God, than have them grow up under communism and one day die no longer believing in God.'

There were thousands of young people in that audience. They came to their feet with shouts of joy. They had instantly recognized the profound truth in what he had said, with regard to the physical and the soul and what was truly important.

Yes, let us pray for the salvation of all of those who live in that totalitarian darkness – pray they will discover the joy of knowing God. But until they do, let us be aware that while they preach the supremacy of the state, declare its omnipotence over individual man, and predict its eventual domination of all peoples on the earth, they are the focus of evil in the modern world.

It was C S Lewis[2] who, in his unforgettable *Screwtape Letters*, wrote: 'The greatest evil is not done now in those sordid "dens of crime" that Dickens loved to paint. It is not even done in concentration camps and labour camps. In those we see its final result. But it is conceived and ordered (moved, seconded, carried and minuted) in clear, carpeted, warmed and well-lighted offices, by quiet men with white collars and cut fingernails and smooth-shaven cheeks who do not need to raise their voices.'

Well, because these 'quiet men' do not 'raise their voices', because they sometimes speak in soothing tones of brotherhood and peace, because, like other dictators before them, they're always making 'their final territorial demand', some would have us accept them at their word and accommodate ourselves to their aggressive impulses. But if history teaches anything, it teaches that simple-minded appeasement, or wishful thinking about our adversaries, is folly. It means the betrayal of our past, the squandering of our freedom.

So I urge you to speak out against those who would place the United States in a position of military and moral inferiority. You know, I've always believed that old Screwtape reserved his best efforts for those of you in the church. So, in your discussions of the nuclear freeze proposals, I urge you to beware the temptation of pride – the temptation of blithely declaring yourselves above it all and labelling both sides equally at fault, to ignore the facts of history and the aggressive impulses of an evil empire, to simply call the arms race a giant misunderstanding and thereby remove yourself from the struggle between right and wrong and good and evil.

I ask you to resist the attempts of those who would have you withhold your support for our efforts, this administration's efforts, to keep America strong and free, while we negotiate real and verifiable reductions in the world's nuclear arsenals and one day, with God's help, their total elimination.

While America's military strength is important, let me add here that I've always maintained that the struggle now going on for the world will never be decided by bombs or rockets, by

---

[2] The Anglo-Irish academic and writer C S Lewis (1898–1963) published *The Screwtape Letters* as a book in 1942. A series of fictional letters addressed by the demon Screwtape to his incompetent nephew Wormwood, this Christian cautionary tale was originally published in instalments in the *Guardian*.

armies or military might. The real crisis we face today is a spiritual one; at root, it is a test of moral will and faith.

Whittaker Chambers, the man whose own religious conversion made him a witness to one of the terrible traumas of our time, the Hiss–Chambers case,[3] wrote that the crisis of the Western world exists to the degree in which the West is indifferent to God, the degree to which it collaborates in communism's attempt to make man stand alone without God. And then he said, for Marxism–Leninism is actually the second oldest faith, first proclaimed in the Garden of Eden with the words of temptation, 'Ye shall be as gods'.[4] …

I believe we shall rise to the challenge. I believe that communism is another sad, bizarre chapter in human history whose last pages even now are being written. I believe this because the source of our strength in the quest for human freedom is not material, but spiritual. And because it knows no limitation, it must terrify and ultimately triumph over those who would enslave their fellow man.

We have it in our power to begin the world over again.

For in the words of Isaiah: 'He giveth power to the faint; and to them that have no might he increaseth strength … But they that wait upon the Lord shall renew their strength; they shall mount up with wings as eagles; they shall run, and not be weary …'[5]

Yes, change your world. One of our Founding Fathers, Thomas Paine, said, 'We have it within our power to begin the world over again.'[6] We can do it, doing together what no one church could do by itself.

God bless you, and thank you very much.

---

[3] In 1948, the US journalist and former communist Whittaker Chambers (1901–61) accused the former US State Department official Alger Hiss (1904–96) of being a communist spy.
[4] Genesis 3:5.

[5] Isaiah 40:29 and 31.
[6] Reagan quotes from the pamphlet 'Common Sense' by the English philosopher Thomas Paine (1737–1809) who advocated American independence and became an American citizen in 1795.

32

Desmond Tutu

South African clergyman

After working as a schoolteacher for about four years Desmond Mpilo Tutu (1931–) attended theological college and became an Anglican parish priest (1961). He rose rapidly to become Bishop of Lesotho (1976–8), Secretary-General of the South African Council of Churches (1978–85), the first black Bishop of Johannesburg (1985–6) and Archbishop of Cape Town (1986–96). A fierce opponent of apartheid, he repeatedly risked imprisonment for his advocacy of punitive international sanctions against South Africa, although he deplored the use of violence. He was awarded the Nobel Peace Prize in 1984, was appointed Chancellor of the University of the Western Cape in Cape Town in 1988, and chaired the post-apartheid Truth and Reconciliation Commission, 1995–9.

'Apartheid's final solution'

11 December 1984, Oslo, Norway

Well known as an outspoken critic of South African apartheid, Archbishop Tutu was awarded the Nobel Peace Prize in 1984. He used this acceptance speech to condemn South Africa's 'racist dream', and to scorn the limited concessions of the country's new constitution, introduced the previous year.

Nelson Mandela (who would receive the Nobel Peace Prize in 1993) once remarked of his ally: 'Sometimes strident, often tender, never afraid and seldom without humour, Desmond Tutu's voice will always be the voice of the voiceless.'

Presenting the award, Egil Aarvik, chairman of the Norwegian Nobel Committee, spoke of Tutu's determination that peace should triumph over violence. He recalled seeing an example of Tutu's ministry during television coverage of a massacre in Johannesburg: 'After the police vehicles had driven away with their prisoners, Desmond Tutu stood and spoke to a frightened and bitter congregation: "Do not hate," he said. "Let us choose the peaceful way to freedom."'

Nonetheless, Tutu is a forceful speaker. Having described individual cases and their tragic consequences for both black and white South Africans, he turns briefly lyrical, before dissecting the iniquities of apartheid.

I come from a beautiful land, richly endowed by God with wonderful natural resources, wide expanses, rolling mountains, singing birds, bright shining stars out of blue skies …

with radiant sunshine, golden sunshine. There is enough of the good things that come from God's bounty, there is enough for everyone, but apartheid has confirmed some in their selfishness, causing them to grasp greedily a disproportionate share, the lion's share, because of their power.

They have taken 87 per cent of the land, though being only about 20 per cent of our population. The rest have had to make do with the remaining 13 per cent. Apartheid[1] has decreed the politics of exclusion. Seventy-three per cent of the population is excluded from any meaningful participation in the political decision-making processes of the land of their birth.

The new constitution[2] … perpetuates by law and entrenches white minority rule. Blacks are expected to exercise their political ambitions in unviable, poverty-stricken, arid, bantustan[3] homelands, ghettoes of misery, inexhaustible reservoirs of cheap black labour, bantustans into which South Africa is being Balkanized.

Blacks are systematically being stripped of their South African citizenship and being turned into aliens in the land of their birth.

This is apartheid's final solution, just as Nazism had its final solution for the Jews in Hitler's Aryan madness. The South African government is smart. Aliens can claim but very few rights, least of all political rights.

In pursuance of apartheid's ideological racist dream, over three million of God's children have been uprooted from their homes, which have been demolished, whilst they have then been dumped in the bantustan homeland resettlement camps. I say dumped advisedly: only things or rubbish is dumped, not human beings. Apartheid has, however, ensured that God's children, just because they are black, should be treated as if they were things, and not as of infinite value as being created in the image of God.

These dumping grounds are far from where work and food can be procured easily. Children starve, suffer from the often irreversible consequences of malnutrition – this happens to them not accidentally, but by deliberate government policy. They starve in a land that could be the bread basket of Africa, a land that normally is a net exporter of food.

The father leaves his family in the bantustan homeland, there eking out a miserable existence, whilst he, if he is lucky, goes to the so-called white man's town as a migrant, to

[1] Apartheid was first introduced in 1948, enshrining racial segregation in South African law, greatly restricting the freedom of movement and residence, and access to education and jobs of the non-white population (including Asians and mixed-race people as well as native Africans), as well as denying them political, civil and legal rights.
[2] The South African constitution was revised in 1983, allowing Asian and 'coloured' (mixed-race) citizens limited participation in subordinate houses of a tricameral

parliament. It decreed that the black majority were to be regarded as citizens of 'independent' 'homelands'.
[3] Bantu is a generic term for over 400 native ethnic groups in the southern part of the African continent. Bantustan refers to the 'homelands' of which black South Africans were designated 'citizens' during the apartheid regime.

live an unnatural life in a single-sex hostel for 11 months of the year, being prey there to prostitution, drunkenness and worse.

This migratory labour policy is declared government policy, and has been condemned … as a cancer in our society.

This cancer, eating away at the vitals of black family life, is deliberate government policy. It is part of the cost of apartheid, exorbitant in terms of human suffering.

Apartheid has spawned discriminatory education, such as Bantu Education, education for serfdom, ensuring that the government spends only about one-tenth on one black child per annum for education what it spends on a white child. It is education that is decidedly separate and unequal. It is wantonly wasteful of human resources, because so many of God's children are prevented, by deliberate government policy, from attaining to their fullest potential …

Apartheid is upheld by a phalanx of iniquitous laws, such as the Population Registration Act, which decrees that all South Africans must be classified ethnically and duly registered according to these race categories. Many times, in the same family one child has been classified white whilst another, with a slightly darker hue, has been classified coloured, with all the horrible consequences for the latter of being shut out from membership of a greatly privileged caste. There have, as a result, been several child suicides.

This is too high a price to pay for racial purity, for it is doubtful whether any end, however desirable, can justify such a means. There are laws such as the Prohibition of Mixed Marriages Act, which regard marriages between a white and a person of another race as illegal. Race becomes an impediment to a valid marriage. Two persons who have fallen in love are prevented by race from consummating their love in the marriage bond. Something beautiful is made to be sordid and ugly …

There are the laws which permit the indefinite detention of persons whom the Minister of Law and Order has decided are a threat to the security of the state. They are detained at his pleasure, in solitary confinement, without access to their family, their own doctor or a lawyer. That is severe punishment when the evidence apparently available to the minister has not been tested in an open court – perhaps it could stand up to such rigorous scrutiny, perhaps not; we are never to know.

It is a far too convenient device for a repressive regime, and the minister would have to be extra-special not to succumb to the temptation to circumvent the awkward process of testing his evidence in an open court, and thus he lets his power under the law to be open to the abuse where he is both judge and prosecutor. Many – too many – have died mysteriously in detention. All this is too costly in terms of human lives.

The minister is able, too, to place people under banning orders without being subjected to the annoyance of the checks and balances of due process. A banned person for three or five years becomes a non-person, who cannot be quoted during the period of her banning order.

She cannot attend a gathering, which means more than one other person. Two persons together talking to a banned person are a gathering! She cannot attend the wedding or funeral of even her own child without special permission. She must be at home from 6pm of one day to 6am of the next and on all public holidays, and from 6pm on Fridays until 6am on Mondays for three years. She cannot go on holiday outside the magisterial area to which she has been confined. She cannot go to the cinema, nor to a picnic.

That is severe punishment, inflicted without the evidence allegedly justifying it being made available to the banned person, nor having it scrutinized in a court of law. It is a serious erosion and violation of basic human rights, of which blacks have precious few in the land of their birth. They do not enjoy the rights of freedom of movement and association. They do not enjoy freedom of security of tenure, the right to participate in the making of decisions that affect their lives. In short, this land, richly endowed in so many ways, is sadly lacking in justice.

Once a Zambian and a South African, it is said, were talking. The Zambian then boasted about their Minister of Naval Affairs. The South African asked, 'But you have no navy, no access to the sea. How then can you have a Minister of Naval Affairs?' The Zambian retorted, 'Well, in South Africa you have a Minister of Justice, don't you?'

It is against this system that our people have sought to protest peacefully since 1912 at least, with the founding of the African National Congress.[4] They have used the conventional methods of peaceful protest – petitions, demonstrations, deputations, and even a passive resistance campaign. A tribute to our people's commitment to peaceful change is the fact that the only South Africans to win the Nobel Peace Prize are both black.[5]

Our people are peace-loving to a fault. The response of the authorities has been an escalating intransigence and violence, the violence of police dogs, tear gas, detention without trial, exile and even death. Our people protested peacefully against the Pass Laws[6] in 1960, and 69 of them were killed on March 21,1960, at Sharpeville, many shot in the back running away.[7]

Our children protested against inferior education, singing songs and displaying placards and marching peacefully. Many in 1976, on June 16 and subsequent times, were killed or imprisoned.[8]

Over 500 people died in that uprising. Many children went into exile. The whereabouts of many are unknown to their parents …

There has been little revulsion or outrage at this wanton destruction of human life in the West. In parenthesis, can somebody please explain to me something that has puzzled me? When a priest goes missing and is subsequently found dead, the media in the West carry his story in very extensive coverage.[9] I am glad that the death of one person can cause so much

[4] The African National Congress (ANC) was formed as the South African Native National Congress in 1912 to defend the rights of South Africa's black majority.
[5] The previous South African to win the Nobel Peace Prize was Albert Lutuli (c.1898–1967), President-General of the African National Congress, who received the award in 1960.
[6] The Pass Laws required black citizens to carry identity documents at all times.
[7] On 21 March 1960, a crowd gathered in the Sharpeville township to demonstrate against the Pass Laws. Estimated numbers vary widely, from 300 to 20,000. As the singing protesters congregated around the police station, the police opened fire, killing 69 and injuring 186. The officer in charge, Colonel J Pienaar, was quoted as saying, 'If they do these things they must learn their lesson the hard way.'
[8] In April 1976, schoolchildren in Soweto (an abbreviation of 'South-Western Townships') on the outskirts of Johannesburg went on strike, refusing to attend classes. At a mass rally on 16 June, children threw stones at police, who responded with bullets, and 566 children were killed.
[9] In October 1984, the Polish priest Father Jerzy Popiełuszko (1947–84) was abducted and murdered by police. The incident sparked an international outcry.

concern. But in the self-same week when this priest is found dead, the South African Police kill 24 blacks who had been participating in the protest, and 6,000 blacks are sacked for being similarly involved, and you are lucky to get that much coverage.

Are we being told something I do not want to believe – that we blacks are expendable and that blood is thicker than water; that when it comes to the crunch, you cannot trust whites, that they will club together against us? I don't want to believe that is the message being conveyed to us.

Be that as it may, we see before us a land bereft of much justice, and therefore without peace and security. Unrest is endemic, and will remain an unchanging feature of the South African scene until apartheid, the root cause of it all, is finally dismantled.

At this time, the army is being quartered on the civilian population. There is a civil war being waged. South Africans are on either side. When the African National Congress and the Pan-Africanist Congress[10] were banned in 1960, they declared that they had no option but to carry out the armed struggle. We in the South African Council of Churches have said we are opposed to all forms of violence – that of a repressive and unjust system, and that of those who seek to overthrow that system. However, we have added that we understand those who say they have had to adopt what is a last resort for them …

I have spoken extensively about South Africa, first because it is the land I know best; but because it is also a microcosm of the world and an example of what is to be found in other lands in differing degree … Because there is global insecurity, nations are engaged in a mad arms race, spending billions of dollars wastefully on instruments of destruction, when millions are starving. And yet, just a fraction of what is expended so obscenely on defence budgets would make the difference in enabling God's children to fill their stomachs, be educated, and given the chance to lead fulfilled and happy lives. We have the capacity to feed ourselves several times over, but we are daily haunted by the spectacle of the gaunt dregs of humanity shuffling along in endless queues, with bowls to collect what the charity of the world has provided, too little too late.

When will we learn? When will the people of the world get up and say, 'Enough is enough'?

God created us for fellowship. God created us so that we should form the human family, existing together because we were made for one another. We are not made for an exclusive self-sufficiency but for interdependence, and we break the law of our being at our peril …

Unless we work assiduously so that all of God's children, our brothers and sisters, members of our one human family, all will enjoy basic human rights, the right to a fulfilled life, the right of movement, of work, the freedom to be fully human, with a humanity measured by nothing less than the humanity of Jesus Christ Himself, then we are on the road inexorably to self-destruction; we are not far from global suicide – and yet it could be so different.

---

[10] A splinter group of the ANC, which sought government 'of the African, by the African, for the African'. The two organizations were banned in the wake of the Sharpeville massacre.

When will we learn that human beings are of infinite value because they have been created in the image of God, and that it is a blasphemy to treat them as if they were less than this, and to do so ultimately recoils on those who do this? In dehumanizing others, they are themselves dehumanized. Perhaps oppression dehumanizes the oppressor as much as, if not more than, the oppressed. They need each other to become truly free, to become human …

Let us work to be peacemakers, those given a wonderful share in Our Lord's ministry of reconciliation. If we want peace, so we have been told, let us work for justice.

Let us beat our swords into ploughshares.[11]

God calls us to be fellow workers with Him, so that we can extend his kingdom of shalom,[12] of justice, of goodness, of compassion, of caring, of sharing, of laughter, joy and reconciliation, so that the kingdoms of this world will become the Kingdom of our God and of his Christ, and he shall reign for ever and ever. Amen. **,,**

[11] Isaiah 2:4.
[12] Hebrew: 'peace'.

'Tear down this wall!'
– *Ronald Reagan*

33

Ronald Reagan

American politician

'*Tear down this wall!*'

12 June 1987, West Berlin, West Germany

On the 750th anniversary of Berlin's foundation, President Reagan spoke from the city's Brandenburg Gate. This was, as he acknowledges in the speech, an echo of the famous Berlin address given by John F Kennedy 24 years earlier, and included in this book.

As in 1963, East was divided from West by the Berlin Wall, but the circumstances had changed. The Soviet premier, Mikhail Gorbachev (1931–), had begun to promote a new policy of glasnost, or openness. Recognizing these developments, Reagan challenged Gorbachev, in possibly the most famous words of his presidency, to 'tear down this wall!'. Just over two years later, the wall did indeed come down.

Ironically, the phrase was nearly omitted from the speech. Many advisers believed it was provocative and would raise false hopes. But Reagan was determined to include it, telling an aide on the morning of his address, 'The boys at State are going to kill me, but it's the right thing to do.'

" Chancellor Kohl,[1] Governing Mayor Diepgen,[2] ladies and gentlemen: 24 years ago, President John F Kennedy visited Berlin, speaking to the people of this city and the world at the City Hall. Well, since then two other presidents have come, each in his turn, to Berlin. And today I myself make my second visit to your city.

We come to Berlin, we American presidents, because it's our duty to speak, in this place, of freedom.

But I must confess, we're drawn here by other things as well: by the feeling of history in this city, more than 500 years older than our own nation; by the beauty of the Grunewald and the Tiergarten; most of all, by your courage and determination. Perhaps the composer, Paul Lincke, understood something about American presidents. You see, like so many presidents before me, I come here today because wherever I go, whatever I do: *ich hab' noch einen Koffer in Berlin*.[3]

Our gathering today is being broadcast throughout western Europe and North America. I understand that it is being seen and heard as well in the East. To those listening throughout eastern Europe, I extend my warmest greetings and the goodwill of the American people. To those listening in East Berlin, a special word: although I cannot be with you, I address my remarks to you just as surely as to those standing here before me. For I join you, as I join your fellow countrymen in the West, in this firm, this unalterable belief: *es gibt nur ein Berlin*.[4]

Behind me stands a wall that encircles the free sectors of this city, part of a vast system of barriers that divides the entire continent of Europe.

From the Baltic south, those barriers cut across Germany in a gash of barbed wire, concrete, dog-runs and guard-towers. Farther south, there may be no visible, no obvious wall. But there remain armed guards and checkpoints all the same – still a restriction on the right to travel, still an instrument to impose upon ordinary men and women the will of a totalitarian state.

Yet it is here in Berlin where the wall emerges most clearly; here, cutting across your city, where the news photo and the television screen have imprinted this brutal division of a continent upon the mind of the world.

Standing before the Brandenburg Gate, every man is a German, separated from his fellow men. Every man is a Berliner, forced to look upon a scar.

President von Weizsäcker[5] has said: 'The German question is open as long as the Brandenburg Gate is closed.' Today I say: as long as this gate is closed, as long as this scar of a wall is permitted to stand, it is not the German question alone that remains open, but the question of freedom for all mankind. Yet I do not come here to lament. For I find in Berlin a message of hope, even in the shadow of this wall, a message of triumph.

---

[1] The German statesman Helmut Kohl (1930–) served as Chancellor of West Germany, and later of Germany, 1982–98.
[2] The German politician Eberhard Diepgen (1941–) served as Mayor of Berlin, 1984–9 and 1991–2001.
[3] German: 'I still have a suitcase in Berlin.'
[4] German: 'There is only one Berlin.'
[5] The German politician Richard, Baron von Weizsäcker (1920–2015) served as president of West Germany, and later of Germany, 1984–94.

In this season of spring in 1945, the people of Berlin emerged from their air-raid shelters to find devastation. Thousands of miles away, the people of the United States reached out to help. And in 1947 Secretary of State George Marshall announced the creation of what would become known as the Marshall Plan. Speaking precisely 40 years ago this month, he said: 'Our policy is directed not against any country or doctrine, but against hunger, poverty, desperation, and chaos.'

In the Reichstag, a few moments ago, I saw a display commemorating this 40th anniversary of the Marshall Plan. I was struck by the sign on a burnt-out, gutted structure that was being rebuilt. I understand that Berliners of my own generation can remember seeing signs like it dotted throughout the western sectors of the city. The sign read simply: 'The Marshall Plan is helping here to strengthen the free world.' A strong, free world in the West, that dream became real. Japan rose from ruin to become an economic giant. Italy, France, Belgium – virtually every nation in western Europe saw political and economic rebirth; the European Community was founded.

In West Germany and here in Berlin, there took place an economic miracle, the *Wirtschaftswunder* … From 1950 to 1960 alone, the standard of living in West Germany and Berlin doubled. Where four decades ago there was rubble, today in West Berlin there is the greatest industrial output of any city in Germany – busy office blocks, fine homes and apartments, proud avenues, and the spreading lawns of parkland. Where a city's culture seemed to have been destroyed, today there are two great universities, orchestras and an opera, countless theatres and museums. Where there was want, today there's abundance – food, clothing, automobiles – the wonderful goods of the Ku'damm.[6] From devastation, from utter ruin, you Berliners have, in freedom, rebuilt a city that once again ranks as one of the greatest on earth …

In the 1950s, Khrushchev[7] predicted: 'We will bury you.' But in the West today, we see a free world that has achieved a level of prosperity and well-being unprecedented in all human history. In the communist world, we see failure, technological backwardness, declining standards of health, even want of the most basic kind – too little food. Even today, the Soviet Union still cannot feed itself. After these four decades, then, there stands before the entire world one great and inescapable conclusion: freedom leads to prosperity. Freedom replaces the ancient hatreds among the nations with comity and peace. Freedom is the victor.

And now the Soviets themselves may, in a limited way, be coming to understand the importance of freedom. We hear much from Moscow about a new policy of reform and openness. Some political prisoners have been released. Certain foreign news broadcasts are no longer being jammed. Some economic enterprises have been permitted to operate with greater freedom from state control …

There is one sign the Soviets can make that would be unmistakable, that would advance dramatically the cause of freedom and peace.

---

[6] The Kurfürstendamm, an upmarket shopping street.
[7] In 1956, the Soviet leader Nikita Khrushchev told Western ambassadors at a reception in Moscow, 'Whether you like it or not, history is on our side. We will bury you!'

General Secretary Gorbachev,[8] if you seek peace, if you seek prosperity for the Soviet Union and eastern Europe, if you seek liberalization: come here to this gate! Mr Gorbachev, open this gate! Mr Gorbachev, tear down this wall!

I understand the fear of war and the pain of division that afflict this continent – and I pledge to you my country's efforts to help overcome these burdens. To be sure, we in the West must resist Soviet expansion. So we must maintain defences of unassailable strength. Yet we seek peace; so we must strive to reduce arms on both sides. Beginning ten years ago, the Soviets challenged the Western alliance with a grave new threat, hundreds of new and more deadly SS-20 nuclear missiles, capable of striking every capital in Europe.[9] The Western alliance responded by committing itself to a counter-deployment unless the Soviets agreed to negotiate a better solution; namely, the elimination of such weapons on both sides.

For many months, the Soviets refused to bargain in earnestness. As the alliance, in turn, prepared to go forward with its counter-deployment, there were difficult days – days of protests like those during my 1982 visit to this city – and the Soviets later walked away from the table.

But through it all, the alliance held firm. And I invite those who protested then – I invite those who protest today – to mark this fact: because we remained strong, the Soviets came back to the table. And because we remained strong, today we have within reach the possibility, not merely of limiting the growth of arms, but of eliminating, for the first time, an entire class of nuclear weapons from the face of the earth. As I speak, NATO ministers are meeting in Iceland[10] to review the progress of our proposals for eliminating these weapons. At the talks in Geneva,[11] we have also proposed deep cuts in strategic offensive weapons …

While we pursue these arms reductions, I pledge to you that we will maintain the capacity to deter Soviet aggression at any level at which it might occur. And in co-operation with many of our allies, the United States is pursuing the Strategic Defence Initiative[12] – research to base deterrence not on the threat of offensive retaliation, but on defences that truly defend; on systems, in short, that will not target populations, but shield them. By these means we seek to increase the safety of Europe and all the world.

But we must remember a crucial fact: East and West do not mistrust each other because we are armed; we are armed because we mistrust each other. And our differences are not about weapons but about liberty. When President Kennedy spoke at the City Hall those 24 years ago, freedom was encircled, Berlin was under siege. And today, despite all the pressures upon this city, Berlin stands secure in its liberty. And freedom itself is transforming the globe …

In Europe, only one nation and those it controls refuse to join the community of freedom. Yet in this age of redoubled economic growth, of information and innovation, the Soviet Union faces a choice. It must make fundamental changes, or it will become obsolete. Today thus represents a moment of hope. We in the West stand ready to co-operate with the East to promote true openness, to break down barriers that separate people, to create a safer, freer world.

[8] Mikhail Gorbachev (1931–) served as General Secretary of the Communist Party of the Soviet Union, 1985–91, and as President of the Soviet Union, 1990–91.
[9] From the late 1970s, the Soviet Union began to replace its arsenal of nuclear warheads with SS-20 missiles, each of which carried three warheads and had the range and accuracy to hit targets anywhere in western Europe in under ten minutes.

[10] The NATO meeting in Reykjavik, Iceland was a follow-up to the summit Reagan and Gorbachev had held there in October 1986 to discuss nuclear arms control.
[11] Strategic arms reduction talks (START) between the USA and the USSR began in Geneva in 1982 and ultimately produced several arms treaties. The talks were also the occasion of the first meeting between Reagan and Gorbachev in November 1985.

And surely there is no better place than Berlin, the meeting place of East and West, to make a start …

And I invite Mr Gorbachev: let us work to bring the eastern and western parts of the city closer together, so that all the inhabitants of all Berlin can enjoy the benefits that come with life in one of the great cities of the world …

In these four decades, as I have said, you Berliners have built a great city. You've done so in spite of threats – the Soviet attempts to impose the East-mark, the blockade.[13] Today the city thrives in spite of the challenges implicit in the very presence of this wall. What keeps you here? Certainly there's a great deal to be said for your fortitude, for your defiant courage. But I believe there's something deeper, something that involves Berlin's whole look and feel and way of life – not mere sentiment … something that speaks with a powerful voice of affirmation, that says yes to this city, yes to the future, yes to freedom. In a word, I would submit that what keeps you in Berlin is love – love both profound and abiding.

Perhaps this gets to the root of the matter, to the most fundamental distinction of all between East and West.

The totalitarian world produces backwardness because it does such violence to the spirit, thwarting the human impulse to create, to enjoy, to worship. The totalitarian world finds even symbols of love and of worship an affront.

Years ago, before the East Germans began rebuilding their churches, they erected a secular structure: the television tower at Alexanderplatz. Virtually ever since, the authorities have been working to correct what they view as the tower's one major flaw, treating the glass sphere at the top with paints and chemicals of every kind. Yet even today when the sun strikes that sphere – that sphere that towers over all Berlin – the light makes the sign of the cross. There in Berlin, like the city itself, symbols of love, symbols of worship, cannot be suppressed.

As I looked out a moment ago from the Reichstag, that embodiment of German unity, I noticed words crudely spray-painted upon the wall, perhaps by a young Berliner, 'This wall will fall. Beliefs become reality.'

Yes, across Europe, this wall will fall. For it cannot withstand faith; it cannot withstand truth. The wall cannot withstand freedom.

And I would like, before I close, to say one word. I have read, and I have been questioned since I've been here, about certain demonstrations against my coming. And I would like to say just one thing to those who demonstrate so. I wonder if they have ever asked themselves that if they should have the kind of government they apparently seek, no one would ever be able to do what they're doing again.

Thank you and God bless you all.

[12] The Strategic Defence Initiative (nicknamed 'Star Wars' by the media) was a system intended to protect the USA from nuclear attack by intercepting incoming missiles from space.

[13] Reagan refers to the crisis of 1948–9, when the Soviet Union attempted to force the Western Allies out of Berlin by imposing an East German currency and blockading communication and transport links between Berlin and the West.

'It is not really important now which party, club or group will prevail in the elections. The important thing is that the winners will be the best of us, in the moral, civic, political and professional sense.'

– Václav Havel

34

Václav Havel

Czech writer and statesman

In 1977, the writer and playwright Václav Havel (1936–2011) was one of the founders of Charter 77, a movement which criticized violations of human and civil rights by the communist regime in Czechoslovakia. Deemed subversive, he was repeatedly arrested and in 1979 was imprisoned for four and a half years. He was again imprisoned in February 1989, but was released three months later. In December 1989, after the overthrow of the Czechoslovak Communist Party during the so-called Velvet Revolution, he was elected president by direct popular vote. He oversaw the peaceful division of Czechoslovakia into separate Czech and Slovak states in 1992 and was elected president of the Czech Republic in 1993. He was re-elected in 1998 and left office in 2003.

'We live in a contaminated moral environment'

1 January 1990, television and radio broadcast from Prague, Czechoslovakia

In November 1989, when the Communist Party relinquished its 41-year monopoly of power in Czechoslovakia, the dissident playwright Václav Havel remarked, 'History has begun to develop very quickly in this country.' He was proved right a month later when, as leader of the Civic Forum party, he became the country's democratically elected president. Two days later, he addressed his compatriots in a broadcast that signalled a dramatic change, not just in governance, but in the national mood.

Havel refers briefly to the environmental contamination caused in Czechoslovakia – as elsewhere in the Eastern Bloc – by thoughtless industrial practices. But his central concern is the moral contamination brought about by communism: corruption, privilege and the deliberate propagation of lies.

In this he echoes the medieval Bohemian martyr Jan Hus (c.1369–1415), whose statue stands in Prague's Old Town Square. An influential church reformer, Hus is best known for his prayer: 'Seek the Truth/Listen to the Truth/Teach the Truth/Love the Truth/Abide by the Truth/And defend the Truth /Unto Death.' Havel urges his listeners not to entertain denial, but to embrace Czechoslovakia's contamination as 'a sin we committed against ourselves'.

These concerns befit a writer concerned with ideological distortions of truth and reality. But, although Havel's plays are abstract and cerebral, his inaugural address is a direct and straight-talking appeal to ordinary people tasting freedom for the first time in a generation.

"My dear fellow citizens: for 40 years, you heard from my predecessors on this day different variations of the same theme: how our country flourished, how many million tons of steel we produced, how happy we all were, how we trusted our government, and what bright perspectives were unfolding in front of us.

I assume you did not propose me for this office so that I, too, would lie to you.

Our country is not flourishing. The enormous creative and spiritual potential of our nations[1] is not being used sensibly. Entire branches of industry are producing goods which are of no interest to anyone, while we are lacking the things we need. A state which calls itself a workers' state humiliates and exploits workers. Our obsolete economy is wasting the little energy we have available. A country that once could be proud of the educational level of its citizens spends so little on education that it ranks today as 72nd in the world. We have polluted our soil, our rivers and forests, bequeathed to us by our ancestors, and we have today the most contaminated environment in Europe. Adult people in our country die earlier than in most other European countries.

Allow me a little personal observation: when I flew recently to Bratislava, I found time during various discussions to look out of the plane window. I saw the industrial complex of Slovnaft chemical factory and the giant Petržalka housing estate right behind it. The view was enough for me to understand that for decades our statesmen and political leaders did not look or did not want to look out of the windows of their planes. No study of statistics available to me would enable me to understand faster and better the situation in which we find ourselves.

But all this is still not the main problem. The worst thing is that we live in a contaminated moral environment. We fell morally ill because we became used to saying something different from what we thought. We learned not to believe in anything, to ignore each other, to care only about ourselves. Concepts such as love, friendship, compassion, humility, or forgiveness lost their depth and dimensions; and for many of us they represented only psychological peculiarities, or they resembled gone-astray greetings from ancient times, a little ridiculous in the era of computers and spaceships. Only a few of us were able to cry out loud that the powers that be should not be all-powerful, and that special farms, which produce ecologically pure and top-quality food just for them, should send their produce to schools, children's homes and hospitals if our agriculture was unable to offer them to all.

The previous regime – armed with its arrogant and intolerant ideology – reduced man to a force of production and nature to a tool of production.

In this it attacked both their very substance and their mutual relationship. It reduced gifted and autonomous people, skilfully working in their own country, to nuts and bolts of some monstrously huge, noisy and stinking machine, whose real meaning is not clear to anyone. It cannot do more than slowly but inexorably wear down itself and all its nuts and bolts.

[1] Havel's use of the plural here acknowledges the existence of the discrete Czech and Slovak nations, which would soon be peacefully separated.

When I talk about contaminated moral atmosphere, I am not talking just about the gentlemen who eat organic vegetables and do not look out of the plane windows. I am talking about all of us. We had all become used to the totalitarian system and accepted it as an unchangeable fact and thus helped to perpetuate it. In other words, we are all – though naturally to differing extents – responsible for the operation of the totalitarian machinery; none of us is just its victim: we are all also its co-creators.

Why do I say this? It would be very unreasonable to understand the sad legacy of the last 40 years as something alien, which some distant relative bequeathed us. On the contrary, we have to accept this legacy as a sin we committed against ourselves. If we accept it as such, we will understand that it is up to us all, and up to us only, to do something about it. We cannot blame the previous rulers for everything, not only because it would be untrue but also because it could blunt the duty that each of us faces today – namely, the obligation to act independently, freely, reasonably and quickly.

Let us not be mistaken: the best government in the world, the best parliament and the best president, cannot achieve much on their own. And it would also be wrong to expect a general remedy from them only. Freedom and democracy include participation and therefore responsibility from us all.

If we realize this, then all the horrors that the new Czechoslovak democracy inherited will cease to appear so terrible. If we realize this, hope will return to our hearts …

We are a small country, yet at one time we were the spiritual crossroads of Europe. Is there any reason why we could not again become one? Would it not be another asset with which to repay the help of others that we are going to need?

Our home-grown Mafia – of those who do not look out of plane windows and who eat specially fed pigs – may still be around and at times may muddy the waters, but they are no longer our main enemy. Even less so is our main enemy the international Mafia.

Our main enemies today are our own bad traits: indifference to the common good, vanity, personal ambition, selfishness and rivalry.

The main struggle will have to be fought on this field.

There are free elections and an election campaign ahead of us. Let us not allow this struggle to dirty the so-far clean face of our gentle revolution. Let us not allow the sympathies of the world, which we have won so fast, to be equally rapidly lost through our becoming entangled in the jungle of skirmishes for power. Let us not allow the desire to serve oneself to bloom once again under the fair mask of the desire to serve the common good.

It is not really important now which party, club or group will prevail in the elections. The important thing is that the winners will be the best of us, in the moral, civic, political and professional sense, regardless of their political affiliations. The future policies and prestige of our state will depend on the personalities we select and later elect to our representative bodies …

In conclusion, I would like to say that I want to be a president who will speak less and work more.

To be a president who will not only look out of the windows of his plane but who, first and foremost, will always be present among his fellow citizens and listen to them well.

You may ask what kind of a republic I dream of. Let me reply: I dream of a republic independent, free and democratic; of a republic economically prosperous and yet socially just; in short, of a humane republic which serves the individual and which therefore holds the hope that the individual will serve it in turn. Of a republic of well-rounded people – because without such it is impossible to solve any of our problems – human, economic, ecological, social or political.

The most distinguished of my predecessors opened his first speech with a quotation from the great Czech educator Komenský.[3] Allow me to round off my first speech with my own paraphrase of the same statement:

People, your government has returned to you! "

[2] The Moravian-born statesman Tomáš Masaryk (1850–1937) was the first president of Czechoslovakia, 1918–35.

[3] The Moravian educationalist John Komenský, or Comenius (1592–1670).

'On this day of my release'
– Nelson Mandela

35

Nelson Mandela

South African lawyer and statesman

The founder of South Africa's first black legal practice, Nelson Rolihlahla Mandela (1918–2013) joined the African National Congress (ANC) in 1944 and for the next 20 years directed a campaign of defiance against the government and its policy of apartheid. In 1964, he was sentenced to life imprisonment for political offences including sabotage and treason, and from his prison cell became an international symbol of resistance. The liberalizing measures of F W de Klerk (1936–), who served as president 1989–94, began the process of dismantling apartheid. De Klerk visited Mandela in prison, lifted the ban on the ANC, removed restrictions on political groups and finally ordered Mandela's release in February 1990. In 1991, Mandela was elected president of the ANC and entered into talks with de Klerk about the country's future. In 1993, Mandela and de Klerk were joint winners of the Nobel Peace Prize. Mandela travelled extensively to win support for continued international pressure to abolish apartheid completely, and on 10 May 1994, following South Africa's first multi-racial elections, he was inaugurated as South Africa's first black president, a post in which he served until 1999.

'On this day of my release'

11 February 1990, Cape Town, South Africa

Sentenced to life imprisonment in 1964, Mandela refused to fade from the world's attention. Instead, he became the focus for a growing international anti-apartheid movement. The slogan 'Free Nelson Mandela' was heard at many demonstrations during the 1970s and 1980s – and even became, in 1984, the refrain of a hit song by the English ska band The Specials.

In the face of international disapproval, however, apartheid endured. There were outbreaks of severe violence in black townships, notably in Soweto, near Johannesburg. By the early 1980s, Prime Minister P W Botha (later president) had accepted a need for change, and announced that whites should 'adapt or die'. Some apartheid laws were repealed, but Mandela refused to renounce armed struggle in return for a conditional offer of release in 1985.

On 10 February 1990, Botha's successor F W de Klerk finally ordered Mandela's release. The following day, the world watched Mandela walk from prison, amazed at the erect, patrician figure who had been hidden from view for so long. Later, he spoke at a rally at Cape Town's Grand Parade. In his speech, he salutes those who have supported him during his imprisonment and who have kept the struggle against apartheid alive. He then insists on the need for a democratic, non-racial South Africa.

" Friends, comrades and fellow South Africans: I greet you all in the name of peace, democracy and freedom for all.

I stand here before you not as a prophet but as a humble servant of you, the people.

Your tireless and heroic sacrifices have made it possible for me to be here today. I therefore place the remaining years of my life in your hands.

On this day of my release, I extend my sincere and warmest gratitude to the millions of my compatriots and those in every corner of the globe who have campaigned tirelessly for my release.

I send special greetings to the people of Cape Town, this city which has been my home for three decades. Your mass marches and other forms of struggle have served as a constant source of strength to all political prisoners.

I salute the African National Congress. It has fulfilled our every expectation in its role as leader of the great march to freedom.

I salute our president, Comrade Oliver Tambo,[1] for leading the ANC even under the most difficult circumstances.

I salute the rank and file members of the ANC. You have sacrificed life and limb in the pursuit of the noble cause of our struggle.

I salute combatants of Umkhonto we Sizwe,[2] like Solomon Mahlangu and Ashley Kriel, who have paid the ultimate price for the freedom of all South Africans.

I salute the South African Communist Party for its sterling contribution to the struggle for democracy. You have survived 40 years of unrelenting persecution. The memory of great communists like Moses Kotane, Yusuf Dadoo, Bram Fischer and Moses Mabhida will be cherished for generations to come.

I salute General Secretary Joe Slovo,[3] one of our finest patriots. We are heartened by the fact that the alliance between ourselves and the party remains as strong as it always was.

I salute the United Democratic Front,[4] the National Education Crisis Committee,[5] the South African Youth Congress, the Transvaal and Natal Indian Congresses and COSATU[6] and the many other formations of the Mass Democratic Movement.

I also salute the Black Sash[7] and the National Union of South African Students. We note with pride that you have acted as the conscience of white South Africa. Even during the darkest days in the history of our struggle you held the flag of liberty high. The large-scale mass

[1] The South African politician Oliver Tambo (1917–93) became acting president of the ANC in 1967, president in 1977 and national chairman in 1991.
[2] The military wing of the ANC, established in 1961.
[3] The Lithuanian-born South African politician Joe Slovo (1926–95) worked in exile after 1963 for the ANC and the South African Communist Party (SACP). He was Chief of Staff of Umkhonto we Sizwe from 1985, and played a leading role in negotiations with the government after 1990.

[4] A coalition of anti-apartheid groups formed in 1983, led by Allan Boesak and Desmond Tutu.
[5] Established in 1986.
[6] The Congress of South African Trade Unions, established in 1985.
[7] An organization of white women, founded in 1955, which promoted non-violent resistance to apartheid.

mobilization of the past few years is one of the key factors which led to the opening of the final chapter of our struggle.

I extend my greetings to the working class of our country. Your organized strength is the pride of our movement. You remain the most dependable force in the struggle to end exploitation and oppression.

I pay tribute to the many religious communities who carried the campaign for justice forward when the organizations for our people were silenced.

I greet the traditional leaders of our country. Many of you continue to walk in the footsteps of great heroes like Hintsa[8] and Sekhukune.[9]

I pay tribute to the endless heroism of youth, you, the young lions. You, the young lions, have energized our entire struggle.

I pay tribute to the mothers and wives and sisters of our nation. You are the rock-hard foundation of our struggle. Apartheid has inflicted more pain on you than on anyone else.

On this occasion, we thank the world community for their great contribution to the anti-apartheid struggle. Without your support our struggle would not have reached this advanced stage. The sacrifice of the front-line states will be remembered by South Africans for ever.

My salutations would be incomplete without expressing my deep appreciation for the strength given to me during my long and lonely years in prison by my beloved wife and family. I am convinced that your pain and suffering was far greater than my own …

Today, the majority of South Africans, black and white, recognize that apartheid has no future. It has to be ended by our own decisive mass action in order to build peace and security. The mass campaign of defiance and other actions of our organization and people can only culminate in the establishment of democracy.

The destruction caused by apartheid on our subcontinent is incalculable. The fabric of family life of millions of my people has been shattered. Millions are homeless and unemployed. Our economy lies in ruins and our people are embroiled in political strife. Our resort to the armed struggle in 1960, with the formation of the military wing of the ANC, Umkhonto we Sizwe, was a purely defensive action against the violence of apartheid. The factors which necessitated the armed struggle still exist today. We have no option but to continue. We express the hope that a climate conducive to a negotiated settlement will be created soon so that there may no longer be the need for the armed struggle.

I am a loyal and disciplined member of the African National Congress. I am therefore in full agreement with all of its objectives, strategies and tactics.

The need to unite the people of our country is as important a task now as it always has been. No individual leader is able to take on this enormous task on his own. It is our task as leaders

---

[8] The African warrior Hintsa (1789–1835) was a Xhosa chief who led his people from 1804. He fought against the British army in the early 19th century and was killed and mutilated by British troops.

[9] The African warrior Sekhukune (1814–82) was King of the Marota people in the Western Transvaal from 1861. He formed the Marota Empire and tried to unite other groups to defend their lands against colonialists.

to place our views before our organization and to allow the democratic structures to decide. On the question of democratic practice, I feel duty-bound to make the point that a leader of the movement is a person who has been democratically elected at a national conference. This is a principle which must be upheld without any exceptions.

Today, I wish to report to you that my talks with the government have been aimed at normalizing the political situation in the country. We have not as yet begun discussing the basic demands of the struggle. I wish to stress that I myself have at no time entered into negotiations about the future of our country except to insist on a meeting between the ANC and the government.

Mr de Klerk has gone further than any other Nationalist president in taking real steps to normalize the situation. However, there are further steps, as outlined in the Harare Declaration,[10] that have to be met before negotiations on the basic demands of our people can begin. I reiterate our call for, *inter alia*, the immediate ending of the State of Emergency and the freeing of all, and not only some, political prisoners. Only such a normalized situation, which allows for free political activity, can allow us to consult our people in order to obtain a mandate.

The people need to be consulted on who will negotiate and on the content of such negotiations. Negotiations cannot take place above the heads or behind the backs of our people. It is our belief that the future of our country can only be determined by a body which is democratically elected on a non-racial basis. Negotiations on the dismantling of apartheid will have to address the overwhelming demand of our people for a democratic, non-racial and unitary South Africa. There must be an end to white monopoly on political power and a fundamental restructuring of our political and economic systems, to ensure that the inequalities of apartheid are addressed and our society thoroughly democratized.

It must be added that Mr de Klerk himself is a man of integrity, who is acutely aware of the dangers of a public figure not honouring his undertakings. But as an organization, we base our policy and strategy on the harsh reality we are faced with. And this reality is that we are still suffering under the policy of the Nationalist government.

Our struggle has reached a decisive moment. We call on our people to seize this moment, so that the process towards democracy is rapid and uninterrupted.

We have waited too long for our freedom. We can no longer wait. Now is the time to intensify the struggle on all fronts. To relax our efforts now would be a mistake which generations to come will not be able to forgive. The sight of freedom looming on the horizon should encourage us to redouble our efforts.

It is only through disciplined mass action that our victory can be assured.

[10] Adopted by the Organization of African Unity in August 1989, the Harare Declaration raised the possibility of negotiating an end to apartheid. It formed the basis of the 'Declaration on Apartheid and its Destructive Consequences in Southern Africa', adopted by the United Nations in December 1989.

We call on our white compatriots to join us in the shaping of a new South Africa. The freedom movement is a political home for you too. We call on the international community to continue the campaign to isolate the apartheid regime. To lift sanctions now would be to run the risk of aborting the process towards the complete eradication of apartheid.

Our march to freedom is irreversible. We must not allow fear to stand in our way.

Universal suffrage on a common voters' roll in a united democratic and non-racial South Africa is the only way to peace and racial harmony.

In conclusion I wish to quote my own words during my trial in 1964. They are true today as they were then: 'I have fought against white domination and I have fought against black domination. I have cherished the ideal of a democratic and free society in which all persons live together in harmony and with equal opportunities. It is an ideal which I hope to live for and to achieve. But if needs be, it is an ideal for which I am prepared to die.' 99

'The lesson history teaches is this: if you believe you are safe, you are at risk. If you do not see this killer stalking your children, look again. There is no family or community, no race or religion, no place left in America that is safe. Until we genuinely embrace this message, we are a nation at risk ...'

— *Mary Fisher*

36

Mary Fisher

American artist, writer and AIDS activist

Since 1992, Mary Fisher (1948–), whose husband, Brian Campbell, died of AIDS-related causes in 1993, has campaigned extensively on HIV/AIDS in America, Europe and Africa. She founded the Family AIDS Network (1992) which in 2000 became the Mary Fisher Center for AIDS Research and Education (CARE) Fund at the University of Alabama, Birmingham. She has frequently given testimony to the US Congress and has twice been named to special presidential councils. She is also a recognized artist whose work in sculpture, printing and fabrics can be found in distinguished public and private collections. In 2006 she became a global emissary for the Joint United Nations Programme on HIV/AIDS.

'AIDS *virus is not a political creature*'

19 August 1992, Houston, Texas, USA

In the summer of 1991, television producer Mary Fisher was diagnosed with HIV, the virus that causes AIDS. After seven months of deliberation – during which she struggled with despair and alcohol abuse – she decided to make her condition public, and to devote her life to campaigning for research, treatment and an end to the stigmatization of AIDS and HIV sufferers.

Soon afterwards, she found a prominent platform at the annual Republican National Convention. She had close links with the party: her father was a leading Republican adviser and she herself had worked for President Gerald Ford.

Her address was delivered with remarkable dignity and composure, and without reference to notes. In this accessible, restrained speech, she calls for awareness, compassion and action, identifying herself – a white, well-to-do, heterosexual mother – with the socially excluded groups often associated with the disease. She also warns against complacency, referring to Pastor Martin Niemöller's famous dictum, 'I was not a Jew, so I did not protest.'

Fisher's straight-talking appeal won warm support from the convention and the speech quickly became famous under the title 'A Whisper of AIDS'. It was an early landmark in Fisher's long and continuing career as an AIDS campaigner.

"Thank you. Thank you. Less than three months ago, at platform hearings in Salt Lake City, I asked the Republican Party[1] to lift the shroud of silence which has been draped over the issue of HIV and AIDS. I have come tonight to bring our silence to an end. I bear a message of challenge, not self-congratulation. I want your attention, not your applause.

I would never have asked to be HIV positive, but I believe that in all things there is a purpose; and I stand before you and before the nation gladly. The reality of AIDS is brutally clear. Two hundred thousand Americans are dead or dying. A million more are infected. Worldwide, 40 million, 60 million, or 100 million infections will be counted in the coming few years. But despite science and research, White House meetings and congressional hearings; despite good intentions and bold initiatives, campaign slogans and hopeful promises, it is – despite it all – the epidemic which is winning tonight.

In the context of an election year, I ask you, here in this great hall, or listening in the quiet of your home, to recognize that AIDS virus is not a political creature. It does not care whether you are Democrat or Republican; it does not ask whether you are black or white, male or female, gay or straight, young or old. Tonight I represent an AIDS community whose members have been reluctantly drafted from every segment of American society …

This is not a distant threat. It is a present danger.

The rate of infection is increasing fastest among women and children. Largely unknown a decade ago, AIDS is the third leading killer of young adult Americans today. But it won't be third for long, because unlike other diseases, this one travels. Adolescents don't give each other cancer or heart disease because they believe they are in love, but HIV is different; and we have helped it along.

We have killed each other with our ignorance, our prejudice and our silence.

We may take refuge in our stereotypes, but we cannot hide there long, because HIV asks only one thing of those it attacks. 'Are you human?' And this is the right question. 'Are you human?' Because people with HIV have not entered some alien state of being. They are human. They have not earned cruelty, and they do not deserve meanness. They don't benefit from being isolated or treated as outcasts …

My call to you, my party, is to take a public stand, no less compassionate than that of the President and Mrs Bush.[2] They have embraced me and my family in memorable ways. In the place of judgement, they have shown affection. In difficult moments, they have raised our spirits. In the darkest hours, I have seen them reaching not only to me, but also to my parents, armed with that stunning grief and special grace that comes only to parents who have themselves leaned too long over the bedside of a dying child.

---

[1] The Republican Party, under President George H W Bush, was then in power.   [2] The First Lady Barbara Bush (1925–) was then engaged in social programmes relating to AIDS.

With the President's leadership, much good has been done. Much of the good has gone unheralded, and as the President has insisted, much remains to be done. But we do the President's cause no good if we praise the American family but ignore a virus that destroys it …

My father has devoted much of his lifetime guarding against another holocaust. He is part of the generation who heard Pastor Niemöller come out of the Nazi death camps to say, 'They came after the Jews, and I was not a Jew, so I did not protest. They came after the trade unionists, and I was not a trade unionist, so I did not protest. Then they came after the Roman Catholics, and I was not a Roman Catholic, so I did not protest. Then they came after me, and there was no one left to protest.'[3]

[Applause.]

The lesson history teaches is this: if you believe you are safe, you are at risk. If you do not see this killer stalking your children, look again. There is no family or community, no race or religion, no place left in America that is safe. Until we genuinely embrace this message, we are a nation at risk …

One of those families is mine. If it is true that HIV inevitably turns to AIDS, then my children will inevitably turn to orphans.

My family has been a rock of support. My 84-year-old father, who has pursued the healing of the nations, will not accept the premise that he cannot heal his daughter. My mother refuses to be broken. She still calls at midnight to tell wonderful jokes that make me laugh. Sisters and friends, and my brother Phillip, whose birthday is today, all have helped carry me over the hardest places. I am blessed, richly and deeply blessed, to have such a family.

[Applause and cheers.]

But not all of you have been so blessed.

> ### *You are HIV positive, but dare not say it. You have lost loved ones, but you dared not whisper the word AIDS. You weep silently; you grieve alone.*

I have a message for you. It is not you who should feel shame; it is we.

We who tolerate ignorance and practise prejudice; we who have taught you to fear.

We must lift our shroud of silence, making it safe for you to reach out for compassion. It is our task to seek safety for our children, not in quiet denial, but in effective action.

Someday our children will be grown. My son Max, now four, will take the measure of his mother. My son Zachary, now two, will sort through his memories. I may not be here to hear their judgements, but I know already what I hope they are. I want my children to know that their mother was not a victim. She was a messenger. I do not want them to think, as I once

---

[3] Recorded in the US Congressional Record, 14 October 1968.

did, that courage is the absence of fear. I want them to know that courage is the strength to act wisely when most we are afraid.

I want them to have the courage to step forward when called by their nation or their party and give leadership, no matter what the personal cost … To my children, I make this pledge: I will not give in, Zachary, because I draw my courage from you. Your silly giggle gives me hope; your gentle prayers give me strength; and you, my child, give me the reason to say to America, 'You are at risk.' And I will not rest, Max, until I have done all I can to make your world safe. I will seek a place where intimacy is not the prelude to suffering. I will not hurry to leave you, my children, but when I go, I pray that you will not suffer shame on my account.

To all within the sound of my voice, I appeal. Learn with me the lessons of history and of grace, so my children will not be afraid to say the word 'AIDS' when I am gone. Then, their children and yours may not need to whisper it at all. God bless the children, and God bless us all.

Good night.

[Standing ovation.] 🙴

37

Elizabeth II

British monarch

Elizabeth II originally Princess Elizabeth Alexandra Mary of York (1926–) was born in London. She was proclaimed Queen Elizabeth II on the death of her father, George VI, in 1952. She is Queen of Great Britain and Northern Ireland, Canada, Australia, New Zealand and of several smaller independent countries, and also head of the Commonwealth. Her husband was created Duke of Edinburgh on the eve of their wedding (1947) and styled Prince Philip (1957). They have three sons – Charles, Prince of Wales; Prince Andrew, the Duke of York; and Prince Edward, the Earl of Wessex – and a daughter, Princess Anne, styled the Princess Royal. The Queen has aimed to modernize the monarchy and make it more informal, instituting luncheon parties for distinguished individuals and pioneering royal walkabouts. She shows a strong personal commitment to the Commonwealth as a voluntary association of equal partners.

'It has turned out to be an annus horribilis'

24 November 1992, London, England

The year 1992 should have been an *annus mirabilis* for Queen Elizabeth. It was the 40th anniversary of her accession, and the previous 40 years had seen peace and increasing prosperity in Britain and throughout the Commonwealth. However, during the months preceding this luncheon at the Guildhall to celebrate the anniversary, she had suffered many harrowing moments. One of these – the fire which had devastated Windsor Castle – had occurred only a few days earlier, on 20 November, her 45th wedding anniversary. The Queen was also troubled by public disquiet over statements that the government would pay for repairs to the castle, as many people considered that the Queen, as a wealthy non-taxpayer, should take responsibility. There had also been well-publicized marital problems in her immediate family during the previous year.

The City of London, in which the Guildhall stands, had itself experienced a difficult year. An IRA bombing in April 1992 had killed three people, destroyed the Baltic Exchange and caused widespread damage to surrounding buildings, and the Lloyd's syndicates had suffered their worst-ever trading results. It was a troubled period, but the Queen managed to make a wryly humorous speech in which she reflected on cherished moments of the preceding 40 years.

The coming months were also to be difficult. Two days after giving the speech, the Queen bowed to the inevitable and agreed to pay tax and to fund most of the Royal Family herself, removing them from the Civil List.

“My Lord Mayor:[1] could I say, first, how delighted I am that the Lady Mayoress is here today.

This great hall has provided me with some of the most memorable events of my life. The hospitality of the City of London is famous around the world, but now here is it more appreciated than among the members of my family. I am deeply grateful that you, my Lord Mayor, and the Corporation, have seen fit to mark the 40th anniversary of my accession with this splendid lunch, and by giving me a picture which I will greatly cherish.

Thank you also for inviting representatives of so many organizations with which I and my family have special connections, in some cases stretching back over several generations. To use an expression more common north of the Border, this is a real 'gathering of the clans'.

Nineteen-ninety-two is not a year on which I shall look back with undiluted pleasure.

In the words of one of my more sympathetic correspondents, it has turned out to be an *annus horribilis*. I suspect that I am not alone in thinking it so. Indeed, I suspect that there are very few people or institutions unaffected by these last months of worldwide turmoil and uncertainty.[2] This generosity and whole-hearted kindness of the Corporation of the City to Prince Philip and me would be welcome at any time, but at this particular moment, in the after math of Friday's tragic fire at Windsor, it is especially so.

And, after this last weekend, we appreciate all the more what has been set before us today. Years of experience, however, have made us a bit more canny than the lady, less well versed than us in the splendours of city hospitality, who, when she was offered a balloon glass for her brandy, asked for 'only half a glass, please'.

It is possible to have too much of a good thing. A well-meaning bishop was obviously doing his best when he told Queen Victoria, 'Ma'am, we cannot pray too often, nor too fervently, for the Royal Family.' The Queen's reply was: 'Too fervently, no; too often, yes.' I, like Queen Victoria, have always been a believer in that old maxim 'moderation in all things'.

I sometimes wonder how future generations will judge the events of this tumultuous year. I dare say that history will take a slightly more moderate view than that of some contemporary commentators. Distance is well known to lend enchantment, even to the less attractive views. After all, it has the inestimable advantage of hindsight.

But it can also lend an extra dimension to judgement, giving it a leavening of moderation and compassion – even of wisdom – that is sometimes lacking in the reactions of those whose task it is in life to offer instant opinions on all things great and small.

No section of the community has all the virtues, neither does any have all the vices.

I am quite sure that most people try to do their jobs as best they can, even if the result is not always entirely successful. He who has never failed to reach perfection has a right to be the harshest critic.

---

[1] Sir Francis McWilliams (1926-).

[2] Abroad, there had been tension in the Gulf, ethnic conflict in an unravelling Yugoslavia, anti-apartheid riots in South Africa, and famine elsewhere in Africa.

There can be no doubt, of course, that criticism is good for people and institutions that are part of public life. No institution – City, monarchy, whatever – should expect to be free from the scrutiny of those who give it their loyalty and support, not to mention those who don't.

But we are all part of the same fabric of our national society and that scrutiny, by one part of another, can be just as effective if it is made with a touch of gentleness, good humour and understanding.

This sort of questioning can also act, and it should do so, as an effective engine for change.

The City is a good example of the way the process of change can be incorporated into the stability and continuity of a great institution. I particularly admire, my Lord Mayor, the way in which the City has adapted so nimbly to what the *Prayer Book*[3] calls 'the changes and chances of this mortal life'.

You have set an example of how it is possible to remain effective and dynamic without losing those indefinable qualities, style and character. We only have to look around this great hall to see the truth of that.

> *Forty years is quite a long time. I am glad to have had the chance to witness, and to take part in, many dramatic changes in life in this country.*

But I am glad to say that the magnificent standard of hospitality given on so many occasions to the sovereign by the Lord Mayor of London has not changed at all. It is an outward symbol of one other unchanging factor which I value above all – the loyalty given to me and to my family by so many people in this country, and the Commonwealth, throughout my reign.

You, my Lord Mayor, and all those whose prayers – fervent, I hope, but not too frequent – have sustained me through all these years, are friends indeed. Prince Philip and I give you all, wherever you may be, our most humble thanks.

And now I ask you to rise and drink the health of the Lord Mayor and Corporation of London. ""

---

[3] The *Book of Common Prayer*, the authorized prayer book of the Church of England since 1544; it has been repeatedly amended since that first version, and the phrase quoted by the Queen dates back to at least the 18th century.

'Women cannot be expected to struggle alone against the forces of discrimination and exploitation. I recall the words of Dante, who reminded us that, "The hottest place in Hell is reserved for those who remain neutral in times of moral crisis."

— *Benazir Bhutto*

38

Benazir Bhutto

Pakistani politician

After the military coup led by General Mohammed Zia ul-Haq – in which her father, the former prime minister Zulfikar Ali Bhutto, was executed (1979) – Benazir Bhutto (1953–2007) was placed under house arrest at frequent intervals until 1984. In 1988, she was elected prime minister after the death of Zia in mysterious circumstances, becoming the first modern-day woman leader of a Muslim nation. Over the following nine years she repeatedly lost and regained power, undermined by the military and by accusations of corruption. Defeated in the 1997 election, she was later sentenced to five years' imprisonment for corruption, disqualified from politics and sent into exile. Having reached an agreement with President Pervez Musharraf, she finally returned to Pakistan in October 2007 and prepared to fight the 2008 general elections as the leading opposition candidate. She was assassinated just two months later, on 27 December, while returning from an election rally at Rawalpindi.

'The ethos of Islam is equality, equality between the sexes'

4 September 1995, Beijing, China

'Action for Equality, Development and Peace' was the mandate of the Fourth United Nations World Conference on Women, held in Beijing between 4 and 15 September 1995. However, disagreement on the role of the family and female sexuality arose between groups of largely Western feminists and a coalition of fundamentalist Christians, Islamists and traditional Catholics. This dispute disrupted meetings convened to prepare the 'Platform of Action', the paper to be discussed at the conference.

The conference's opening ceremony was held at the Great Hall of the People in Tiananmen Square, and representatives from 189 countries sat through a display of dancing, music, fashion and gymnastics felt by many to have been more suited to an Olympic opening ceremony than a conference discussing the role of women. Following this extravaganza and the formal opening of the conference, Benazir Bhutto addressed the first plenary meeting, speaking in a dazzling style honed during her tenure as President of the Oxford Union debating society. In her speech she defended Islam while condemning fundamentalism, and although she conformed with the Islamic requirement to cover her head in public, her headscarf continually slipped from her head as she spoke.

As the female leader of an Islamic nation, educated in the West, Bhutto exemplified the tension between the opposite sides at the conference, and her speech trod a careful line between these extremes.

" As the first woman ever elected to head an Islamic nation, I feel a special responsibility about issues that relate to women.

In addressing the new exigencies of the new century, we must translate dynamic religion into a living reality.

We must live by the true spirit of Islam, not only by its rituals.

And for those of you who may be ignorant of Islam, cast aside your preconceptions about the role of women in our religion. Contrary to what many of you may have come to believe, Islam embraces a rich variety of political, social, and cultural traditions. The fundamental ethos of Islam is tolerance, dialogue, and democracy.

Just as in Christianity and Judaism, we must always be on guard for those who will exploit and manipulate the Holy Book[1] for their own narrow political ends, who will distort the essence of pluralism and tolerance for their own extremist agendas.

To those who claim to speak for Islam but who would deny to women our place in society, I say:

The ethos of Islam is equality, equality between the sexes. There is no religion on earth that, in its writing and teachings, is more respectful of the role of women in society than Islam.

My presence here, as the elected woman prime minister of a great Muslim country, is testament to the commitment of Islam to the role of women in society.

It is this tradition of Islam that has empowered me, has strengthened me, has emboldened me. It was this heritage that sustained me during the most difficult points in my life, for Islam forbids injustice; injustice against people, against nations, against women. It denounces inequality as the gravest form of injustice. It enjoins its followers to combat oppression and tyranny. It enshrines piety as the sole criterion for judging humankind. It shuns race, colour, and gender as a basis of distinction amongst fellow men.

When the human spirit was immersed in the darkness of the Middle Ages, Islam proclaimed equality between men and women.

When women were viewed as inferior members of the human family, Islam gave them respect and dignity. When women were treated as chattels, the Prophet of Islam (peace be upon him) accepted them as equal partners.

Islam codified the rights of women. The Koran elevated their status to that of men. It guaranteed their civic, economic, and political rights. It recognized their participative role in nation building.

Sadly, the Islamic tenets regarding women were soon discarded. In Islamic society, as in other parts of the world, their rights were denied. Women were maltreated, discriminated against, and subjected to violence and oppression, their dignity injured and their role denied.

[1] The Koran.

Women became the victims of a culture of exclusion and male dominance. Today more women than men suffer from poverty, deprivation, and discrimination.

Half a billion women are illiterate. Seventy per cent of the children who are denied elementary education are girls.

The plight of women in the developing countries is unspeakable. Hunger, disease, and unremitting toil is their fate. Weak economic growth and inadequate social support systems affect them most seriously and directly. They are the primary victims of structural adjustment processes, which necessitate reduced state funding for health, education, medical care and nutrition. Curtailed resource-flows to these vital areas impact most severely on the vulnerable groups, particularly women and children.

This, Madam Chairperson, is not acceptable. It offends my religion. It offends my sense of justice and equity. Above all, it offends commonsense.

That is why Pakistan, the women of Pakistan, and I personally have been fully engaged in recent international efforts to uphold women's rights. The Universal Declaration of Human Rights enjoins the elimination of discrimination against women.

The Nairobi Forward-looking Strategies[2] provide a solid framework for advancing women's rights around the world. But the goal of equality, development and peace still eludes us.

Sporadic efforts in this direction have failed. We are satisfied that the Beijing Platform of Action[3] encompasses a comprehensive approach toward the empowerment of women. This is the right approach and should be fully supported.

Women cannot be expected to struggle alone against the forces of discrimination and exploitation. I recall the words of Dante, who reminded us that, 'The hottest place in Hell is reserved for those who remain neutral in times of moral crisis.'[4]

Today in this world, in the fight for the liberation of women, there can be no neutrality.

My spirit carries many a scar of along and lonely battle against dictatorship and tyranny. I witnessed, at a young age, the overthrow of democracy, the assassination of an elected prime minister,[5] and a systematic assault against the very foundations of a free society.

But our faith in democracy was not broken. The great Pakistani poet and philosopher Dr Allam Iqbal[6] says, 'Tyranny cannot endure for ever'. It did not. The will of our people prevailed against the forces of dictatorship.

But, my dear sisters, we have learned that democracy alone is not enough. Freedom of choice alone does not guarantee justice. Equal rights are not defined only by political values. Social justice is a triad of freedom, an equation of liberty.

---

[2] 'The Nairobi Forward-looking Strategies for the Advancement of Women' was a document produced by the United Nations as the outcome of a conference held in Nairobi in July 1985.
[3] A document signed by 189 governments in 1995, which analysed and prioritized issues and strategies relating to women's rights.
[4] The Florentine poet Durante degli Alighieri, or Dante (1265–1321), is best known for his Divine Comedy trilogy. Bhutto quotes from the Inferno section, which deals with damnation.

[5] Bhutto refers to her father.
[6] The Punjab-born poet and philosopher Allam Iqbal (1877–1938) was one of Muslim India's cultural figureheads. Although he died before the creation of Pakistan as a state, he was one of the first Indians to call for partition.

Justice is political liberty. Justice is economic independence. Justice is social equality.

Delegates, sisters, the child who is starving has no human rights. The girl who is illiterate has no future. The woman who cannot plan her life, plan her family, plan a career, is fundamentally not free.

I am determined to change the plight of women in my country. More than 60 million of our women are largely sidelined. It is a personal tragedy for them. It is a national catastrophe for my nation. I am determined to harness their potential to the gigantic task of nation-building.

I dream of a Pakistan in which women contribute to their full potential.

I am conscious of the struggle that lies ahead. But, with your help, we shall persevere. Allah willing, we shall succeed. "

Bill Clinton

American politician

William Jefferson Clinton (1946–) taught law at the University of Arkansas (1973–6), marrying Hillary Clinton (née Rodham) in 1975. He was elected Attorney General (1976), then governor (1978) of Arkansas, in which role he served for five terms (1979–81, 1983–92). In 1992, he defeated President George H W Bush and was elected president, thus ending a 12-year Republican hold on the office. He was a popular and charismatic figure, and his presidency saw economic prosperity, with low inflation and unemployment, and a focus on promoting peace on the international stage. However, it was also marked by scandal, most notably in 1998 with his affair with White House intern Monica Lewinsky. Despite such troubles, by the time he stepped down in January 2001, he had the highest approval rating of any outgoing president since records began.

'I have sinned'

11 September 1998, Washington, DC, USA

In January 1998, it was reported in the *Washington Post* that President Bill Clinton had been involved in a sexual relationship with the former White House intern Monica Lewinsky. Months of denials and smokescreens followed, including First Lady Hillary Clinton's assertion, in a television interview, that there had been a 'vast right-wing conspiracy' against her husband.

Finally, on 17 August, Clinton admitted to an 'improper physical relationship' with Lewinsky, in taped testimony to the Office of Independent Counsel and the grand jury. That evening, he made a brief televised address to the nation, in which he offered a rather bullish apology, adding: 'I intend to reclaim my family life for my family. It's nobody's business but ours.'

It soon became apparent that Clinton's approval ratings had not been impaired, but many commentators were not satisfied with his limited contrition. The public apologies continued, but it was not until the annual Religious Leaders' Breakfast at the White House on 11 September that Clinton finally hit the right tone.

The *Time* magazine columnist Lance Morrow wrote that Clinton had 'performed miserably' on 17 August, but reported watching the Dow Jones index steadily rise during the 11 September speech. Clinton had been nicknamed 'Slick Willy' for his polished handling of potential embarrassments – including the much-publicized investigation of the Clintons' failed Whitewater Development Corporation. Yet here his delivery is notably awkward and clumsy. Was this brought on by the shame of a 'broken spirit', or merely – as cynics suspected – a disingenuous show of penitence?

" Thank you very much, ladies and gentlemen. Welcome to the White House, and to this day, to which Hillary and the Vice President and I look forward so much every year.

This is always an important day for our country … It is an unusual and, I think, unusually important day today. I may not be quite as easy with my words today as I have been in years past, and I was up rather late last night thinking about and praying about what I ought to say today. And rather unusual for me, I actually tried to write it down. So if you will forgive me, I will do my best to say what it is I want to say to you – and I may have to take my glasses out to read my own writing.

First, I want to say to all of you that, as you might imagine,

I have been on quite a journey these last few weeks to get to the end of this, to the rock-bottom truth of where I am and where we all are.

I agree with those who have said that in my first statement after I testified I was not contrite enough. I don't think there is a fancy way to say that I have sinned.

It is important to me that everybody who has been hurt know that the sorrow I feel is genuine: first and most important, my family; also my friends, my staff, my Cabinet, Monica Lewinsky and her family, and the American people. I have asked all for their forgiveness.

But I believe that to be forgiven, more than sorrow is required – at least two more things. First, genuine repentance – a determination to change and to repair breaches of my own making. I have repented. Second, what my Bible calls a 'broken spirit'; an understanding that I must have God's help to be the person that I want to be; a willingness to give the very forgiveness I seek; a renunciation of the pride and the anger which cloud judgement, lead people to excuse and compare and to blame and complain.

Now, what does all this mean for me and for us? First, I will instruct my lawyers to mount a vigorous defence, using all available appropriate arguments.

But legal language must not obscure the fact that I have done wrong. Second, I will continue on the path of repentance, seeking pastoral support and that of other caring people so that they can hold me accountable for my own commitment.

Third, I will intensify my efforts to lead our country and the world toward peace and freedom, prosperity and harmony, in the hope that with a broken spirit and a still strong heart I can be used for greater good, for we have many blessings and many challenges and so much work to do.

In this, I ask for your prayers and for your help in healing our nation. And though I cannot move beyond or forget this – indeed, I must always keep it as a caution light in my life – it is very important that our nation move forward.

I am very grateful for the many, many people – clergy and ordinary citizens alike – who have written me with wise counsel.

I am profoundly grateful for the support of so many Americans, who somehow through it all seem to still know that I care about them a great deal, that I care about their problems and their dreams. I am grateful for those who have stood by me and who say that in this case and many others, the bounds of presidency have been excessively and unwisely invaded. That may be.

Nevertheless, in this case, it may be a blessing, because I still sinned. And if my repentance is genuine and sustained, and if I can maintain both a broken spirit and a strong heart, then good can come of this for our country as well as for me and my family.

[Applause.]

The children of this country can learn in a profound way that integrity is important and selfishness is wrong, but God can change us and make us strong at the broken places. I want to embody those lessons for the children of this country – for that little boy in Florida who came up to me and said that he wanted to grow up and be president and to be just like me.[1] I want the parents of all the children in America to be able to say that to their children.

A couple of days ago, when I was in Florida, a Jewish friend of mine gave me this liturgy book called Gates of Repentance.[2] And there was this incredible passage from the Yom Kippur[3] liturgy. I would like to read it to you: 'Now is the time for turning. The leaves are beginning to turn from green to red to orange. The birds are beginning to turn and are heading once more toward the south. The animals are beginning to turn to storing their food for the winter. For leaves, birds and animals, turning comes instinctively. But for us, turning does not come so easily. It takes an act of will for us to make a turn. It means breaking old habits. It means admitting that we have been wrong, and this is never easy. It means losing face. It means starting all over again. And this is always painful. It means saying I am sorry. It means recognizing that we have the ability to change. These things are terribly hard to do.

'But unless we turn, we will be trapped for ever in yesterday's ways.

Lord help us to turn, from callousness to sensitivity, from hostility to love, from pettiness to purpose, from envy to contentment, from carelessness to discipline, from fear to faith. Turn us around, O Lord, and bring us back toward you. Revive our lives as at the beginning, and turn us toward each other, Lord, for in isolation there is no life.'

I thank my friend for that. I thank you for being here. I ask you to share my prayer, that God will search me and know my heart, try me and know my anxious thoughts, see if there is any hurtfulness in me, and lead me toward the life everlasting. I ask that God give me a clean heart, let me walk by faith and not sight.

I ask once again to be able to love my neighbour – all my neighbours – as myself, to be an instrument of God's peace; to let the words of my mouth and the meditations of my heart and, in the end, the work of my hands, be pleasing.[4] This is what I wanted to say to you today.

Thank you. God bless you.

[1] Two days before he gave this speech, Clinton had spoken at Hillcrest School in Orlando, Florida. Later that day, he reported a young boy telling him, 'Mr President, I want to grow up to be president. I want to be a president like you.'
[2] A classic text by Rabbi Yonah of Gerona (1180–1263).
[3] In Judaism, Yom Kippur is the annual Day of Atonement festival, which falls on the tenth day of the month of Tishri, i.e. sometime between mid-September and mid-October.
[4] See Psalms 19:14.

'Today, our nation saw evil'
– *George W Bush*

40

George W Bush

American politician

George Walker Bush (1946–) was the son of the American politician George H W Bush, who became the 41st US president. He was elected governor of Texas in 1994 and proved popular, winning re-election four years later. In 2000, he stood as the Republican presidential candidate against Al Gore, winning by the tightest margin for more than a century. In contrast to the left-leaning presidency of Bill Clinton, Bush led a swing to the right and was closely associated with the Neoconservative movement and the Christian Right. In September 2001, following the terrorist strikes on New York and Washington, Bush was plunged into the international arena and became committed to military action against perceived enemies in the Middle East. In 2004, Bush was re-elected president but faced a rising tide of popular criticism, especially for his handling of the ongoing Iraq War, Hurricane Katrina (2005) and the so-called 'Great Recession' that began in 2007. He left office in 2009.

'Today, our nation saw evil'

11 September 2001, television broadcast from Washington, DC, USA

The terrorist strikes of 11 September 2001 were unquestionably a turning point in history, though their significance may not be fully understood for some years. They led to war in Afghanistan and a raft of security measures and legislation under the umbrella title the 'War on Terror'. They were also used to justify the 2003 invasion of Iraq.

Bush was in a classroom at Emma Booker Elementary School in Florida when he was told about the attacks in New York. Photographs and film footage show anguish settling over his features as he clutches the children's book *My Pet Goat*. He made a brief media announcement from the school, then travelled to Louisiana, where he made a further announcement. By now, the World Trade Center had collapsed, and two further hijacked planes had crashed, one destroying part of the Pentagon in Washington.

Bush returned to the White House and by 8.30pm he was ready to address the nation, which he did in this televised address from the Oval Office. Visibly rattled, and stumbling on a few words, he gave a competent performance nonetheless. This disaster was, in a sense, a gift for Bush: his hawkish response propelled a president formerly considered inward-looking into the international arena.

" Good evening. Today, our fellow citizens, our way of life, our very freedom came under attack in a series of deliberate and deadly terrorist acts. The victims were in airplanes, or in their offices; secretaries, businessmen and women, military and federal workers; moms and dads, friends and neighbours. Thousands of lives were suddenly ended by evil, despicable acts of terror.

The pictures of airplanes flying into buildings, fires burning, huge structures collapsing, have filled us with disbelief, terrible sadness and a quiet, unyielding anger.

These acts of mass murder were intended to frighten our nation into chaos and retreat. But they have failed; our country is strong.

A great people has been moved to defend a great nation.

Terrorist attacks can shake the foundations of our biggest buildings, but they cannot touch the foundation of America. These acts shattered steel, but they cannot dent the steel of American resolve.

America was targeted for attack because we're the brightest beacon for freedom and opportunity in the world. And no one will keep that light from shining.

Today, our nation saw evil, the very worst of human nature. And we responded with the best of America – with the daring of our rescue-workers, with the caring of – for strangers and neighbours who came to give blood and help in any way they could.

Immediately following the first attack, I implemented our government's emergency response plans. Our military is powerful, and it's prepared. Our emergency teams are working in New York City and Washington, DC to help with local rescue efforts. Our first priority is to get help to those who have been injured, and to take every precaution to protect our citizens at home and around the world from further attacks.

The functions of our government continue without interruption. Federal agencies in Washington which had to be evacuated today are reopening for essential personnel tonight, and will be open for business tomorrow. Our financial institutions remain strong, and the American economy will be open for business, as well.

The search is under way for those who are behind these evil acts. I've directed the full resources of our intelligence and law-enforcement communities to find those responsible and to bring them to justice. We will make no distinction between the terrorists who committed these acts and those who harbour them.

I appreciate so very much the members of Congress who have joined me in strongly condemning these attacks.

And on behalf of the American people, I thank the many world leaders who have called to offer their condolences and assistance.

America and our friends and allies join with all those who want peace and security in the world, and we stand together to win the war against terrorism. Tonight, I ask for your prayers for all those who grieve, for the children whose worlds have been shattered, for all whose sense of safety and security has been threatened. And I pray they will be comforted by a power greater than any of us, spoken through the ages in Psalm 23:'Even though I walk through the valley of the shadow of death, I fear no evil, for you are with me.'

This is a day when all Americans from every walk of life unite in our resolve for justice and peace.

America has stood down enemies before, and we will do so this time. None of us will ever forget this day. Yet we go forward to defend freedom and all that is good and just in our world.

Thank you. Good night, and God bless America. 🙶

41

Saddam Hussein

Iraqi dictator

A member of the Ba'ath Socialist Party since 1957, Saddam Hussein (1937–2006) took a leading part in the 1968 Iraqi revolution and established a Revolutionary Command Council (RCC), of which he became vice president, then chairman and state president (1979). He waged a bitter war against Iran (1980–8) and dealt harshly with Kurdish rebels. In July 1990, he ordered the invasion of Kuwait, which led to United Nations sanctions and later the Gulf War, in which he was opposed by a UN-backed force involving US, European and Arab troops. Saddam's army surrendered in February 1991. Tensions continued with the West, and following the terrorist strikes in the USA in 2001, President George W Bush identified Iraq as a member of the 'axis of evil' and renewed demands for regime change. In March 2003, amid widespread controversy over the legality of war, an invasion was launched by a US-led alliance of 35 countries. Decisive victory was accomplished within three weeks, though insurgency has persisted. Saddam went into hiding but was captured in December 2003. His trial for crimes against humanity began in July 2004. He was convicted in November 2006 and executed by hanging just under two months later.

'Iraq will be victorious'

20 March 2003, Baghdad, Iraq

Following the terrorist attacks of 11 September 2001 in the USA, American fears of overseas threats were heightened and the anti-American rhetoric of Saddam reinforced a perception of his regime as a sponsor of international terrorism. His continued obstruction of the work of UN weapons inspection teams hardened international attitudes towards him and strengthened calls for President George W Bush to complete his father's 'unfinished business'. Allied forces were assembled on Iraq's borders in the early months of 2003 and US bombers struck Baghdad on 20 March.

Saddam appeared on Iraqi television two hours after these initial 'decapitation' bombings, which announced the onset of the expected war. Wearing military uniform – and citing the date, to prove that the speech had not been pre-recorded and that he was still in control – Saddam conceded no suggestion of defeat, despite the overwhelming odds.

The fierce defiance, pious religious language and promises of humiliation for the enemy are all characteristic features of his bullish oratorical style.

" In the name of God, the merciful, the compassionate … Those who are oppressed are permitted to fight and God is capable of making them victorious. God is greatest.

To the great people of Iraq, to our brave strugglers, to our men in the heroic armed forces, to our glorious nation: at dawn prayers today on 20 March 2003, the criminal, reckless little Bush and his aides committed this crime which he was threatening to commit against Iraq and humanity. He executed his criminal act with his allies; thereby he and his followers have added to the series of shameful crimes committed against Iraq and humanity.

To the Iraqis and the good people of our nation: your country, your glorious nation and your principles are worth the sacrifices of yourself, your souls, your family and your sons.

In this context, I don't need to repeat to you what each and every one of you must and needs to do to defend our precious nation, our principles and sanctities. I say to every single member of the patient and faithful Iraqi family which is oppressed by the evil enemy to remember and not to forget everything that he has said and pledged. These days, and according to God's will, will add to the eternal history of glorious Iraq.

You brave men and women of Iraq: you deserve victory and glory and everything that elevates the stature of the faithful before their God and defeats the infidels, enemies of God and humanity at large. You, Iraqis, will be victorious along with the sons of the nation. You are already victorious, with the help of God. Your enemies will be in disgrace and shame …

To you friends, opposed to the evil in the world, peace upon you. Now that you have seen how the reckless Bush belittled your positions and views against the war and your sincere call for peace, he has committed his despicable crime today …

They will be defeated, a defeat that is wished for them by the good, faithful and lovers of peace and humanity. Iraq will be victorious, God willing, and with Iraq our nation and humanity will be victorious and the evil ones will be hit in a way that will make them unable to achieve their crime in the way that they, the American and Zionist coalition, have planned for nations and peoples, above all our glorious Arab nation.

God is greatest. Long live Iraq and Palestine. God is greatest. Long live our glorious nation; long live human brotherhood; long live lovers of peace and security and those who seek the right of people to live in freedom, based on justice. God is greatest. Long live Iraq; long live jihad[1] and long live Palestine. God is greatest. God is greatest. God is greatest. "

---

[1] Holy war waged by Muslims in defence of their faith.

'... it is very clear who is the one benefiting from igniting this war and from the shedding of blood. It is the warlords, the bloodsuckers, who are steering the world policy from behind a curtain.'

– *Osama bin Laden*

42

Osama bin Laden

Saudi Arabian terrorist

The son of a Yemeni-born construction billionaire, Osama bin Mohammad bin Laden (1957–2011) founded the al-Qaeda organization in 1988 to support Islamic opposition movements across the world. In 1998, he called upon Muslims everywhere to attack Americans and US interests and was strongly suspected of being involved in various terrorist attacks against the West. He rose to global notoriety after 11 September 2001, when four commercial airliners were hijacked by terrorists, two of which were used to destroy the World Trade Center in New York. In total, almost 3,000 people were killed. Soon afterwards, bin Laden was identified as the chief culprit. US president George W Bush responded by declaring an international 'war on terrorism', organizing assaults against Bin Laden's bases in Afghanistan and against the Taliban regime, which was accused of sheltering him. Considered the world's most wanted criminal, for a decade he consistently eluded capture. On 2 May 2011, he was assassinated during a controversial covert operation ordered by President Barack Obama at what seems to have been his long-standing home in Abbottabad, Pakistan.

'Our acts are reaction to your own acts'

15 April 2004, sound recording made in an undeclared location

After the attacks of 2001, Osama bin Laden taunted his enemies with taped audio and video messages, delivered to broadcasting organizations. In April 2004, one such audio tape, believed to be a recording of his voice, was broadcast by the pan-Arab satellite channels al-Arabiya and al-Jazeera.

On the tape, bin Laden outlines his view of the global security situation. He argues that his followers are targeting the West because Western nations have harmed Muslim interests, denying them power and security. This, he suggests, is morally equivalent to the acts of terrorism pursued by al-Qaeda – 'your commodity that was returned to you'.

He points specifically to the plight of the Palestinians displaced and dispossessed by Israel, with the support of the USA. Westerners who desire peace, he says, should promote the cause of Palestinians and other oppressed Muslim people. He emphasizes this message with a blunt threat: 'stop shedding our blood so as to preserve your blood'.

This 'peace offer' was interpreted by most Western commentators as propaganda designed to appeal to Western intellectuals, who might influence their governments to reduce support for Israel and withdraw troops from Iraq.

" Praise be to Almighty God; peace and prayers be upon our Prophet Muhammad, his family, and companions. This is a message to our neighbours north of the Mediterranean, containing a reconciliation initiative as a response to their positive reactions.

Praise be to God; praise be to God; praise be to God who created Heaven and earth with justice and who allowed the oppressed to punish the oppressor in the same way.

Peace upon those who followed the right path. In my hands there is a message to remind you that justice is a duty towards those whom you love and those whom you do not. And people's rights will not be harmed if the opponent speaks out about them.

The greatest rule of safety is justice, and stopping injustice and aggression. It was said: oppression kills the oppressors and the hotbed of injustice is evil. The situation in occupied Palestine is an example. What happened on 11 September and 11 March[1] is your commodity that was returned to you.

It is known that security is a pressing necessity for all mankind. We do not agree that you should monopolize it only for yourselves. Also, vigilant people do not allow their politicians to tamper with their security.

Having said this, we would like to inform you that labeling us and our acts as terrorism is also a description of you and of your acts. Reaction comes at the same level as the original action. Our acts are reaction to your own acts, which are represented by the destruction and killing of our kinfolk in Afghanistan, Iraq and Palestine. The act that horrified the world – that is, the killing of the old, handicapped Sheikh Ahmed Yassin,[2] may God have mercy on him – is sufficient evidence.

We pledge to God that we will punish America for him, God willing.

Which religion considers your killed ones innocent and our killed ones worthless? And which principle considers your blood real blood and our blood water? Reciprocal treatment is fair and the one who starts injustice bears greater blame.

As for your politicians and those who have followed their path, who insist on ignoring the real problem of occupying the entirety of Palestine and exaggerate lies and falsification regarding our right in defence and resistance: they do not respect themselves. They also disdain the blood and minds of peoples. This is because their falsification increases the shedding of your blood instead of sparing it.

Moreover, the examining of the developments that have been taking place – in terms of killings in our countries and your countries – will make clear an important fact; namely, that injustice is inflicted on us and on you by your politicians, who send your sons – although you are opposed to this – to our countries to kill and be killed.

---

[1] On 11 March 2004, ten bombs were detonated on commuter trains in Madrid, Spain, killing 191 people and wounding over 1,800. Spain had been a member of the US-led coalition that invaded Iraq in 2003, and had been cited as a target in a bin Laden broadcast of October 2003.

[2] The Palestinian activist Ahmed Yassin (c.1937–2004) was the founder and spiritual leader of Hamas, the Palestinian Islamic Resistance Movement. He was assassinated by Israeli security forces on 22 March 2004.

Therefore, it is in both sides' interest to curb the plans of those who shed the blood of peoples for their narrow personal interest and subservience to the White House gang.

The Zionist lobby is one of the most dangerous and most difficult figures of this group.

God willing, we are determined to fight them. We must take into consideration that this war brings billions of dollars in profit to the major companies, whether it be those that produce weapons or those that contribute to reconstruction, such as the Halliburton Company,[3] its sisters and daughters.

Based on this, it is very clear who is the one benefiting from igniting this war and from the shedding of blood. It is the warlords, the bloodsuckers, who are steering the world policy from behind a curtain.

As for President Bush: the leaders who are revolving in his orbit, the leading media companies and the United Nations, which makes laws for relations between the masters of veto[4] and the slaves of the General Assembly – these are only some of the tools used to deceive and exploit peoples. All these pose a fatal threat to the whole world.

Based on the above, and in order to deny war merchants a chance – and in response to the positive interaction shown by recent events and opinion polls, which indicate that most European peoples want peace – I ask honest people … to form a permanent committee to enlighten European peoples of the justice of our causes, above all Palestine. They can make use of the huge potential of the media.

The door of reconciliation is open for three months from the date of announcing this statement. I also offer a reconciliation initiative to them, whose essence is our commitment to stopping operations against every country that commits itself to not attacking Muslims or interfering in their affairs – including the US conspiracy on the greater Muslim world …

The reconciliation will start with the departure of its last soldier from our country.

The door of reconciliation is open for three months from the date of announcing this statement. For those who reject reconciliation and want war, we are ready …

Stop shedding our blood so as to preserve your blood. It is in your hands to apply this easy, yet difficult, formula. You know that the situation will expand and increase if you delay things. If this happens, do not blame us – blame yourselves. A rational person does not relinquish his security, money and children to please the liar of the White House …

It is said that prevention is better than cure. A happy person is he who learns a lesson from the experience of others. Heeding right is better than persisting in falsehood.

Peace be upon those who follow guidance.

[3] The Halliburton Company, whose chief executive 1995–2000 was Dick Cheney (US vice president, 2001–9) was awarded reconstruction contracts in Iraq after the 2003 invasion without a competitive tender process taking place. A US government inquiry into the contracts was established in 2004.

[4] The voting procedures of the 15-member UN Security Council give the five permanent members (China, France, Russia, the UK and the USA) the power of veto over Security Council resolutions. Although the General Assembly can adopt resolutions, authorization of external action must come from the Security Council, unless in exceptional circumstances.

43

Steve Jobs

American IT entrepreneur/pioneer

In 1976, Steven Paul Jobs (1955–2011) formed Apple Computers with his friend, electronics engineer Steve Wozniak. Known for his drive and charisma, Jobs developed Apple to become one of the world's leading brands in IT and consumer electronics. In 1985 he quit Apple and founded a new IT company, NeXT. In 1986, he helped found the pioneering computer animation company Pixar. Apple purchased NeXT in 1997, and Jobs became its chief executive again, spearheading a major revival in the company's fortunes. He oversaw the development and launch of key products and services, including the iMac, iPod, iPhone and iPad, iTunes and the OSX operating system. Diagnosed with pancreatic cancer in 2003, he died from the disease in 2011.

'You are already naked. There is no reason not to follow your heart.'

12 June 2005, Stanford, California, USA

The development of personal computing has had a revolutionary effect on almost every area of human life – and, as he points out in this speech, Steve Jobs had a key role in that process. He also pioneered several other key areas of global culture, including the smart phone, music downloads and computerized animation.

The speech was delivered as a commencement address – a lecture to new graduates – at Stanford University in California, where his wife, Laurene Powell, was studying when he met her. The event was held in a sports stadium, where a large crowd was assembled, most wearing mortar boards, some using them to shield their eyes from the sun.

Jobs' showmanship at product launches and technology, entertainment, design (TED) conferences was legendary. This speech was written and presented with aplomb and understated humour, but without grandstanding: Jobs merely stood still, referring frequently to his notes and pacing himself carefully through a brief speech of 15 minutes. Laurene later revealed that he had practised it many times in front of his family, but had woken that morning 'with butterflies in his stomach'.

"I am honoured to be with you today for your commencement from one of the finest universities in the world. *[Applause.]* Truth be told, I never graduated from college, *[Laughter]* and this is the closest I've ever gotten to a college graduation. *[Laughter.]* Today I want to tell you three stories from my life. That's it. No big deal. Just three stories.

The first story is about connecting the dots.

I dropped out of Reed College[1] after the first six months, but then stayed around as a drop-in for another 18 months or so before I really quit. So why did I drop out? *[Commotion and laughter.]*

It started before I was born. My biological mother was a young, unwed college graduate student, and she decided to put me up for adoption. She felt very strongly that I should be adopted by college graduates, so everything was all set for me to be adopted at birth by a lawyer and his wife. Except that when I popped out they decided at the last minute that they really wanted a girl. So my parents, who were on a waiting list, got a call in the middle of the night, asking: 'We've got an unexpected baby boy – do you want him?'

They said: 'Of course.'

My biological mother found out later that my mother had never graduated from college and that my father had never graduated from high school. She refused to sign the final adoption papers. She only relented a few months later when my parents promised that I would go to college. This was the start in my life.

And 17 years later I did go to college. But I naïvely chose a college that was almost as expensive as Stanford *[ripple of laughter]* and all of my working-class parents' savings were being spent on my college tuition. After six months, I couldn't see the value in it. I had no idea what I wanted to do with my life and no idea how college was going to help me figure it out. And here I was spending all of the money my parents had saved their entire life.

So I decided to drop out and trust that it would all work out okay. It was pretty scary at the time, but looking back, it was one of the best decisions I ever made. *[Laughter.]* …

I loved it [dropping out]. And much of what I stumbled into by following my curiosity and intuition turned out to be priceless later on.

Let me give you one example. Reed College at that time offered perhaps the best calligraphy instruction in the country. Throughout the campus, every poster, every label on every drawer, was beautifully hand calligraphed. Because I had dropped out and didn't have to take the normal classes, I decided to take a calligraphy class to learn how to do this … It was beautiful, historical, artistically subtle in a way that science can't capture, and I found it fascinating.

None of this had even a hope of any practical application in my life. But ten years later, when we were designing the first Macintosh computer, it all came back to me. And we designed it all into the Mac. It was the first computer with beautiful typography. If I had never dropped

[1] A liberal arts college in Portland, Oregon.

in on that single course in college, the Mac would have never had multiple typefaces or proportionally spaced fonts.

And since Windows[2] just copied the Mac *[laughter and applause]* … it's likely that no personal computer would have them. If I had never dropped out, I would have never dropped in on that calligraphy class, and personal computers might not have the wonderful typography that they do. Of course, it was impossible to connect the dots looking forward when I was in college. But it was very, very clear looking backwards ten years later.

Again, you can't connect the dots looking forward; you can only connect them looking backward.

So you have to trust that the dots will somehow connect in your future. You have to trust in something – your gut, destiny, life, karma, whatever. Because believing that the dots will connect down the road will give you the confidence to follow your heart, even when it leads you off the well-worn path, and that will make all the difference.

[Pause.]

My second story is about love and loss.

I was lucky – I found what I loved to do early in life. Woz[3] and I started Apple in my parents' garage when I was 20. We worked hard, and in ten years Apple had grown from just the two of us in a garage into a $2 billion company with over 4,000 employees. We had just released our finest creation – the Macintosh – a year earlier, and I had just turned 30. And then I got fired.

How can you get fired from a company you started?

[Laughter.] Well, as Apple grew we hired someone who I thought was very talented to run the company with me,[4] and for the first year or so things went well. But then our visions of the future began to diverge and eventually we had a falling out. When we did, our board of directors sided with him. So at 30 I was out. And very publicly out. What had been the focus of my entire adult life was gone, and it was devastating …

I didn't see it then, but it turned out that getting fired from Apple was the best thing that could have ever happened to me. The heaviness of being successful was replaced by the lightness of being a beginner again, less sure about everything. It freed me to enter one of the most creative periods of my life.

During the next five years, I started a company named NeXT[5], another company named Pixar, and fell in love with an amazing woman who would become my wife. Pixar went on to create the world's first computer-animated feature film, *Toy Story*, and is now the most successful animation studio in the world. *[Cheers* and *applause.]* In a remarkable turn of

[2] Microsoft Windows has for many years been the chief rival to Apple's operating systems.

[3] Steve Wozniak (1950–), known as 'Woz', founded Apple Computer (later Apple, Inc.) with Steve Jobs and Ronald Wayne in 1976, and demonstrated the first Apple Mac computer the same year.

[4] John Sculley (1939–) left his job as president of Pepsi-Cola in 1983 to become chief executive officer of Apple, Inc. By 1985, his relationship with Jobs had soured and Jobs left Apple, though Sculley has denied that this was at his behest.

[5] NeXT, Inc. was a computer company founded by Jobs in 1985, initially specialising in computer workstations.

events, Apple bought NeXT, and I returned to Apple, and the technology we developed at NeXT is at the heart of Apple's current renaissance. And Laurene and I have a wonderful family[6] together.

I'm pretty sure none of this would have happened if I hadn't been fired from Apple. It was awful tasting medicine, but I guess the patient needed it. Sometimes life's going to hit you in the head with a brick. Don't lose faith. I'm convinced that the only thing that kept me going was that I loved what I did. You've got to find what you love. And that is as true for your work as it is for your lovers. Your work is going to fill a large part of your life, and the only way to be truly satisfied is to do what you believe is great work. And the only way to do great work is to love what you do. If you haven't found it yet, keep looking – and don't settle. As with all matters of the heart, you'll know when you find it. And like any great relationship, it just gets better and better as the years roll on. So keep looking. Don't settle.

[Applause.]

My third story is about death.

When I was 17, I read a quote that went something like: 'If you live each day as if it was your last, someday you'll most certainly be right.' *[Laughter.]* It made an impression on me, and since then, for the past 33 years, I have looked in the mirror every morning and asked myself: 'If today were the last day of my life, would I want to do what I am about to do today?' And whenever the answer has been 'No' for too many days in a row, I know I need to change something.

Remembering that I'll be dead soon is the most important tool I've ever encountered to help me make the big choices in life.

Because almost everything – all external expectations, all pride, all fear of embarrassment or failure – these things just fall away in the face of death, leaving only what is truly important. Remembering that you are going to die is the best way I know to avoid the trap of thinking you have something to lose. You are already naked. There is no reason not to follow your heart.

About a year ago, I was diagnosed with cancer. I had a scan at 7.30 in the morning, and it clearly showed a tumour on my pancreas. I didn't even know what a pancreas was. The doctors told me this was almost certainly a type of cancer that is incurable, and that I should expect to live no longer than three to six months …

I lived with that diagnosis all day. Later that evening I had a biopsy, where they stuck an endoscope down my throat, through my stomach and into my intestines, put a needle into my pancreas and got a few cells from the tumour. I was sedated, but my wife, who was there, told me that when they viewed the cells under a microscope, the doctors started crying, because it turned out to be a very rare form of pancreatic cancer that is curable with surgery. I had the surgery and thankfully I'm fine now.

---

[6] Steve and Laurene Jobs had three children: Reed (1991–), Erin (1995–) and Eve (1998–). Jobs also had a daughter, Lisa (1978–) with an earlier partner.

[7] Stewart Brand (1938–) is a California-based author and editor who became a key figure in the hippie counterculture and later wrote on business and ecological issues.

[Applause.]

This was the closest I've been to facing death, and I hope it's the closest I get for a few more decades. Having lived through it, I can now say this to you with a bit more certainty than when death was a useful but purely intellectual concept:

No one wants to die. Even people who want to go to Heaven don't want to die to get there.

[Ripple of laughter.]

And yet death is the destination we all share. No one has ever escaped it. And that is as it should be, because Death is very likely the single best invention of Life. It is Life's change agent. It clears out the old to make way for the new.

Right now the new is you, but someday not too long from now, you will gradually become the old and be cleared away. Sorry to be so dramatic, but it's quite true.

Your time is limited, so don't waste it living someone else's life.

Don't be trapped by dogma — which is living with the results of other people's thinking. Don't let the noise of others' opinions drown out your own inner voice. And most important, have the courage to follow your heart and intuition. They somehow already know what you truly want to become. Everything else is secondary.

[Applause.]

When I was young, there was an amazing publication called *The Whole Earth Catalog*, which was one of the bibles of my generation. It was created by a fellow named Stewart Brand[7] not far from here in Menlo Park[8], and he brought it to life with his poetic touch … It was sort of like Google in paperback form, 35 years before Google came along: It was idealistic, and overflowing with neat tools and great notions.

Stewart and his team put out several issues of *The Whole Earth Catalog*, and then, when it had run its course, they put out a final issue. It was the mid-1970s, and I was your age. On the back cover of their final issue was a photograph of an early morning country road, the kind you might find yourself hitchhiking on, if you were so adventurous.

Beneath it were the words: 'Stay Hungry. Stay Foolish.' It was their farewell message as they signed off. Stay Hungry. Stay Foolish. And I have always wished that for myself. And now, as you graduate to begin anew, I wish that for you.

Stay Hungry. Stay Foolish.

Thank you all very much. **99**

---

[8] A city in northern California.

'Heroism is here, in the hearts of so many of our fellow citizens' – Barak Obama

44

Barack Obama

American politician

Barack Hussein Obama II (1961–) is the 44th President of the United States, the first African-American to hold the office. Obama's political career began in the 1990s. From 1997 to 2004, he served three terms in the Illinois Senate, and in 2004 he ran a successful campaign to represent Illinois in the US Senate. In 2008, he received the presidential nomination of the Democratic Party, and after defeating the Republican nominee, John McCain, in the general election, was sworn in as president on 20 January 2009. His campaign the previous year had been accompanied by a surge of popular optimism among liberal and left-leaning voters, especially the young, as well as globally. Obama's struggle to carry through reforms and his failure to fulfil election promises such as the closure of the detention centre at Guantanamo Bay led to a degree of disillusion. Nonetheless, he was re-elected president in November 2012 and inaugurated for a second term on 20 January 2013. In his second term, he foregrounded key liberal issues such as LGBT rights, global warming and gun control, but his policy initiatives were often blocked by a hostile Congress dominated by the Republican Party. This led to some domestic disaffection, although Obama has enjoyed high approval ratings overseas.

'Heroism is here, in the hearts of so many of our fellow citizens'

12 January 2011, McKale Center, University of Arizona, Tucson

Barack Obama's power as a political orator is widely recognized and has undoubtedly played a significant role in his political career. A measured but impassioned delivery, combined with an almost lyrical quality often present in the speechwriting, have resulted in masterly, crowd-pleasing oratory, as seen in the iconic 'Yes, we can' New Hampshire primary speech of January 2008.

This speech was delivered as part of the memorial for the victims of the 2011 Tucson shooting. On 8 January 2011 US Representative Gabrielle Giffords and 18 others were shot by Jared Lee Loughner during a constituent meeting held in a supermarket parking lot in the Tucson suburb Casas Adobes. Six people died, including the District Court Chief Judge John Roll, Gabe Zimmerman, one of Giffords' aides, and a nine-year-old girl, Christina-Taylor Green. The primary target, Giffords, who was shot in the head at point-blank range, survived and made a slow recovery. Loughner's motivation was unclear, although he had been recently diagnosed with schizophrenia.

The speech was written by Obama in collaboration with his speechwriter Cody Keenan and was viewed by some 30 million Americans on television. Its dignity and restraint, together with its powerful statement of the value of community and mutual responsibility, won Obama widespread praise.

Thank you. Please. Please, be seated.

To the families of those we've lost, to all who called them friends, to the students of this university, the public servants who are gathered here, the people of Tucson and the people of Arizona:

> *I have come here tonight as an American who, like all Americans, kneels to pray with you today and will stand by you tomorrow.*

There is nothing I can say that will fill the sudden hole torn in your hearts. But know this: the hopes of a nation are here tonight. We mourn with you for the fallen. We join you in your grief. And we add our faith to yours that Representative Gabrielle Giffords[1] and the other living victims of this tragedy will pull through …

On Saturday morning, Gabby, her staff, and many of her constituents gathered outside a supermarket to exercise their right to peaceful assembly and free speech.

They were fulfilling a central tenet of the democracy envisioned by our founders: representatives of the people answering questions to their constituents, so as to carry their concerns back to our nation's capital. Gabby called it 'Congress on Your Corner,' just an updated version of government of and by and for the people.

And that quintessentially American scene, that was the scene that was shattered by a gunman's bullets. And the six people who lost their lives on Saturday: they, too, represented what is best in us, what is best in America.

Judge John Roll[2] served our legal system for nearly 40 years.

A graduate of this university and a graduate of this law school, Judge Roll was recommended for the federal bench by John McCain 20 years ago, appointed by President George H W Bush, and rose to become Arizona's chief federal judge … John is survived by his loving wife, Maureen, his three sons, and his five beautiful grandchildren.

George and Dorothy Morris – 'Dot' to her friends – were high school sweethearts who got married and had two daughters. They did everything together, traveling the open road in their R.V., enjoying what their friends called a 50-year honeymoon.

Saturday morning, they went by the Safeway to hear what their congresswoman had to say. When gunfire rang out, George, a former marine, instinctively tried to shield his wife.

Both were shot. Dot passed away.

A New Jersey native, Phyllis Schneck retired to Tucson to beat the snow. But in the summer, she would return east, where her world revolved around her three children, her seven

---

[1] Gabrielle ('Gabby') Giffords (1970–) was Democratic member of the US House of Representatives for Arizona's 8th Congressional District, 2007–12. A year after the shooting she resigned her seat to focus on her recovery, but with the promise to return to politics.

[2] John McCarthy Roll (1947–2011) served on the US District Court for the District of Arizona, from 1991 until his death, serving as chief judge from 2006.

grandchildren, and two-year-old great-granddaughter … A Republican, she took a liking to Gabby and wanted to get to know her better.

Dorwan and Mavy Stoddard grew up in Tucson together about 70 years ago. They moved apart and started their own respective families, but after both were widowed, they found their way back here, to, as one of Mavy's daughters put it, 'be boyfriend and girlfriend again' … His final act of selflessness was to dive on top of his wife, sacrificing his life for hers.

Everything – everything Gabe Zimmerman[3] did, he did with passion, but his true passion was helping people. As Gabby's outreach director, he made the cares of thousands of her constituents his own, seeing to it that seniors got the Medicare[4] benefits that they had earned, that veterans got the medals and the care that they deserved, that government was working for ordinary folks …

And then there is nine-year-old Christina-Taylor Green. Christina was an A student … She showed an appreciation for life uncommon for a girl her age. She'd remind her mother, 'We are so blessed. We have the best life.' And she'd pay those blessings back by participating in a charity that helped children who were less fortunate …

Our hearts are full of hope and thanks for the 13 Americans who survived the shooting, including the congresswoman many of them went to see on Saturday.

I have just come from the University Medical Center, just a mile from here, where our friend Gabby courageously fights to recover even as we speak.

And I want to tell you – her husband, Mark, is here, and he allows me to share this with you. Right after we went to visit, a few minutes after we left her room and some of her colleagues from Congress were in the room, Gabby opened her eyes for the first time.

Gabby opened her eyes for the first time.

Gabby opened her eyes.

Gabby opened her eyes, so I can tell you, she knows we are here, she knows we love her, and she knows that we are rooting for her through what is undoubtedly going to be a difficult journey. We are there for her.

Our hearts are full of thanks for that good news, and our hearts are full of gratitude for those who saved others.

We are grateful to Daniel Hernandez, a volunteer in Gabby's office. And Daniel, I'm sorry, you may deny it, but we've decided you are a hero, because you ran through the chaos to minister to your boss and tended to her wounds and help keep her alive.

We are grateful to the men who tackled the gunman as he stopped to reload.

They're right over there.

---

[3] Gabriel Matthew ('Gabe') Zimmerman (1980–2011) had worked for Congresswoman Giffords for the previous five years.

[4] US national programme that guarantees access to health insurance for the over-65s and other vulnerable groups.

We – we are grateful for petite Patricia Maisch, who wrestled away the killer's ammunition and undoubtedly saved some lives.

And we are grateful for the doctors and nurses and first responders[5] who worked wonders to heal those who'd been hurt. We are grateful to them.

These men and women remind us that heroism is found not only on the fields of battle. They remind us that heroism does not require special training or physical strength. Heroism is here, in the hearts of so many of our fellow citizens, all around us, just waiting to be summoned, as it was on Saturday morning …

Already, we've seen a national conversation commence, not only about the motivations behind these killings, but about everything from the merits of gun safety laws[6] to the adequacy of our mental health system. And much – much of this process of debating what might be done to prevent such tragedies in the future is an essential ingredient in our exercise of self-government.

But at a time when our discourse has become so sharply polarized, at a time when we are far too eager to lay the blame for all that ails the world at the feet of those who happen to think differently than we do, it's important for us to pause for a moment and make sure that we're talking with each other in a way that – that heals, not in a way that wounds …

Bad things happen, and we have to guard against simple explanations in the aftermath.

For the truth is, none of us can know exactly what triggered this vicious attack. None of us can know with any certainty what might have stopped these shots from being fired or what thoughts lurked in the inner recesses of a violent man's mind.

Yes, we have to examine all the facts behind this tragedy. We cannot and will not be passive in the face of such violence. We should be willing to challenge old assumptions in order to lessen the prospects of such violence in the future.

But what we cannot do is use this tragedy as one more occasion to turn on each other.

That we cannot do.

That we cannot do.

As we discuss these issues, let each of us do so with a good dose of humility. Rather than pointing fingers or assigning blame, let's use this occasion to expand our moral imaginations, to listen to each other more carefully, to sharpen our instincts for empathy, and remind ourselves of all the ways that our hopes and dreams are bound together. After all, that's what most of us do when we lose somebody in our family, especially if the loss is unexpected. We're shaken out of our routines. We're forced to look inward. We reflect on the past …

[5] In the US, 'first responder' is a person qualified to give pre-hospital care in emergencies. Most US policemen and all firefighters are first responders.
[6] Mass shootings had become a depressingly familiar feature of contemporary America society and the issue of fire arms had long been a matter of high-profile and bitter debate. The right to bear arms is enshrined in the Second Amendment to the US Constitution and is vigorously defended by such groups as the National Rifle Association. In the wake of the Sandy Hook Elementary School shooting (2012), Obama would put forward moderate proposals for improving gun control, in which he was backed by the vast majority of the US public.

So sudden loss causes us to look backward, but it also forces us to look forward, to reflect on the present and the future, on the manner in which we live our lives and nurture our relationships with those who are still with us.

We may ask ourselves if we've shown enough kindness and generosity and compassion to the people in our lives. Perhaps we question whether we're doing right by our children, or our community, whether our priorities are in order. We recognize our own mortality. And we are reminded that, in the fleeting time we have on this Earth, what matters is not wealth, or status, or power, or fame, but rather how well we have loved and what small part we have played in making the lives of other people better.

And that process – that process of reflection, of making sure we align our values with our actions … that, I believe, is what a tragedy like this requires …

If this tragedy prompts reflection and debate, as it should, let's make sure it's worthy of those we have lost.

Let's make sure it's not on the usual plane of politics and point-scoring and pettiness that drifts away in the next news cycle.

The loss of these wonderful people should make every one of us strive to be better, to be better in our private lives, to be better friends and neighbors and co-workers and parents.

And if, as has been discussed in recent days, their death helps usher in more civility in our public discourse, let us remember it is not because a simple lack of civility caused this tragedy – it did not – but rather because only a more civil and honest public discourse can help us face up to the challenges of our nation in a way that would make them proud.

We should be civil because we want to live up to the example of public servants like John Roll and Gabby Giffords, who knew first and foremost that we are all Americans, and that we can question each other's ideas without questioning each other's love of country, and that

> ### *… our task, working together, is to constantly widen the circle of our concern, so that we bequeath the American dream to future generations.*

They believe – they believe and I believe that we can be better. Those who died here, those who saved lives here, they help me believe. We may not be able to stop all evil in the world, but I know that how we treat one another, that's entirely up to us.

And I believe that, for all our imperfections, we are full of decency and goodness and that the forces that divide us are not as strong as those that unite us.

That's what I believe, in part because that's what a child like Christina-Taylor Green believed.

Imagine – can you imagine for a moment? – here was a young girl who was just becoming aware of our democracy, just beginning to understand the obligations of citizenship, just starting to glimpse the fact that someday she, too, might play a part in shaping her nation's future.

She had been elected to her student council. She saw public service as something exciting and hopeful. She was off to meet her congresswoman, someone she was sure was good and important and might be a role model. She saw all this through the eyes of a child, undimmed by the cynicism or vitriol that we adults all too often just take for granted.

I want us to live up to her expectations.

I want our democracy to be as good as Christina imagined it …

… Christina was given to us on September 11th, 2001, one of 50 babies born that day to be pictured in a book called *Faces of Hope*.[7] On either side of her photo in that book were simple wishes for a child's life: 'I hope you help those in need,' read one. 'I hope you know all of the words to the National Anthem and sing it with your hand over your heart. I hope – I hope you jump in rain puddles.'

If there are rain puddles in Heaven, Christina is jumping in them today.

And here on this Earth, here on this Earth, we place our hands over our hearts and we commit ourselves as Americans to forging a country that is forever worthy of her gentle, happy spirit.

May God bless and keep those we've lost in restful and eternal peace. May he love and watch over the survivors. And may he bless the United States of America. **"**

---

[7] Christine Naman, *Faces of Hope: 50 Babies Born on 9/11* (HCI, 2002).

'Countries that geographically are distant have shown that they are close to Burma in what really matters: they are close to the aspirations of the people of Burma …'

— Aung San Suu Kyi

45

Aung San Suu Kyi

Burmese political leader

Aung San Suu Kyi (1945–) was the daughter of the nationalist hero General Aung San (1915–47), who led Burma's fight for independence until his assassination a few months before it was achieved. She began her career as an academic, eventually settling in Oxford, UK, with her British husband, Michael Aris (1946–99). In 1988, she returned to Burma, which was in a state of extreme political unrest under a new military junta, and helped found the National League for Democracy (NLD), becoming its general secretary. Over the following two decades, despite winning wide popular support, both at home and abroad, she was subjected to long periods of house arrest. She was finally released on 13 November 2010, and in 2012 the NLD successfully contested that year's by-elections, with Suu Kyi assuming a seat in the lower house of the Burmese Parliament and the position of Leader of the Opposition. In 2012, she announced her candidacy for the presidential elections of 2015. The NLD won a clear majority, but under the constitution of 2008 Suu Kyi was barred from becoming president as the widow and mother of foreigners. Instead, she assumed a number of key ministerial positions and was appointed by President Htin Kyaw as state counsellor – a post equivalent to prime minister.

'My country today stands at the start of a journey'

21 June 2012, Westminster Hall, London

In June 2012, Aung San Suu Kyi visited the UK and four other European countries during her first visit overseas in many years. She had been leader of Burma's National League for Democracy almost continuously since 1988, but only recently elected as an MP. On 21 June, she addressed the joint Houses of Commons and Lords in Westminster Hall, giving this impassioned plea for Britain to assist her country as it struggled to recreate itself as a parliamentary democracy.

At the heart of her speech is a comparison between the hard-won, fledgling democracy of Burma and the British parliamentary system on which it was modelled, 'perhaps the pre-eminent symbol to oppressed peoples around the world of freedom of speech'. In her appeal for support and assistance, she warns against complacency, suggesting that many in the West take their democracy for granted.

A calm but undemonstrative speaker, she referred closely to her notes throughout the speech, and made few hand gestures – though the solemnity of her speech is leavened with anecdotes and gentle humour. More than charisma and panache, she relies on two factors: the simple, common-sense imperatives embedded in the content of her speech, and the personal authority accorded to her by much of the world.

" Lord Speaker, Mr Speaker, Mr Prime Minister,[1] My Lords and Members of the House of Commons. Thank you for inviting me to speak to you here in this magnificent hall. I am very conscious of the extraordinary nature of this honour …

I have just come from Downing Street.[2] It was my first visit there, and yet for me it was a familiar scene – not just from television broadcasts, but from my own family history. As some of you may be aware, the best-known photograph of my father, Aung San, taken shortly before his assassination in 1947, was of him standing in Downing Street with Clement Attlee[3] and others, with whom he had been discussing Burma's transition to independence …

A couple of hours ago I was photographed in the same place where my father was photographed, together with Prime Minister David Cameron, and it was raining. Very British! *[Laughter.]*

My father was a founding member of the Burmese Independence Army[4] in World War II. He took on this responsibility out of a desire to see democracy established in his homeland. It was his view that democracy was the only political system worthy of an independent nation. It is a view of course that I have long shared.

General Slim,[5] commander of the 14th Army, who led the Allied Burmese campaign, wrote about his first encounter with my father in his memoir Defeat until Victory. The meeting came towards the end of the war, shortly after my father had decided that the Burmese Independence Army should join forces with the Allies. General Slim said to my father: 'You've only come to us because we are winning.' To which my father replied, 'It wouldn't be much good coming to you if you weren't!' Slim saw in my father a practical man with whom he could do business. Six decades later, I strive to be as practical as my father was.

And so I am here, in part, to ask for practical help. Help as a friend and as an equal. In support of the reforms which can bring better lives and greater opportunities to the people of Burma who have been for so long deprived of their rights and place in the world.

As I said yesterday in Oxford,[6] my country today stands at the start of a journey toward I hope a better future. So many hills remain to be climbed, chasms to be bridged, obstacles to be breached.

Our own determination can get us so far. The support of the people of Britain and of peoples around the world can get us so much further.

In a speech about change and reform, it is very appropriate to be in Westminster Hall, because at the heart of this process must be the establishment of a strong, parliamentary institution in my own country. The British Parliament is perhaps the pre-eminent symbol to oppressed peoples around the world of freedom of speech. I would imagine that some people here, to some extent, take this freedom for granted.

[1] David Cameron (1966–), British prime minister, 2010–16. In April 2012, he had become the first British prime minister to visit Burma since the 1950s, and the first leader of a major international power to visit her.
[2] No. 10 Downing Street in Westminster has been the official residence of the British prime minister since 1733.
[3] Clement Attlee later 1st Earl Attlee (1883–1967) served as British prime minister, 1945–51.

[4] The Burmese Independence Army was established in 1941. Initially, it fought in collaboration with the Japanese as they sought to end British colonial rule in Burma, but many of its members later joined the Allies against Japan.
[5] William Slim later 1st Viscount Slim (1891–1970), commander of the 14th Army, 1943–5, which comprised multinational forces drawn from Commonwealth countries.
[6] On the previous day Suu Kyi had given a speech at her former university when receiving an honorary doctorate.

For us in Burma, what you take for granted, we have had to struggle for long and hard. So many people in Burma gave up so much, gave up everything, in Burma's ongoing struggle for democracy, and we are only now just beginning to see the fruits of our struggle.

Westminster has long set a shining example of realizing the people's desire to be part of their own legislative process. In Burma our parliament is in its infancy, having been established only in March 2011. As with any new institution, especially an institution which goes against the cultural grain of 49 years of direct military rule, it will take time to find its feet and time to find its voice.

Our new legislative processes, which undoubtedly are an improvement on what has gone before, are not as transparent as they might be. I would like to see us learn from established examples of parliamentary democracies elsewhere, so that we might deepen our own democratic standards over time.

> *Perhaps the most critical moment in establishing the credibility of the parliamentary process happens before parliament even opens – namely the people's participation in a free, fair, inclusive electoral process.*

Earlier this year I myself participated in my first election as a candidate. To this day, however, I have not yet had the chance to vote freely in any election. In 1990 I was allowed to cast an advance vote while under house arrest.

But I was prevented from contesting as a candidate for my party, the National League for Democracy. I was disqualified on the grounds that I had received help from foreign quarters. This amounted to BBC broadcasts that the authorities considered to be biased in my favour. What struck me most, ahead of this year's by-elections, was how quickly people in the constituencies around Burma grasped the importance of participating in the political process. They understood first hand that the right to vote was not something given to all. They understood that they must take advantage when the opportunity arose, because they understood what it meant to have that opportunity taken away from them …

It has been less than 100 days, since I, together with my fellow National League for Democracy candidates, was out on the campaign trail across Burma. Our by-elections were held on April 1st, and I was conscious there was a certain scepticism that this would turn out to be an elaborate April Fool's joke. In fact, it turned out to be an April of new hope.

The voting process was largely free and fair, and I would like to pay tribute to President Thein[7] for this and for his commitment and his sincerity in the reform process.

As I have long said, it is through dialogue and through cooperation that political differences can best be resolved, and my own commitment to this path remains as strong as ever.

Elections in Burma are very different to those in many more established democracies such as yours. Apathy, especially among the young, is certainly not an issue. For me, the most

[7] Thein Sein (1945–) is a Burmese politician and former military commander, who served as prime minister, 2007–11, and president, 2011–16. He is considered by many as a moderate who has led the way in the post-junta reforms.

encouraging and rewarding aspect of our own elections was the participation, in such vast numbers and with such enthusiasm, of our young people. Often, our biggest challenge was in restraining the crowds of university students, schoolchildren and flag-waving toddlers who greeted us on the campaign, blocking the roads throughout the length of towns …

The passion of the electorate was a passion born of hunger for something long denied.

Following Burma's independence in 1948, our parliamentary system was of course based on that of the United Kingdom. The era became known in Burmese as the Parliamentary Era, a name which, by the mere necessity of its application, speaks of the unfortunate changes which followed.

Our parliamentary era, which lasted more or less until 1962, could not be said to have been perfect. But it was certainly the most progressive and promising period until now in the short history of independent Burma. It was at this time that Burma was considered the nation most likely to succeed in South-East Asia. Things did not, however, go entirely to plan. They often don't in Burma and indeed in the rest of the world.

Now, once again, we have an opportunity to re-establish true democracy in Burma. It is an opportunity for which we have waited many decades. If we do not use this opportunity, if we do not get things right this time around, it may be several decades more before a similar opportunity arises again.

And so it is for this reason that I would ask Britain, as one of the oldest parliamentary democracies, to consider what it can do to build the sound institutions needed to support our nascent parliamentary democracy.

The reforms taking place, led by President Thein Sein, are to be welcomed. But this cannot be a personality-based process. Without strong institutions, this process will not be sustainable. Our legislature has much to learn about the democratization process, and I hope that Britain and other democracies can help by sharing your own experiences with us …

… What is most important is to empower the people, the essential ingredient of democracy. Britain is living proof that a constitution does not need to be written down to be effective. It is more important that a constitution should be accepted by the people, that the people should feel it belongs to them, that it is not an external document imposed on them.

One of the clearly stated aims of my party, the National League for Democracy, is constitutional reform. Britain's[8] original constitution was drawn up following the meeting between my father Aung San and Clement Attlee here in London in 1947. This constitution may not have been perfect, but at its core was a profound understanding of and respect for the aspirations of the people.

The current constitution, drawn up by the military government in 2008, must be amended to incorporate the basic rights and aspirations of Burma's ethnic nationalities. In over 60 years of independence, Burma has not yet known a time when we could say that there is peace throughout the land …

---

[8] The context makes it clear that Aung Sang Suu Kyi intended to say 'Burma's' at this point.

We need to address the problems that lie at the root of conflict. We need to develop a culture of political settlement through negotiation and to promote the rule of law, that all who live in Burma may enjoy the benefits of both freedom and security.

In the immediate term, we also need humanitarian support for the many peoples in the north and west, largely women and children, who have been forced to flee their homes.

> *As the long history of the United Kingdom shows clearly, people never lose their need to preserve their national or ethnic identity. This is something which goes beyond, which supersedes economic development.*

And that is why I hope that in working for Burma's national reconciliation, the international community will recognize that it is political dialogue and political settlement which must be given precedence over short-term economic development.

If differences remain unresolved, if basic aspirations remain unfulfilled, there cannot be an adequate foundation for sustainable development of any kind – economic, social or political.

Britain has for so long, under successive governments – including the present Conservative / Liberal Democratic coalition, and the previous Labour government – been a staunch and unshakeable supporter of aid efforts in Burma. I hope that you can continue to help our country through targeted and coordinated development assistance.

Britain has been until now the largest bilateral donor to Burma. It is in education in particular that I hope the British can play a major role …

Vocational training and creation of employment opportunities to help address Burma's chronic youth unemployment are particularly important. Longer term, Burma's education system is desperately weak. Reform is needed, not just of schools and the curriculum and the training of teachers, but also of our attitude to education, which at present is too narrow and rigid.

I hope also that British businesses can play a role in supporting the democratic reform process, through what I have termed democracy-friendly investment. By this I mean investment that prioritizes transparency, accountability, workers' rights and environmental sustainability. Investment particularly in labour-intensive sectors, when carried out responsibly and with positive intent, can offer real benefits to our people.

One test will be whether new players will benefit from the investment coming in. Britain has played an important role in facilitating the forthcoming visit, next month, of the Extractive Industries Transparency Initiative Secretariat.[9] I hope this will be the start of many similar initiatives in the months ahead.

It was through learning, while at Oxford, about two great British leaders, Gladstone[10] and Disraeli,[11] that I first developed my understanding of parliamentary democracy. I learnt the

---

[9] The Extractive Industries Transparency Initiative (EITI), whose secretariat is based in Oslo, Norway, works to promote transparency in the exploitation of countries' oil, gas and mineral resources. Burma has rich gas and oil resources and is the world's biggest producer of rubies.

[10] William Ewart Gladstone (1809–98), served as prime minister in 1853–5, 1859–66, 1873–4 and 1880–2.

[11] Benjamin Disraeli 1st Earl of Beaconsfield (1804–81), served as prime minister in 1874–80.

basics: that one accepts the decision of the voters; that the governing power is gained and relinquished in accordance with the desires of the electorate, that it is a system which goes on, and that ultimately everyone gets another chance.

These are things taken for granted here in Britain, but in 1990 in Burma, the winner of the elections was never allowed even to convene parliament. I hope that we can leave such days behind us, and that as we look forward to the future, it will be the will of the people that is reflected faithfully in Burma's changing political landscape.

This journey out of Burma has not been a sentimental pilgrimage to the past, but an exploration of the new opportunities at hand for the people of Burma. I have been struck throughout my trip by how extraordinarily warm-hearted and open the world has been to us.

To experience this first-hand, after so long physically separated from the world, has been very moving.

Countries that geographically are distant have shown that they are close to Burma in what really matters: they are close to the aspirations of the people of Burma …

During the years of my house arrest, it was not just the BBC and other broadcasting stations that kept me in touch with the world outside. It was the music of Mozart and Ravi Shankar and the biographies of men and women of different races and religions that convinced me I would never be alone in my struggle. The prizes and honours I received were not so much a personal tribute as a recognition of the basic humanity that unites one isolated person to the rest of the world.

During our dark days in the 1990s, a friend sent me a poem by Arthur Hugh Clough.[12] It begins … 'Say not the struggle nought availeth'. I understand that Winston Churchill, one of the greatest parliamentarians this world has known, used this poem himself as a plea to the United States of America to step in against Nazi Germany.

Today I want to make a rather different point: that we can work together, combining political wisdom from East and West to bring the light of democratic values to all peoples in Burma and beyond …

I would like to emphasize in conclusion that this is the most important time for Burma; that this is the time of our greatest need. And so I would ask that our friends, both here in Britain and beyond, participate in and support Burma's efforts towards the establishment of a truly democratic and just society.

Thank you for giving me this opportunity to address the members of one of the oldest democratic institutions in the world. Thank you for letting me into your midst. My country has not entered the ranks of truly democratic societies, but I am confident that we will get there before too long, with your help. Thank you. 〝

---

[12] Arthur Hugh Clough (1819–61) was a prominent poet of the Victorian era. Aung San Suu Kyi quotes the fourth stanza of 'Say Not the Struggle Nought Availeth' – a rousing call to weary soldiers to keep up their struggle.

'They thought that the bullets would silence us. But they failed'
– *Malala Yousafzai*

46

Malala Yousafzai

Pakistani activist

Malala Yousafzai (1997–) was born in the Swat Valley, in the Khyber Pakhtunkhwa province of northern Pakistan. Her parents were Sunni Muslims of Pashtun ethnicity, who ran schools in the region. At an early age, she emerged as a campaigner for human rights, particularly in relation to women and education. At the age of 11, she began writing a blog for the BBC about life in a region controlled by the Taliban, a militant Sunni movement, which uses violence to impose a harsh interpretation of Islamic sharia law, including the denial of education to girls. She featured prominently in *Class Dismissed*, a *New York Times* documentary of 2010, and soon became widely known, giving media interviews throughout the world. In October 2012, a Taliban gunman boarded her school bus and shot her in the head. Although critically injured, she made a full recovery following treatment in Birmingham, UK, where she later returned to attend school. On 12 July 2013, her 16th birthday, she was the keynote speaker at a 'Youth Takeover' event held by the United Nations in New York. In 2014, she became the youngest ever recipient of the Nobel Peace Prize (jointly with Kailash Satyarthi).

'They thought that the bullets would silence us. But they failed.'

12 July 2013, New York, USA

The world already knew about the extraordinary courage and determination of Malala Yousafzai long before the 'Youth Takeover' event at the United Nations headquarters, dubbed Malala Day in her honour. But few can have imagined that she would deliver this speech with such composure and clarity, just nine months after a near-fatal injury. Standing almost perfectly still, she spoke with quiet confidence and dignity under the world's gaze. Her key message – delivered in support of the United Nations' 'Education First' initiative – was the importance of education and the right of everyone to receive it.

She establishes her credentials as a devout Muslim at the beginning of her speech, but later cites the figureheads of other world religions, as well as secular figures who have espoused non-violent activism. Islam, she insists, is a peaceful religion which encourages learning for all children. She repudiates hatred for her cowardly would-be assassin, instead calling on the Taliban to allow their children to be educated.

"In the name of God, the Most Beneficent, The Most Merciful.[1]

Honourable UN Secretary General Mr Ban Ki-moon,[2]

Respected President General Assembly Vuk Jeremić,[3]

Honourable UN envoy for global education Mr Gordon Brown,[4]

Respected elders and my dear brothers and sisters;

As-salamu alaykum.[5] *[Repeated in response by some audience members.]*

Today, it is an honour for me to be speaking again after a long time.[6] Being here with such honourable people is a great moment in my life, and it's an honour for me that today I am wearing today a shawl of Benazir Bhutto Shaheed.[7]

I don't know where to begin my speech. I don't know what people would be expecting me to say.

But first of all, thank you to God for whom we all are equal and thank you to every person who has prayed for my fast recovery and a new life. I cannot believe how much love people have shown me. I have received thousands of good wish cards and gifts from all over the world. Thank you to all of them. Thank you to the children whose innocent words encouraged me. Thank you to my elders whose prayers strengthened me.

I would like to thank my nurses, doctors and the staff of the hospitals in Pakistan and the UK, and the UAE government,[8] who have helped me get better and recover my strength. I fully support Mr Ban Ki-moon, the Secretary-General, in his Global Education First Initiative and the work of the UN Special Envoy, Mr Gordon Brown, and the respected President General Assembly Vuk Jeremić. I thank all of them for the leadership they continue to give. They continue to inspire all of us to action.

Dear brothers and sisters, do remember one thing. Malala Day is not my day. Today is the day of every woman, every boy and every girl who have raised their voice for their rights.

There are hundreds of human rights activists and social workers who are not only speaking for their rights, but who are struggling to achieve their goals of peace, education and equality. Thousands of people have been killed by the terrorists and millions have been injured. I am just one of them.

---

[1] A form of words known as Bismillah, used by Muslims during prayers and in other contexts.
[2] Ban Ki-moon (1944–) is a South Korean statesman who served as Secretary-General of the United Nations, 2007–16.
[3] Vuk Jeremić (1975–) is a Serbian politician and journalist who served as President of the 67th session of the General Assembly of the United Nations (2012–13).
[4] Gordon Brown (1951–) is a prominent Scottish politician who served as leader of the Labour Party and prime minister of the UK in 2007–10. In 2012, he was appointed as United Nations Special Envoy on Global Education.
[5] An Arabic greeting, which translates as 'Peace be with you'.
[6] This was Yousafzai's first public speech since she was attacked.
[7] Benazir Bhutto (1953–2007) was a Pakistani stateswoman who served as Prime Minister in 1988–90 and 1993–6. She was assassinated in 2007. The Arabic honorific Shaheed translates as 'martyr'.
[8] The aeroplane carrying Yousafzai to the UK for treatment refuelled at Abu Dhabi in the United Arab Emirates.

So here I stand … so here I stand, one girl among many.

I speak not for myself, but for those without voice can be heard.

Those who have fought for their rights:

Their right to live in peace. Their right to be treated with [slight fluff] dignity. Their right to equality of opportunity. Their right to be educated.

Dear friends, on the 9th of October 2012, the Taliban shot me on the left side of my forehead. They shot my friends too. They thought that the bullets would silence us. But they failed. And out of that silence came thousands of voices.

The terrorists thought that they would change my aims and stop my ambitions but nothing changed in my life except this: weakness, fear and hopelessness died. Strength, power and courage was born.

[Prolonged applause and cheers.] I am the same Malala. My ambitions are the same. My hopes are the same. And my dreams are the same.

Dear sisters and brothers, I'm not against anyone. Neither am I here to speak in terms of personal revenge against the Taliban or any other terrorist group. I am here to speak up for the right of education of every child.

[Applause.] I want education for the sons and daughters of the Taliban and all terrorists and extremists.

I do not even hate the Talib who shot me. Even if there is a gun in my hand and he stands in front of me, I would not shoot him. This is the compassion that I have learnt from Muhammad, the prophet of mercy, and Jesus Christ and Lord Buddha. This is the legacy of change that I have inherited from Martin Luther King, Nelson Mandela and Muhammad Ali Jinnah.[9] This is … [Interrupted by applause.] This is the philosophy of non-violence that I have learnt from Gandhiji,[10] Bacha Khan[11] and Mother Teresa.[12] And this is the forgiveness that I have learned from my father and from my mother [Applause.] This is what my soul is telling me: be peaceful and love everyone.

Dear sisters and brothers, we realise the importance of light when we see darkness. We realise the importance of our voice when we are silenced. In the same way, when we were in Swat[13], the north of Pakistan, we realised the importance of pens and books when we saw the guns.

The wise saying, 'The pen is mightier than sword'[14] was true. The extremists were and they are afraid of books and pens.

---

[9] Muhammad Ali Jinnah (1876–1948) was a lawyer and politician, instrumental in the creation of Pakistan in 1947, and served as the country's first Governor-General until his death the following year.
[10] A popular nickname for Mohandas Karamchand Gandhi.
[11] Bacha Khan (officially Khan Abdul Ghaffar Khan) (1890–1988) was a Pashtun political and spiritual leader who led non‑violent opposition to British rule in India.

[12] Mother Teresa (originally Anjezë Gonxhe Bojaxhiu) (1910–97) was an Albanian nun known for her missionary work among the poor and sick of India.
[13] Swat is a district in the north of Pakistan, centred on the Swat River valley. Yousafzai's family was displaced from the region by fighting in May 2009.
[14] An axiom attributed to the English author Edward Bulwer-Lytton (1803–73), who included it in his play *Richlieu; or The Conspiracy* (1839).

The power of education, the power of education frightens them. They are afraid of women. The power of the voice of women frightens them. And that is why they killed 14 innocent students in the recent attack in Quetta.[15] And that is why they killed female teachers and polio workers in Khyber Pakhtunkhwa. That is why they are blasting schools every day. Because they were and they are afraid of change, afraid of equality that we will bring into our society.

And I remember that there was a boy in our school who was asked by a journalist, 'Why are the Taliban against education?' He answered very simply, by pointing to his book. He said, 'A Talib doesn't know what is written inside this book.' They think that God is a tiny, little conservative being who would send girls to the Hell just because of going to school. The terrorists are misusing the name of Islam and Pashtun society for their own personal benefits. *[Applause.]*

Pakistan is peace-loving, democratic country. Pashtuns want education for their daughters and sons. And Islam is a religion of peace, humanity and brotherhood. Islam says it's not only each child's right to get education, rather it's their duty and responsibility.

Honourable Secretary-General, peace is necessary for education. In many parts of the world, especially Pakistan and Afghanistan, terrorism, wars and conflicts stop children to go to their schools. We are really tired of these wars. Women and children are suffering in many ways in many parts of the world. In India, innocent and poor children are victims of child labour. Many schools have been destroyed in Nigeria.[16] People in Afghanistan have been affected by the hurdles of extremism for decades. Young girls have to do domestic child labour and are forced to get married at early age. Poverty, ignorance, injustice, racism and the deprivation of basic rights are the main problems faced by both men and women.

Dear fellows, today I am focusing on women's rights and girls' education because they are suffering the most. There was a time when women social activists asked men to stand up for their rights. But, this time, we will do it by ourselves. *[Cheers and applause.]* I'm not telling men to step away from speaking for women's rights; rather I am focusing on women to be independent to fight for themselves.

So, dear sisters and brothers, now it's time to speak up.

So today, we call upon the world leaders to change their strategic policies in favour of peace and prosperity.

We call upon the world leaders that all the peace deals must protect women's and children's rights. A deal that goes against the rights of women is unacceptable.

We call upon all governments to ensure free compulsory education all over the world for every child. *[Applause.]*

---

[15] A city in north–central Pakistan, where a terrorist bus bombing killed 14 students at a women's university on 15 June 2013.

[16] The Islamic extremist organisation Boko Haram is based in north-eastern Nigeria, and has carried out attacks and kidnappings in the region since 2009, with schools among its targets.

We call upon all the governments to fight against terrorism and violence, to protect children from brutality and harm.

We call upon the developed nations to support the expansion of educational opportunities for girls in the developing world.

We call upon all the communities to be tolerant, to reject prejudice based on caste, creed, sect, religion or gender. To ensure freedom and equality for women so that they can flourish. We cannot all succeed when half of us are held back.

We call upon our sisters around the world to be brave – to embrace the strength within themselves and realise their full potential.

Dear brothers and sisters, we want schools and education for every child's bright future. We will continue our journey to our destination of peace and education. No one can stop us. We will speak up for our rights and we will bring change through our voice. We must believe in the power and the strength of our words. Our words can change the whole world, because we are all together, united for the cause of education.

And if we want to achieve our goal, then let us empower ourselves with the weapon of knowledge and let us shield ourselves with unity and togetherness.

Dear brothers and sisters, we must not forget that millions of people are suffering from poverty, injustice and ignorance. We must not forget that millions of children are out of their schools. We must not forget that our sisters and brothers are waiting for a bright, peaceful future.

So let us wage … so let us wage a global struggle against illiteracy, poverty and terrorism. Let us pick up … let us pick up our books and our pens. They are our most powerful weapons.

[Holding up a finger.]

One child, one teacher, one book and one pen can change the world.

Education is the only solution. Education First.

Thank you.

[Cheers and prolonged standing ovation.]

'The most important drivers of extreme inequality are well known – technological progress and financial globalization ...'

– *Christine Lagarde*

47

Christine Lagarde

French lawyer, politician and economist

Christine Lagarde (1956–) studied English, law and politics in France and began work as a lawyer in Chicago, USA in 1981, becoming her firm's chairman in 1999. She became France's trade minister in 2005 and in 2007 the country's first female finance minister. Since July 2011, she has been the managing director of the International Monetary Fund (IMF) which seeks to 'foster global monetary cooperation, secure financial stability, facilitate international trade, promote high employment and sustainable economic growth, and reduce poverty around the world'. In 2014, she faced a charge of criminal negligence during her tenure as finance minister. This was over her handling of a €400 million legal battle between the tycoon Bernard Tapie and the bank Crédit Lyonnais over the sale of the sportswear firm Adidas. In July 2016, a French court confirmed that she must stand trial in relation to this charge, which carries a possible jail sentence. In 2014, she was named in *Forbes* magazine as the fifth most influential woman in the world.

'Reducing excessive inequality is not just morally and politically correct, but it is good economics'

17 June 2015, Brussels, Belgium

This speech was given to the Grandes Conférences Catholiques, a high-profile lecture series which has run since 1931. In its own words, it is 'animated by a spirit of openness, curiosity and free thinking'. As head of the IMF, Christine Lagarde would naturally be expected to lecture on economics. Her chosen theme was economic inequality: its causes, its damaging effects and how it can be addressed.

The IMF has at times faced criticism for favouring the interests of the developed world over poorer countries, but Lagarde's focus is firmly on global concerns, and she draws numerous examples from developing nations. However, her overriding argument is that the most pressing problem is internal inequality: within rather than between individual nations.

Lagarde is a highly polished and engaging speaker, who can convey complex ideas with a persuasive lightness of touch. Here, she draws on a cynical joke about the luxury yachts owned by Wall Street bankers for her central metaphor of 'small boats', which she defines as 'the livelihoods and economic aspirations of the poor and the middle class'.

" Good evening! I am absolutely delighted to participate again in this prestigious conference, and I would like to thank Vice Premier Reynders[1] for his kind introduction.

Last month, on May 6, I almost choked on my morning yoghurt when I saw the front page of a leading business newspaper. There it was – a league table of the world's best paid hedge fund managers.[2] It showed that the highest earner was able to pocket $1.3 billion in 2014. One man, $1.3 billion!

Together, the 25 best-paid hedge fund managers earned a combined $12 billion last year, even as their industry suffered from largely mediocre investment performance.

This reminded me of a famous Wall Street joke – about a visitor to New York who admired the gorgeous yachts of the richest bankers and brokers. After gazing long and thoughtfully at these beautiful boats, the visitor asked wryly: 'Where are the customers' yachts?' Of course, the customers could not afford yachts, even though they dutifully followed the advice of their bankers and brokers.

Why is this relevant right now? Because the theme of growing and excessive inequality is not only back in the headlines, it has also become a problem for economic growth and development. I would like to take an economic perspective on this with you tonight. I will not focus on the gorgeous yachts of the super-rich, who have become the face of a new Gilded Age. It is not immoral to enjoy one's financial success.

But I would like to bring into the discussion what I would call the 'small boats' – the livelihoods and economic aspirations of the poor and the middle class.

In too many countries, economic growth has failed to lift these small boats – while the gorgeous yachts have been riding the waves and enjoying the wind in their sails.

In too many cases, poor and middle-class households have come to realise that hard work and determination alone may not be enough to keep them afloat …

My key message tonight is this: reducing excessive inequality – by lifting the 'small boats' – is not just morally and politically correct, but it is good economics.

You do not have to be an altruist to support policies that lift the incomes of the poor and the middle class. Everybody will benefit from these policies, because they are essential to generate higher, more inclusive and more sustainable growth.

In other words, if you want to see more durable growth, you need to generate more equitable growth. With this in mind, I would like to focus on three issues:

---

[1] Didier Reynders (1958–) is a Belgian politician who was leader of the Reform Movement party, 2004–11. He became deputy prime minister in 2004. He also served as finance minister in 2008–11, becoming foreign minister in 2011.

[2] Hedge fund managers operate highly complex and profitable investment schemes for an exclusive clientele of investors.

1   The global economic outlook.

2   The causes and consequences of excessive inequality.

3   The policies needed for stronger, more inclusive and more sustainable growth.

Let me start by describing the global economic weather map, as we see it. According to the IMF's spring forecast, the global economy will grow 3.5 per cent this year – about the same as last year – and 3.8 per cent in 2016.

Advanced economies are doing slightly better than last year. In the US, the outlook still is for a strong expansion – the weak first quarter was just a temporary setback. Prospects in the Euro Area are improving, partly because of monetary easing by the European Central Bank. And Japan seems to finally reap the first rewards of its 'three arrows' recovery strategy (monetary, fiscal and structural).

Forecasts for most emerging and developing economies are slightly worse than last year, mainly because commodity exporters are affected by price declines, especially for oil … But there is a tremendous diversity of national trends – from still strong growth in India to recession in Brazil and Russia.

So the good news remains that the global recovery continues. But growth remains moderate overall and uneven across countries.

What about the years beyond 2016, the second half of this decade? Well, here is where I have to share some not-so-good news with you. Our view at the IMF is that the growth potential of both advanced and emerging economies is likely to be lower in the years to come. This is partly because of changing demographics and lower productivity. Our concern is that this will bring more challenges in the labour markets, less-solid public finances and slower improvements in living standards.

This is the 'new mediocre' about which I have been warning. For the 'small boats', it means that the wind is picking up, but it is not strong enough to reduce high unemployment. It is not strong enough to bolster middle-class incomes and drive poverty reduction. It is simply not strong enough to lift the 'small boats' – even as the yachts are enjoying the breeze out on the high seas.

So, what is going on? Are we to resign in the face of unfavourable weather? Is there no hope for the captains of the 'small boats' …?

The short answer is: there is hope, but to see it, we need to step back and look at the global picture before we zoom in on the country level.

Imagine lining up the world's population from the poorest to the richest, each standing behind a pile of money that represents his or her annual income.

You will see that the world is a very unequal place. There is obviously a vast gulf between the richest and the poorest. But if you look at the changes in this line-up over time, you will notice that global income inequality – that is, inequality between countries – has actually fallen steadily over the past few decades.

Why? Because average incomes in emerging market economies, such as China and India, have risen much faster than those in richer countries. This shows the transformative power of international trade and investment. The massive global flows of products, services, people, knowledge and ideas have been good for global equality of income – and we need more of that. So we can further reduce the gap between countries.

But – and this is a big 'but' – we have also seen growing income inequality within countries …

In advanced economies, for example, the top 1 percent of the population now account for about 10 per cent of total income. And the gap between rich and poor is even wider when it comes to wealth. Oxfam[3] estimates that, in 2016, the combined wealth of the world's richest 1 per cent will overtake that of the other 99 percent of people …

If you put all this together, you see a striking divergence between a positive global trend and mostly negative trends within countries.

China, for example, has been at the sharp end of both trends. By lifting more than 600 million people out of poverty over the past three decades, China has made a remarkable contribution to greater global equality of income. But in the process, it has become one of the world's most unequal societies – because many rural areas remain poor and because income and wealth have risen sharply in the cities and at the top levels of Chinese society.

In fact, economies like China and India seem to fit neatly into a traditional narrative, which says that extreme inequality is an acceptable price to pay for economic growth …

But there is a growing new consensus that countries should not accept this Faustian trade-off. For example, analysis by my colleagues at the IMF has shown that excessive income inequality actually drags down the economic growth rate and makes growth less sustainable over time.

Earlier this week, we released our latest IMF analysis,[4] which provides the hard numbers for my key message – that you need to lift the 'small boats' to generate stronger and more durable growth.

Our research shows that, if you lift the income share of the poor and middle class by one percentage point, then GDP growth increases by as much as 0.38 percentage points in a country over five years. By contrast, if you lift the income share of the rich by one percentage point, then GDP growth decreases by 0.08 percentage points. One possible explanation is that the rich spend a lower fraction of their incomes, which could reduce aggregate demand and undermine growth.

In other words, our findings suggest that – contrary to conventional wisdom – the benefits of higher income are trickling up, not down.

This, of course, shows that the poor and the middle class are the main engines of growth. Unfortunately, these engines have been stalling …

This kind of inequality holds back growth because it discourages investment in skills and human capital – which leads to lower productivity in a large part of the economy.

So, the consequences of excessive income inequality are increasingly clear – but what about its causes?

---

[3] Founded in Oxford in 1942, Oxfam is an international confederation of organizations devoted to tackling poverty and injustice.

[4] A paper entitled 'Causes and Consequences of Income Inequality: A Global Perspective' was published by the IMF on 15 June 2015.

The most important drivers of extreme inequality are well known – technological progress and financial globalization …

Another factor is the over-reliance on finance in major economies such as the United States and Japan. Of course, finance – especially credit – is essential to any prosperous society. But there is growing evidence, including from IMF staff,[5] that too much finance can distort the distribution of income, corrode the political process and undermine economic stability and growth.

In emerging and developing economies, extreme income inequality is largely driven by an inequality of access – to education, health care and financial services …

With these kinds of disadvantages – with this kind of inequality of opportunity – millions of people have little or no chance of earning higher incomes and building up wealth. This is – in the words of Pope Francis – an 'economy of exclusion'.[6]

Policy makers can, in our view, generate a swell under the bow of the 'small boats'. There are recipes for stronger, more inclusive and more sustainable growth in all countries.

The first priority – the number one item on the list – should be macroeconomic stability. If you do not apply good monetary policies, if you indulge in fiscal indiscipline, if you allow your public debt to balloon, you are bound to see slower growth, rising inequality and greater economic and financial instability …

The second priority should be prudence. We all know that actions need to be taken to reduce excessive inequality. But we also know that a certain level of inequality is healthy and helpful. It provides incentives for people to compete, innovate, invest and seize opportunities – to upgrade their skills, start new businesses and make things happen …

The next priority should be to adjust policies to country-specific drivers of inequality, including political, cultural and institutional settings. No more one-size-fits-all, but smart policies – potential game changers – that could help reverse the trend towards greater inequality.

One potential game changer is smart fiscal policy.

The challenge here is to design tax and spending measures that have minimal adverse effects on incentives to work, save and invest. The objective must be to promote both greater equality and greater efficiency.

This means widening the tax revenue base by – for example – clamping down on tax evasion; reducing tax relief on mortgage payments from which the rich benefit most;[6] and reducing or removing tax relief on capital gains, stock options and the profits of private equity investments funds, known as 'carried interest'.

In many European countries, it also means reducing high labour taxes … This would provide a strong incentive to create more jobs and more full-time positions – which would help stem the tide of part-time and temporary jobs that have contributed to rising income inequality.

[5] An IMF paper entitled 'Rethinking Financial Deepening: Stability and Growth in Emerging Markets', published in May 2015, argued that excessive financial development had the potential to damage growth.

[6] An 'Apostolic Exhortation' issued by Pope Francis on 24 November 2013 stated: 'Just as the commandment "Thou shalt not kill" sets a clear limit in order to safeguard the value of human life, today we also have to say "thou shalt not" to an economy of exclusion and inequality.'

On the expenditure side, it means expanding access to education and health care. In many emerging and developing economies, it means reducing energy subsidies – which are costly and inefficient – and using the freed-up resources for better education, training and stronger safety nets …

Promoting greater equality and efficiency also means relying more on so-called conditional cash transfers. These are immensely successful anti-poverty tools that have contributed significantly to the reduction in income inequality in countries such as Brazil, Chile and Mexico.

During my recent visit to Brazil,[8] I had the opportunity to visit a favela[9] and witness first-hand the so-called Bolsa Familia[10] programme. This programme provides aid to poor families – in the form of pre-paid debit cards – on condition that their children go to school and take part in government vaccination programmes.

Bolsa Familia has proven to be both efficient and cost-effective: for expenditure of 0.5 percent of GDP per year, 50 million people are being supported – that's one in every four Brazilians.

In addition to these smart fiscal policies, there is another potential game changer – smart reforms in vital areas such as education, health care, labour markets, infrastructure and financial inclusion. These structural reforms are essential to lift potential economic growth and boost income and living standards over the medium term.

> ### *If I had to pick the three most important structural tools to reduce excessive income inequality, it would be education, education, education.[7] …*

Higher incomes require higher human capital and policies that bring together more teachers and students in 21st-century class rooms, with better books and access to online resources. Emerging and developing economies need to promote more equal access to basic education, while advanced economies need to focus more on the quality and affordability of university education …

Another important tool is labour market reform. Think of well-calibrated minimum wages and policies to support job search and skill matching. Think of reforms to protect workers rather than jobs …

Labour market reforms also have an important gender dimension. Across the globe, women have been facing a triple disadvantage. They are less likely than men to have a paid job, especially in the Middle East and North Africa. If they do find paid employment, it is more likely to be in the informal sector. And if they eventually get a job in the formal sector, they earn just three-quarters as much as men – even with the same level of education and in the same occupation.

Countries like Chile and the Netherlands have shown that you can sharply increase female labour force participation through smart policies that emphasise affordable childcare,

---

[6] About half of the governments of the developed world allow mortgage holders to deduct the interest from their taxable income.
[8] Lagarde visited Brazil in May 2015.
[9] A Brazilian Portuguese term for an urban slum district.
[10] Portuguese: 'family purse'.
[7] This phrase was coined by the British Labour Party leader Tony Blair during a manifesto speech in November 1997. Soon afterwards, he was elected as prime minister.

maternity leave and workplace flexibility. You also need to remove legal barriers and tax discrimination that continue to hold back women in many countries.

Worldwide, there are about 865 million women who have the potential to contribute more fully to the economy.

So the message is clear: if you care about greater shared prosperity, you need to unleash the economic power of women.

You also need to foster greater financial inclusion, especially in developing economies. Think of microcredit initiatives that turn poor people – mostly women – into successful micro-entrepreneurs – as I could recently see in Peru.[8] Think of initiatives to build credit histories for people without bank accounts. Think of the transformative impact of cellphone-based banking, especially in Sub-Saharan Africa.

By improving their access to basic financial services, poor families in developing economies can invest more in health and education, which leads to higher productivity and higher income potential …

All these policies and reforms require leadership, courage and collaboration. This is why I am calling on politicians, policymakers, business leaders and all of us here to translate good intentions into bold and lasting actions.

In particular, policy makers need to take advantage of what I think is a once-in-a generation opportunity for development …

I sincerely hope that, by the end of this year, we will be able to look back and say, 'we did it'. 'We re-energised global economic growth.' 'We reached a historic agreement on climate change.' 'And we launched a brand new development agenda with ambitious goals and solid financing.'

On all these issues, I see an important role for the IMF. Our key mandate is to promote global economic and financial stability. This is why we have been deeply involved in development – by helping our 188 member countries to design and implement policies and by lending to countries in times of distress, so they can get back on their feet …

Consider the latest migrant tragedies in the Mediterranean[9] and on South-East Asian shores.[10] These cramped migrant boats represent the most fragile states and communities. They are the smallest of the 'small boats' – a powerful reminder of the most extreme inequality of wealth and income. The economy of exclusion is staring us right in the face.

It is often said that we should measure the health of our society not at its apex, but at its base. By lifting the 'small boats' of the poor and the middle class, we can build a fairer society and a stronger economy. Together, we can create greater shared prosperity – for all.

Thank you. **"**

---

[8] Lagarde visited Peru in November 2014.

[9] In 2015, the number of refugees and economic migrants seeking to enter Europe rapidly increased. Thousands attempted the journey via the Mediterranean on boats inadequate for the crossing, often after paying extortionate fees to people-traffickers. Many died in the attempt.

[10] A similar crisis developed in South-East Asia, where migrants mainly from Bangladesh and Burma attempted to reach Indonesia, Thailand and Malaysia by crossing the Indian Ocean.

'And we are here faced by fascists. Not just their calculated brutality, but their belief that they are superior to every single one of us here tonight, and all of the people that we represent.'

– *Hilary Benn*

48

Hilary Benn

British politician

Hilary James Wedgwood Benn (1953–) is the second son of the Labour Cabinet Minister Tony Benn (1925–2014). He read Russian and East European studies at Sussex University, then worked at two trade unions and served as deputy leader of Ealing Borough Council. He stood unsuccessfully as a Labour candidate in the 1983 and 1987 general elections. He distanced himself from his father's famously far-left stance, describing himself as 'a Benn, not a Bennite' and was elected as MP for Leeds Central in 1999. He was a Cabinet Secretary in the governments led by Tony Blair and Gordon Brown. Under Ed Miliband's leadership of the Labour Party he became Shadow Leader of the House of Commons. He was appointed as Shadow Foreign Secretary in 2015, but was dismissed from the post by the Labour leader, Jeremy Corbyn, in 2016. Like his father, he is a teetotaller and vegetarian; unlike his father, he supports the UK's retention of a nuclear deterrent.

'We never have and we never should walk by on the other side of the road'

2 December 2015, London, England

This was the final speech in a long and passionate debate in the House of Commons. Under discussion was a government motion to extend air strikes in the Middle East. This was a response the growing might of Daesh – also known as ISIS, ISIL or Islamic State. This highly organized group uses violence and terror in pursuit of its goal of a 'global caliphate' – political and military control of the world's Muslim populations. The British government, led by Conservative Prime Minister David Cameron, had already ordered bombing raids on Daesh-held regions in Iraq. The proposal was to extend air strikes into Syria, where Daesh also holds swathes of territory.

As Shadow Foreign Secretary, Benn supported the motion. In doing so, he disagreed with his party leader, Jeremy Corbyn, the left-wing Leader of the Opposition, who had reluctantly allowed his party a free vote on the issue. Concerned over an 'ill-thought-out rush to war', Corbyn had refused to back the government motion. Cameron had criticized opponents of the motion as 'a bunch of terrorist sympathizers', a slur which he refused to withdraw.

Benn's speech was greeted with cheers and applause – not normally permitted in the House of Commons. The motion was passed by 397 votes to 223, a comfortable majority of 174. The media response was mostly very positive, though in some quarters, Benn was compared unfavourably to his father, the late Tony Benn, a left-wing pacifist who would almost certainly have opposed the motion.

“ Thank you very much, Mr Speaker. Before I respond to the debate, I would like to say this directly to the Prime Minister: although my right honourable friend the Leader of the Opposition and I will walk into different division lobbies[1] tonight, I am proud to speak from the same Despatch Box as him. My right honourable friend is not a terrorist sympathizer. He is an honest, a principled, a decent and a good man, and I think the Prime Minister must now regret what he said yesterday and his failure to do what he should have done today, which is simply to say, 'I am sorry.'

Now, Mr Speaker, we have had an intense and impassioned debate – and rightly so, given the clear and present threat from Daesh, the gravity of the decision that rests upon the shoulders and the conscience of every single one of us, and the lives that we hold in our hands tonight. And whatever decision we reach, I hope we will treat one another with respect …[2]

The question which confronts us in a very, very complex conflict is at its heart very simple.

What should we do with others to confront this threat to our citizens, our nation, other nations and the people who suffer under the yoke, the cruel yoke, of Daesh?

The carnage in Paris[3] brought home to us the clear and present danger we face from them. It could just as easily have been London or Glasgow or Leeds or Birmingham – and it could still be. And I believe that we have a moral and a practical duty to extend the action we are already taking in Iraq to Syria. And I am also clear – and I say this to my colleagues – that the conditions set out in the emergency resolution passed at the Labour Party conference in September[4] have been met. We now have a clear and unambiguous UN Security Council resolution 2249, paragraph five of which specifically calls on member states to take all necessary measures; to redouble and co-ordinate their efforts to prevent and suppress terrorist acts committed specifically by ISIL and to eradicate the safe haven they have established over significant parts of Iraq and Syria.

So the United Nations is asking us to do something. It is asking us to do something now …

So given that the United Nations has passed this resolution, given that such action would be lawful under Article 51 of the UN Charter[5] – because every state has the right to defend itself – why would we not uphold the settled will of the United Nations, particularly when there is such support from within the region, including from Iraq?

We are part of a coalition of over 60 countries standing together shoulder to shoulder to oppose their ideology and their brutality. Now, Mr Speaker, all of us understand the

---

[1] Members of Parliament vote by walking from the debating chamber into one of two annexes known as division lobbies.

[2] At this point, Benn pays tribute to a number of other speakers on both sides of the debate.

[3] On 13 November 2015, 137 people (including seven perpetrators) died in a series of coordinated suicide bombings and shootings in Paris, France. The targets included a football stadium, restaurants, cafés and the Bataclan music venue, where 89 of the victims were killed.

[4] During an emergency debate on defence policy at the Labour Party's annual conference in September 2015, agreement was reached on four tests to be passed before military action in Syria would be approved. These included a United Nations authorization.

[5] Article 51 of the United Nations Charter permits member states to undertake self defence against armed attack.

importance of bringing an end to the Syrian civil war,[6] and there is now some progress on a peace plan because of the Vienna talks.[7] They are the best hope we have of achieving a ceasefire. Now that would bring an end to Assad's bombing, leading to a transitional government and elections. And why is that vital? Both because it will help in the defeat of Daesh and because it would enable millions of Syrians who have been forced to flee to do what every refugee dreams of: they just want to be able to go home.

Now, Mr Speaker, no one in this debate doubts the deadly serious threat we face from Daesh and what they do – although sometimes we find it hard to live with the reality …

We know they have killed 30 British tourists in Tunisia,[8] 224 Russian holidaymakers on a plane,[9] 178 people in suicide bombings in Beirut, Ankara and Suruç,[10] 130 people in Paris – including those young people in the Bataclan, whom Daesh, in trying to justify their bloody slaughter, called them apostates engaged in prostitution and vice. If it had happened here, they could have been our children. And we know they are plotting more attacks.

So the question for each of us and for our national security is this: given that we know what they are doing, can we really stand aside and refuse to act fully in our self-defence against those who are planning these attacks? Can we really leave to others the responsibility for defending our national security when it is our responsibility? And if we do not act, what message would that send about our solidarity with those countries that have suffered so much, including Iraq and our ally France? …

Now, Mr Speaker, it has been argued in the debate that air strikes achieve nothing. Not so. Look at how Daesh's forward march has been halted in Iraq

The house will remember that 14 months ago people were saying, 'They are almost at the gates of Baghdad.' And that is why we voted to respond to the Iraqi government's request for help to defeat them. Look at how their military capacity and their freedom of movement has been put under pressure. Ask the Kurds about Sinjar and Kobanî[11] …

And so to suggest, Mr Speaker, that air strikes should not take place until the Syrian civil war has come to an end is, I think, to miss the urgency of the terrorist threat that Daesh poses to us and others and I think misunderstands the nature and objectives of the extension to air strikes that is being proposed.

And of course we should take action – it is not a contradiction between the two – to cut off Daesh's support in the form of money and fighters and weapons. And of course we should give humanitarian aid, and of course we should offer shelter to more refugees, including in this country, and yes we should commit to play our full part in helping to rebuild Syria when the war is over.

---

[6] Since 2011, Syria has been in a state of civil war, with a large number of rival factions engaged, among them the brutally repressive regime of President Bashar al-Assad (1965–), who assumed power on his father's death in 2000.
[7] Peace talks for Syria, known as the International Syria Support Group, began in Vienna, Austria in October 2015. The principles proposed were endorsed in December 2015 by UN Resolution 2254.
[8] On 26 June 2015, 38 people were massacred by a gunman on a beach at the Tunisian resort of Sousse. Thirty British tourists were among the 38 victims.

[9] On 31 October 2015, a Metrojet airliner blew up over Egypt with the loss of 224 lives. The passengers were Russian holidaymakers returning from the Egyptian resort of Sharm el-Sheikh. Evidence of explosives was found among the wreckage.
[10] A city and district in south-central Turkey, near the border with Syria, with a predominantly Kurdish population.
[11] In northern Iraq and Syria, respectively.

Now I accept that there are legitimate arguments, and we've heard them in the debate, for not taking this form of action now, and it is also clear that many members have wrestled – and who knows, in the time that is left may still be wrestling – with what the right thing to do is. But I say the threat is now and there are rarely if ever perfect circumstances in which to deploy military forces.

Now we heard very powerful testimony from the honourable member for Eddisbury earlier when she quoted that passage,[12] and I just want to read what Karwan Jamal Tahir, the Kurdistan regional government high representative in London, said last week, and I quote: 'Last June, Daesh captured one third of Iraq overnight, and a few months later attacked the Kurdistan region. Swift air strikes by Britain, America and France, and the actions of our own Peshmerga[13] saved us. We now have a border of 650 miles with Daesh. We have pushed them back and recently captured Sinjar. Again, Western air strikes were vital. But the old border between Iraq and Syria does not exist. Daesh fighters come and go across this fictional boundary.'

And that is the argument, Mr Speaker, for treating the two countries as one if we are serious about defeating Daesh.

Now, Mr Speaker, I hope the House will bear with me if I direct my closing remarks to my Labour friends and colleagues on this side of the House.

> *As a party, we have always been defined by our internationalism. We believe we have a responsibility one to another. We never have and we never should walk by on the other side of the road.[14]*

And we are here faced by fascists. Not just their calculated brutality, but their belief that they are superior to every single one of us here tonight, and all of the people that we represent. They hold us in contempt. They hold our values in contempt. They hold our belief in tolerance and decency in contempt. They hold our democracy, the means by which we will make our decision tonight, in contempt.

And what we know about fascists is that they need to be defeated. And it is why, as we have heard tonight, socialists and trade unionists and others joined the International Brigade[15] in the 1930s to fight against Franco. It's why this entire House stood up against Hitler and Mussolini. It is why our party has always stood up against the denial of human rights and for justice. And my view, Mr Speaker, is that we must now confront this evil. It is now time for us to do our bit in Syria. And that is why I ask my colleagues to vote for this motion tonight. 🙶

---

[12] Earlier in the debate, Antoinette Sandbach, MP had cited the famous dictum, 'All that is necessary for the triumph of evil is that good men do nothing,' usually attributed to the Irish philosopher Edmund Burke (1729–97).
[13] The militia of Iraqi Kurdistan, whose name translates as 'Those who face death'.

[14] A reference to the Parable of the Good Samaritan (Luke 10:25–37), in which the victim of a violent robbery is ignored by all those who might be expected to come to his aid.
[15] A loose alliance of volunteer militias, allegedly from 53 countries, formed to resist the fascist coup led by General Francisco Franco during the Spanish Civil War (1936–9).

'And, yes, our next president has to bring our country together so we can all share in the promise of America. We should be breaking down barriers, not building walls. We're not going to succeed by dividing this country between us and them.'

– *Hillary Clinton*

49

Hillary Clinton

American lawyer and politician

Hillary Clinton (née Rodham) (1947–) graduated from Yale Law School in 1973 and became a successful lawyer. In 1975, she married Bill Clinton, who became governor of Arkansas in 1979 and president of the USA in 1993. She stood by him through scandals surrounding his marital infidelity and also survived numerous allegations about her own legal and financial probity. At the end of Bill Clinton's second term as president, she stood for election as Senator from New York, serving in that post 2001–9, and campaigned for the Democratic presidential nomination in 2008. The nomination and the presidency were won by Barack Obama, and she served as Secretary of State during his first term, 2009–13. In April 2015, she formally announced her candidacy for the Democratic presidential nomination and was chosen to run against the Republican candidate, Donald Trump, in July 2016.

'You voted for our tomorrow to be better than our yesterday'

15 March 2016, West Palm Beach, Florida

This speech was given by a hoarse but buoyant presidential candidate enjoying an early taste of success. The occasion was her victory in three 'primaries' – part of the selection process for the Democratic Party's candidate – and her anticipated victory in two others. Beaming, triumphant and clad in blue – the colour of the Democrats – she addressed a large and voluble crowd of her supporters. Confident of a rapturous response, she used simple hand gestures, rhythm and emphasis to cue their cheers.

Like many seasoned speakers, she adopts a 'rule of three' structure, identifying the three key challenges facing the next president. The first is making positive changes – a theme neatly summarized in the 'tomorrow better than yesterday' motif. The second is national security, which allows her to make several digs at Donald Trump, her adversary in the November 2016 election. The third is a call for unity – often deployed by candidates in a divisive leadership contest.

The speech marked an important milestone in Clinton's bid to become the first female president of the USA. The job is a notoriously challenging one, and throughout her campaign she presented herself as tough and determined. On this occasion, she was playing to an easy crowd, but both content and delivery were designed to portray her as a woman steeled for combat.

" Thank you! Thank you so much! Thank you! Thank you all so very much! Well, I'll tell you, this is another Super Tuesday[1] for our campaign … *[Cheers.]*

You voted for our tomorrow to be better than our yesterday, tomorrow where all of us do our part and everyone has a chance to live up to his or her God-given potential. *[Cheers.]*

Because that's how America can live up to its potential too.

Now we need you to keep working, keep volunteering, keep contributing at hillaryclinton. com. *[Cheers.]* Please, please join the 950,000 supporters who already have contributed – most less than $100 – because our campaign depends on small donations for the majority of our support …

You know, tonight it's clearer than ever that this may be one of the most consequential campaigns of our lifetimes. The next president will walk into the Oval Office[2] next January, sit down at that desk, and start making decisions that will affect the lives and the livelihoods of everyone in this country – indeed everyone on this planet. *[Cheers.]*

Now I know, I know that easy decisions don't make it to the president's desk – only the hardest choices and the thorniest problems. I saw President Obama wrestle with the decision to send Navy Seals after Osama bin Laden,[3] the decision to rescue the auto industry,[4] to fight for the Affordable Care Act[5] and so many more.

And so our next president has to be ready to face three big tests. First: can you make positive differences in people's lives? Second: can you keep us safe? Third: can you bring our country together again? *[Cheers.]*

Now, now making differences in people's lives comes first because Americans everywhere are hungry for solutions. They want to break down the barriers holding them back so we can all rise together. Ask any parent. You'll hear nothing is more important than making sure their kids have a good school and a good teacher, no matter what ZIP code[6] they live in. They deserve a president who understands that when we invest in our children's education, we're investing in all of our futures *[Cheers.]* and young people … young people across America struggling under the weight of student debt find it difficult to imagine the futures they want, and they deserve a president who will help relieve them of that burden and help future generations go to college without borrowing a dime for tuition. *[Cheers.]*

And you know, grandparents … grandparents who worry about retirement deserve a president who will protect and then expand social security for those who need it most – not cut or privatise it. *[Cheers.]*

---

[1] Super Tuesday is a significant point during the selection process for a US political party's presidential nominee. It is the day when the largest number of US states hold primary elections – conducted as caucuses in some states. On Tuesday 1 March 2016, the Democratic Party held primaries or caucuses in 11 states, and Clinton won in seven of them.
[2] The Oval Office is the US president's official office in the White House, the presidential residence in Washington, DC.
[3] In April 2011, Obama ordered a raid by US Navy Seals (Sea, Air and Land Team) on a residential compound in Abbottabad, Pakistan, where the terrorist leader Osama bin Laden was found to be living. Bin Laden was shot dead during the raid on 2 May.

[4] In spring 2009, Obama took various measures to improve the US economy by boosting its failing car industry.
[5] Passed in March 2010, the Patient Protection and Affordable Care Act (known as 'Obamacare') was the outcome of a key policy of Obama's presidency, and the most important change in US health policy in 45 years.
[6] The Zone Improvement Plan introduced postal codes in 1963, providing a simple indicator of residential address.

Families deserve a president who will fight for the things that are priorities at home but too often aren't priorities in Washington: affordable childcare; paid family leave; and something we have waited for long enough: equal pay for equal work for women. *[Prolonged cheers.]*

And above all … above all, hardworking Americans across our country deserve a president with both the ideas and the know-how to create good jobs with rising incomes right here in our country. And I am absolutely convinced that we have the tools to do that. That's why I've laid out a programme to do what can be done. More good jobs in infrastructure, more good jobs in manufacturing, *[Cheers]* more good jobs in small businesses, more good jobs in clean, renewable energy. *[Cheers.]* Good-paying jobs are the ticket to the middle class and we're going to stand up for the American middle class again. We're going to stand up for American workers and make sure no one takes advantage of us. Not China, not Wall Street and not overpaid corporate executives. *[Cheers.]*

Now look, look, of course every candidate, every candidate makes promises like this. But every candidate owes it to you to be clear and direct about what our plans will cost and how we're going to make them work. That's the difference between running for president and being president. *[Cheers.]*

And I'll tell you … *[interrupted by chants of 'Hill-a-ry! Hill-a-ry!']* … Let me tell you that … that the second big test for our next president is keeping us safe.

We live in a complex and, yes, a dangerous world. Protecting America's national security can never be an afterthought. Our commander in chief[7] has to be able to defend our country, not embarrass it. *[Cheers.]* Engage our allies, not alienate them. Defeat our adversaries, not embolden them.

When we hear a candidate for president call for rounding up 12 million immigrants, banning all Muslims from entering the United States … When he embraces torture, that doesn't make him strong. It makes him wrong.[8] *[Prolonged cheers.]*

And, yes, our next president has to bring our country together so we can all share in the promise of America. We should be breaking down barriers, not building walls.[9] We're not going to succeed by dividing this country between us and them.

You know, to be great, we can't be small.

We can't lose what made America great in the first place, and this isn't just about Donald Trump. All of us have to do our part. We can't just talk about economic inequality, we have to take on all forms of inequality and discrimination.

Together, we have to defend all of our rights. Civil rights and voting rights. Workers' rights and women's rights. LGBT[10] rights and rights for people with disabilities. *[Cheers.]*

---

[7] The US Constitution designates the president as Commander in Chief of the Armed Forces.
[8] Clinton refers here to some of the more outlandish statements made by Donald Trump during his campaign to secure the Republican Party's presidental nomination.

[9] One of Trump's pledges was to build a wall along the US–Mexican border, to deter illegal immigration. He also promised to compel the Mexican government to pay for it. This proposal was widely considered preposterous.
[10] Clinton has been an outspoken advocate for improved rights for Lesbian, Gay, Bisexual and Transgender people.

And that starts by standing with President Obama when he nominates a justice to the Supreme Court.[11] Our next president will face all these challenges and more.

You know, running for president is hard, but being president is harder. It is the hardest, most important job in the world and no one person can succeed at the job without seeking and finding common ground to solve the problems we face.

If we work together, we can make a real difference in people's lives. If we reach out and treat each other with respect, kindness and even love instead of bluster and bigotry.

[Cheers.] If we lift each other up instead of tearing each other down, there's nothing we can't accomplish together ....

Eight years ago … eight years ago on the night of the Ohio primary, I said I was running for everyone who's ever been counted out but refused to be knocked out, for everyone who has stumbled but stood right back up, for everyone who works hard and never gives up. Well, that is still true.

Our campaign is for the steel worker I met in Ohio on Sunday night, who's laid off but hoping to get back to work. It's for the mother I met in Miami whose five children haven't seen their father since he was deported. She dreams of a day when deportations end and families are reunited, on a path to citizenship in America. *[Cheers.]* And it is for the mothers I stood with in Chicago yesterday who have lost children to gun violence. They're turning their sorrow into a strategy and their mourning into a movement.

Let's stand with people who have courage, who have resilience.

Let's stand with everyone who believes America's best days are ahead of us.

For all of our challenges, I've never had more faith in our future – and if we work together, if we go forward in this campaign, if we win in November, I know our future will be brighter tomorrow than yesterday. Thank you all so very much. **"**

---

[11] Clinton refers to Obama's intention to nominate the senior judge, Merrick Garland, to serve on the Supreme Court of the United States. A vacancy had been created by the death of Antonin Scalia in February 2016. However, Garland's nomination was controversial because he was considered much less conservative than Scalia; and because Obama was a Democratic president, requesting confirmation of the appointment from a hostile, Republican-controlled Senate. Obama nominated Garland the following day, but the Senate has so far refused to vote on the nomination until after the inauguration of a new president.

'We are living through an important moment in our country's history. Following the referendum, we face a time of great national change.'

— *Theresa May*

50

Theresa May

British politician

Theresa Mary May (1956–) was born in Eastbourne, Sussex. After studying at Oxford University and starting her working career at the Bank of England, May moved into politics first as a councillor for the London Borough of Merton from 1986 to 1994. She was elected as the Conservative Party Member of Parliament for Maidenhead in 1997, became the first female to become chairman of her party in 2002 and served in the Shadow Cabinet from 1999 until she assumed the role of Home Secretary in 2010, which she held for six years. Following the resignation of Prime Minister David Cameron following the result of the EU referendum, May won the Conservative Party leadership election and was appointed Prime Minister on 13 July 2016, becoming the second woman to lead the United Kingdom.

'As we leave the European Union, we will forge a bold new positive role for ourselves in the world'

13 July 2016, London, England

After a nationwide referendum on 23 June 2016, the United Kingdom voted to leave the European Union after 42 years as a member state. The 'Brexit' vote followed increasing growing disenchantment with Brussels but it still came as something of a shock when the UK electorate voted by 51.9 per cent to 48.9 per cent to leave. The campaigning prior to the vote was prickly and contentious, with issues centred on the economy, immigration and national sovereignty.

Cameron resigned the day after the vote, sparking a series of leadership bids from Remain and Leave campaigners from within the Conservative Party. Battling through the pack came Home Secretary Theresa May, a Remain campaigner and longtime member of Cameron's cabinet, who maintained popular support from the backbenches to secure the nomination and become the second woman to become UK Prime Minster.

May's first statement as Prime Minister, delivered outside 10 Downing Street, reveals her vision for Britain under her premiership. Her primary intention was to appeal for unity and to direct that appeal to the widest possible audience. After first praising Cameron, May briskly addresses a broad cross-section of British society, listing typical challenges faced by the public on a day-to-day basis and outlining a mission to improve the prospects of everyone in the United Kingdom. The inclusive principles she espouses are essentially those of 'one-nation' Toryism – a phrase coined by the Victorian Tory prime minister Benjamin Disraeli.

" I have just been to Buckingham Palace, where Her Majesty The Queen has asked me to form a new government, and I accepted.

In David Cameron, I follow in the footsteps of a great, modern prime minister. Under David's leadership, the government stabilised the economy, reduced the budget deficit, and helped more people into work than ever before.

But David's true legacy is not about the economy but about social justice. From the introduction of same-sex marriage,[1] to taking people on low wages out of income tax altogether; David Cameron has led a one-nation government, and it is in that spirit that I also plan to lead.

Because not everybody knows this, but the full title of my party is the Conservative and Unionist Party, and that word 'unionist' is very important to me.

It means we believe in the Union: the precious, precious bond between England, Scotland, Wales and Northern Ireland.[2] But it means something else that is just as important; it means we believe in a union not just between the nations of the United Kingdom but between all of our citizens, every one of us, whoever we are and wherever we're from.

That means fighting against the burning injustice that, if you're born poor, you will die on average nine years earlier than others.

If you're black, you're treated more harshly by the criminal justice system than if you're white.

If you're a white, working-class boy, you're less likely than anybody else in Britain to go to university.

If you're at a state school, you're less likely to reach the top professions than if you're educated privately.

If you're a woman, you will earn less than a man. If you suffer from mental health problems, there's not enough help to hand.

If you're young, you'll find it harder than ever before to own your own home.

But the mission to make Britain a country that works for everyone means more than fighting these injustices. If you're from an ordinary working-class family, life is much harder than many people in Westminster realize. You have a job but you don't always have job security. You have your own home, but you worry about paying a mortgage. You can just about manage but you worry about the cost of living and getting your kids into a good school.

If you're one of those families, if you're just managing, I want to address you directly.

[1] The Marriage (Same Sex Couples) Act 2013 was passed on 13 March 2013 in England and Wales.
[2] The Union of nations had been a political talking point since the Scottish independence referendum of 2014 where the electorate voted to remain part of the United Kingdom. The Scottish National Party called for a second referendum on independence in the aftermath of the EU referendum result. Scotland had voted by 62 per cent to 38 per cent to remain part of the EU.

I know you're working around the clock, I know you're doing your best, and I know that sometimes life can be a struggle. The government I lead will be driven not by the interests of the privileged few, but by yours.

We will do everything we can to give you more control over your lives. When we take the big calls, we'll think not of the powerful, but you. When we pass new laws, we'll listen not to the mighty but to you. When it comes to taxes, we'll prioritize not the wealthy, but you. When it comes to opportunity, we won't entrench the advantages of the fortunate few. We will do everything we can to help anybody, whatever your background, to go as far as your talents will take you.

We are living through an important moment in our country's history. Following the referendum, we face a time of great national change.

And I know because we're Great Britain, that we will rise to the challenge. As we leave the European Union, we will forge a bold new positive role for ourselves in the world, and we will make Britain a country that works not for a privileged few, but for every one of us.

That will be the mission of the government I lead, and together we will build a better Britain. ❞

Acknowledgements

I am indebted to the following people, whose time, knowledge and expertise were crucial to the development and completion of this book: Libby Bassett, Women's Environment & Development Organization; Dr Douglas Cairns; Angus Calder; Julie Christensen, Mary Fisher CARE Fund; Louise Clarke, Cambridge University Library; Dr Frank Cogliano, University of Edinburgh; Chris Collins, Margaret Thatcher Foundation; Dr Markus Daechsel, University of Edinburgh; Dr John Doyle, Dublin City University; Barry Eaden, Cambridge University Library; Owen Dudley Edwards, University of Edinburgh; Bashabi Fraser, University of Edinburgh/ Open University; Diane S Gianelli, the President's Council on Bioethics; Professor Robert F Goheen, Princeton University; Ieuan Hopkins, Churchill Archives Centre, Cambridge; Lord Howard; Ami Isseroff, mideastweb.org; Prof Rhodri Jeffreys-Jones, University of Edinburgh; Helen Langley, Bodleian Library, Oxford; Michael McManus; Joyce McMillan; Aurelie Martot; Dr Jolyon Mitchell, University of Edinburgh; Alan Morrison; Dr Graeme Morton, University of Edinburgh; Judy Nokes, the Office of Public Sector Information; Barry Pateman, University of California, Berkeley; Patrick Price, The Northern Ireland Assembly; Elaine Steel, literary agent; Emily Tarrant, Bodleian Library, Oxford; Alan Taylor; Martin Tod, MP; Darren Treadwell, the People's History Museum, Manchester; Barbara Walker; Colin Webb, Palazzo Editions; John Wells, Cambridge University Library; Louise Weston, BBC Written Archives Office; Prof Philip Williamson, University of Durham; the staff of the National Library of Scotland, Edinburgh City Libraries and Edinburgh University Library.

AB

Sources

Thanks are due to the following for their kind permission to reproduce copyright material: Daniel Barenboim: to Daniel Barenboim; David Ben-Gurion: to Philosophical Library, New York (reprinted from Rebirth and Destiny of Israel, copyright © 1954 by Philosophical Library);

Benazir Bhutto: to The Wylie Agency (UK) Ltd, copyright © 1995 Benazir Bhutto; Sir Winston Churchill: to Curtis Brown Ltd, London, on behalf of the Estate of Winston Churchill, copyright © Winston S Churchill; Anthony Eden: to the BBC; Edward VIII: to the Royal Household; Elizabeth II: to the Royal Household; Mary Fisher: to the Mary Fisher Clinical AIDS Research and Education (CARE) Fund at the University of Alabama at Birmingham (copyright © 1992 The Mary Fisher CARE Fund at the University of Alabama at Birmingham); Betty Friedan: to Curtis Brown Ltd (reprinted from *It Changed My Life*, Dell 1991); Mahatma Gandhi; to the Navajivan Trust on behalf of the Estate of M K Gandhi; Joseph Goebbels: to Cordula Schacht, translation by Randall Bytwerk; Dag Hammarskjöld: to Marlene Hagstrom; Edward Heath: to the Conservative Party Archive and the Estate of Sir Edward Heath; Heinrich Himmler: to Stéphane Bruchfeld (translator), Uppsala University, translation reproduced from www.scrapbookpages.com; Ho Chi Minh: to The Gioi (World) Publishers, Hanoi, Vietnam (reprinted from *Ho Chi Minh: Selected Works*, copyright © 1977 by Foreign Languages Publishing House, Hanoi); Nikita Khrushchev: reproduced by permission of Andrew Nurnberg Associates Ltd on behalf of the copyright holder; Martin Luther King, Jr.: to the Estate of Martin Luther King, Jr. (reprinted by arrangement with the Heirs to the Estate of Martin Luther King, Jr., c/o Writers House as agent for the proprietor, New York, NY); Patrice Lumumba: to Little, Brown and Co., Inc. (reprinted from *Lumumba Speaks* by Patrice Lumumba. Copyright © 1963 by Éditions Présence Africaine; copyright © 1972 by Little, Brown and Company, Inc. (translation). By permission of Little, Brown and Co., Inc. All rights reserved); Harold Macmillan: to the Trustees of the Harold Macmillan Book Trust (reproduced from the archive of the Harold Macmillan Book Trust); Malcolm X: to CMG Worldwide, Inc., www.CMG Worldwide.com (TM 2006 Malcolm X); Nelson Mandela: to Nelson Mandela (copyright © Nelson Mandela); Richard Nixon: to the Richard Nixon Foundation; La Pasionaria (Dolores Ibarruri): to Lawrence and Wishart, London (reprinted from *Speeches and Articles 1936–1938*, copyright © 1938 by Lawrence and Wishart); Margaret Thatcher: Copyright estate of Lady Thatcher, reproduced with permission from www.margaretthatcher.org, the website of the Margaret Thatcher Foundation; Desmond Tutu: to The Nobel Foundation (copyright © The Nobel Foundation 1984)

While every effort has been made to contact copyright holders, the publishers will be glad to rectify, in future editions, any errors or omissions brought to their attention.